ENGAGING MODERNITY

ENGAGING MODERNITY

Methods and Cases for Studying African Independent Churches in South Africa

Edited by Dawid Venter

PRAEGER

Westport, Connecticut
London

Library of Congress Cataloging-in-Publication Data

Engaging modernity : methods and cases for studying African independent churches in
South Africa / edited by Dawid Venter.
p. cm.
Includes bibliographical references and index.
ISBN 0–275–96903–7 (alk. paper)
1. Independent churches—South Africa. 2. Religion and sociology—South Africa. 3.
South Africa—Economic conditions. 4. Globalization. I. Venter, Dawid J.
BR1450.E54 2004
306.6'8993'0968—dc22 2003060069

British Library Cataloguing in Publication Data is available.

Library of Congress Catalog Card Number: 2003060069
ISBN: 0–275–96903–7

First published in 2004

Praeger Publishers, 88 Post Road West, Westport, CT 06881
An imprint of Greenwood Publishing Group, Inc.
www.praeger.com

Printed in the United States of America

The paper used in this book complies with the
Permanent Paper Standard issued by the National
Information Standards Organization (Z39.48–1984).

10 9 8 7 6 5 4 3 2 1

Copyright Acknowledgments

The editor and publisher gratefully acknowledge permission for use of the folowing materials:

Chapter 2 originally appeared as "African Independent Churches and Modernity" in *The Journal of African Christian Thought* 2 (1), 1999. Reprinted by permission of the editor of *The Journal of African Christian Thought.*

Sections of Chapters 3 and 4 first appeared in "Safe Sects? Dynamic Religion and AIDS in South Africa" in *Journal of Modern African Studies* 38 (1), 2000. Reprinted by permission of Cambridge University Press. Some of the data in these chapters previously appeared in "Religion as as Source of Social Change in the New South Africa" by Robert Garner in *Journal of Religion in Africa* 30 (3), 2000, and in "AIDS and Theologies of Discipline" by Robert Garner in *Bulletin of Contextual Theology* (Special Edition on the Church and AIDS), 2001. Reprinted by permission of the editor and of Brill Academic Publishers, respectively.

Chapter 7 is updated and adapted from "Globalisation and African Indigenous Churches" in *Missionalia* 26 (3), 1998. Reprinted by permission of the editor of *Missionalia.*

Dedicated to Ansie, Cara, and Simon.

Contents

Introduction

Dawid Venter

The title of this book takes its cue from the controversial claim by Bengt Sundkler (1948) that African Independent Churches (AICs) were bridges that led back to tradition. By implication, membership of an AIC would hinder Africans from full incorporation into modernity. The opposite would also apply: affiliation with a mainstream denomination would enhance modernization. A third implication is that a decline in religious beliefs would also presumably lead to modernity. Thirteen years after his original claim, Sundkler (1961) retracted his statement in the second edition of his book. Regardless, his claim and counterclaim continue to reverberate among those who research AICs.

In contrast to Sundkler's earlier assertion, Inus Daneel (1987) and G. C. Oosthuizen (1986) argued that AICs in general facilitate modernization, as membership orients individuals away from older historical practices towards a modern present. Daneel (1987) pointed to Zimbabwean AIC members who insist that their children have a modern education. Recently, Oosthuizen returned to a theme that he had brought up earlier (1987), to conclude that AIC members exhibit a potential for participation in development projects (Oosthuizen and Clark 1994). This suggests that AIC members are open to engage in inherently modernizing activities.

MODERNITY DEFINED

Like Sundkler's claim, our title begs modernity to be defined, if not operationalized, and so I will briefly indicate its major aspects in relation to our work. A fuller discussion remains well beyond the scope of this book, as can be clearly demonstrated by the sheer volume of literature on the subject. The Open University's editors, for instance, apparently could not fit their discussion of the contours of modernity into fewer than four volumes (Allen, Braham, and Lewis 1992; Bocock and Thompson 1992; Hall and Gieben 1992; Hall, Held, and McGrew 1992).

Alan Swingewood (1998, 138, 140) argues that modernity is commonly understood in three ways. He indicates that the origins of the concept can be traced back to the use in the Middle Ages of *modernitus* (modern times) and *modernity* (men of today).

In the first understanding, modernity is defined as a *literary-aesthetic* orientation towards the new—characterised as fleeting, dynamic, and constantly changing. A central feature of this definition is that of a decisive break—rather than continuity—with the past. Consequently, all periods "have their own modernity, as all epochs seek to represent the new" (Swingewood 1998, 142). Therefore, an analysis of the whole is rejected for an atomistic view that favours the micrological scale. Enlightenment beliefs in the inevitability of historical progress and in the autonomy of reason are rebuffed. The French poet and critic Charles Baudelaire already defined modernity in this manner in 1863 (141). Michel Foucault similarly suggested that modernity is a way of comprehending the present that does not refer to anything (such as transcendent principles) beyond the present (143). Modernity conceptualised as the fleeting, unfinished present tries to answer the question, "what does the present mean?"

Georg Simmel and others applied the literary-aesthetic understanding to devise a social theory of modernity. The development of capitalism was seen to lead to cultural and social upheavals, in tandem with associated changes in perceptions of time and space. The inherent danger is that this approach contains a tendency towards static and ahistorical analysis (Swingewood 1998, 142, 144). Some would argue that the refusal by theorists like Simmel to reify the social should count as an advantage of this conceptualisation of modernity (145). Yet, as Swingewood (147) argues, Simmel's description of modernity lacks attention to historical momentum, historical time, or structural analysis.

In the second understanding, modernity is characterised in *sociological-historical* terms. Different fields increasingly become autonomous from one another; yet autonomy is threatened by the growth of specialists that augurs the triumph of formal rationality. This approach is exemplified by the work of Max Weber, who develops a concept of modernity with structural and normative elements (Swingewood 1998, 147).

In a third view, modernity refers to a *structural* process that operates at the macrological level, although with the active contributions of agents. The emphasis here is on the transformation of "whole societies, ideologies, social structures and culture" (Swingewood 1998, 140).

In addition, we can theoretically distinguish between *objective* and *subjective* features of modernity. The subjective traits of modernity include "increased purposiveness, conscious collective action and the ability to engage in 'reflexive monitoring' in relation to possible alternatives" (Swingewood 1998, 140).

A discussion of the objective features of modernity is usually situated in a wider discourse of societal change. The objective aspects of modernity are seen to refer to an outcome produced by historical processes that operate under unique conditions (see Hall, Held, and McGrew 1992, 2). This conclusion forms a relatively potent and common understanding of modernity. The historical dynamics of modernity are perceived to substantively change the political, cultural, economic, and social structures of post-fifteenth-century societies. Anthony Giddens (1991, 15) and David Held (1992, 32) suggest that modernity derives from globalization, and contains four institutional complexes, each with its own separate logic: capitalism, industrialism, supervisory surveillance, and military power. Andrew McGrew (1992, 65) verifies capitalism and industrialism as "the primary institutions of Western modernity," but prefers to include the nation-state.

Another commonly held understanding is that the processes leading to modernity are inherently *secularising*, with multiple effects. Societies soaked in religious values and ruled by religious polities—or by rulers legitimated by religious leaders—eventually became secular states, with secular cultures, governed by secular polities. Barter-based precapitalist exchange systems, whether functioning within local areas or stretching across regional zones, were ultimately overrun by a global capitalist economy. Kinship-based forms of social organization made way for societies exhibiting class formation. Simple, gender-based divisions of labor were usurped by more advanced forms (Hall, Held, and McGrew 1992, 2). Such descriptions recall Emile Durkheim's premise that premodern societies exhibited simple institutions that assumed more complex forms in modern states.

Commentators tend to synthesize these various conceptualisations into a perception that modern societies are marked by constant and continuous change, and so to be discontinuous with traditional societies; whose members tend to interpret change in terms of continuity with the past (Hall 1992, 278–79). Modern institutions are seen as either radically new "(e.g., the nation-state or the commodification of products and forms of labor)," or as having "a specious continuity with earlier forms (e.g., the city)" (279).

One broad way of operationalizing the notion is to regard modernity as a measure of convergence with certain indicators that apply to particular institutions. Consequently, low levels of religious affiliation could indicate a modernizing trend in the cultural domain. Other indicators could include rejection of older for more recent traditions, and relinquishment of indigenous for European cultural forms (such as languages). The replacement of traditional forms of education by Western forms would serve as an example, as would the jettisoning of ancestral beliefs for secular orientations.

Unfortunately, scholars seldom—if ever—address the issue of how to operationalize modernity, and most contributors to this volume follow suit. The exception is Lawrencia Kwark, who sifts her data for evidence of modernity.

In chapter 6, Kwark rejects the often-assumed opposition of modernity to tradition in favour of a more nuanced understanding in which she links the two concepts. She identifies the traits and processes of modernity in a manner that recalls Swingewood's analysis. For Kwark, modernity entails the increasing autonomy of subjects from older forms of tradition alongside the proliferation of value systems. Similarly, Swingewood (1998, 137) argues that modernism is "built on the principles of differentiation and autonomy." Modernity, he asserts, is "the cultural logic of an urban-based industrial capitalism in which highly differentiated structures—political, economic, cultural—increasingly separate themselves from centralised institutions." Kwark argues that the growth of AICs in South Africa urgently calls sociologists to radically rethink the implicit causal link that many tend to assume between modernization and secularization.

Kwark's position represents an alternative to the dominant approach—that modernity opposes tradition—which has recently been put forward with increasing vigor. The dominant position has existed since at least the end of the nineteenth century, as Swingewood confirms. For example, a character in Bram Stoker's novel *Dracula* (1897) opposes 'modernity' to the powers of old centuries. Modernity here "signifies a culture of innovation, a rational ethos challenging traditions and rituals in the name of critical thought, empirical knowledge and humanism" (Swingewood 1998, 138–39). Kwark draws on an equally venerable alternative perspective, which suggests that the archaic is used in the construction of modernity.

But each contributor does deal *indirectly* with one of the empirical attributes of modernity. For example, in chapter 4, Garner's neoeconomic inclination leads him innovatively to compare the costs of older traditional practices to modern forms of education. He concludes that in the current South African context older traditional practices are financially more expensive to maintain.

Discussions of the nature of modernity tend to either ignore or reject links between modernity and modernization, which I believe is shortsighted. A similar problem arises with definitions of modernism and modernization, which may be the consequence of a rejection of holism in social theory. Subsequently, modernism is viewed from an aesthetic perspective, while modernization is viewed as a structural societal process.

I detect an implicit link between modernity and modernization that should be made explicit. *Modernity*, the condition of being modern, is surely an *outcome* of processes of *modernization* and implies a reflexive awareness of this condition. In similar fashion, globality—a feature of the world system—should be viewed as the outcome of processes of globalization. Swingewood (1998, 137) notes that modernity "is not merely about ideas but embraces intellectual, political and social forms linked historically with capitalist modernisation." Yet modernity—"a process of cultural differentiation"—is distinct from the modernizing infrastructure of capitalism (137). The exploration of the linkages between modernity and modernization is therefore inherently somewhat problematic, as Swingewood points out.

An issue not raised so far is the violence with which processes of modernization were often enforced on others. Scholarship outside of world-economy writings tends to ignore the dimensions of violence and inherent differences in power that effected modernization. Modernization included rapacious extractions of raw material by labor that was coerced to varying extents. Simultaneously, modernization proceeded from—and contributed to—unequal distributions of power in the world system.

THE STRUCTURE OF THIS VOLUME

Our book is structured to provide insights into methodologies for those who desire to conduct primary or secondary research on South African AICs. Extended case studies demonstrate how these methods were put into practice. Contributors engage previous researchers and move beyond them in the light of firsthand empirical research and secondary literature studies.

The book advances existing scholarship by presenting new data and fresh perspectives on AICs. The various contributors mount specific challenges to existing data and theories. For example, the empirical work carried out in 1997 by Robert Garner apparently contradicts findings that associate low educational levels with membership in certain types of AICs. Garner also demonstrates that retention of traditional practices among non-AIC church members in his sample is higher than previously reported.

None of the existing books on AICs has yet retrospectively synthesised and challenged preceding conceptualizations as we intend to do. Nor has any book—yet—provided detailed descriptions of exactly how the research was conducted. Our book contains explicit outlines of three research methods, and demonstrates, through three extended case studies at four different analytical levels, the results that can be obtained. Our emphasis on explicit research strategies means that while we target potential and existing researchers in this field, scholars from other fields will also benefit. Our book not only represents an aid to teachers of research methodology but also to those who study religion. In addition, the case studies by themselves will be attractive to lecturers and students who may not intend to do fieldwork themselves.

The contributors to this volume are researchers from France, Britain, and South Africa—each of whom spent several years since 1994 to study some aspect of AICs in South Africa. As befits an anthology, the different contributions represent varying and contending lines of argumentation, rather than homogeneous conclusions. This is clear from their contrasting conclusions about the relation of AICs to modernity. In chapters 5 and 6, Kwark argues that AICs represent a means of engaging modernity—as I do in chapter 8. Garner, like Kiernan in chapter 2, maintains in chapter 4 that different AICs exhibit a range of responses to modernity. But Garner proceeds beyond Kiernan in distinguishing between Zionist churches that exhibit little integration, adaptation, or conscious resistance to modernity, and Apostolics, which do.

TOWARDS RESOLVING THE MODERNITY-TRADITION DILEMMA

Despite their diverging conclusions, the contributors imply three possible avenues of escape from the modernity-tradition dilemma.

One avenue would be to allow that differing types of AICs exhibit contrasting stances towards modernity. Some could be more open to it, others more closed. Future research should examine why this is so, using the internal characteristics of AICs as well as their location in a country increasingly drawn into economic globalization. South Africa's incorporation into the world system reproduces core and peripheries inside the country as much as it does across the globe. For these reasons, mixtures of openness and closure to modernity are to be expected, and researchers should be encouraged to explore the empirical dimensions of both attitudes.

A second avenue would be to view the data by using hybridity as analytical lens. From this perspective, AICs represent both the preservation of selected traditional practices alongside a more rationalised urbanism within the same individual or group. The extent to which AICs emphasise one or the other of these intertwined dimensions determines the kind and shape of the raft with which they navigate the socioeconomic flows produced by a modernizing environment.

Finally, the third avenue is to view the emergence of the AICs against the backdrop of the global system. Then the modernity-tradition debate can be evaluated against the contributions that AICs make to the antisystemic movement. This approach can also be used to find empirical evidence to support or contradict Roland Robertson's proposal that globalization simultaneously spurs on greater homogeneity *and* heterogeneity. Empirical data can also help to outline the difficulties or advantages of Robertson's idea.

Situating AICs within a discussion of hybridity in the context of globalization within a world system will allow scholars to pay proper attention to power relations. In addition, globalization can be viewed as operating along two contradictory flows that occur simultaneously. Accordingly, under certain historical and structural conditions, trends towards a hybrid social formation in which cultural homogeneity feature more strongly occur alongside a weaker movement towards heterogeneity.

Similarly, Hall (1992, 304) suggests that alongside the tendency towards cultural homogenization there is a new articulation between the global and the local, which produces new global and new local identifications. The uneven and unequal forces of globalization bring about a greater proliferation of identity choices at the centre of the world system than at its peripheries (305). For example, in choices of cuisine, you would find more variety in New York or London "than in Calcutta or Delhi." He notes that globalization "is very unevenly distributed around the globe, between regions and between different strata of the population *within* regions." Such uneven and unequal dynamics means that

> global capitalism has in reality been about Westernization—the export of Western commodities, values, priorities, ways of life. In a process of unequal cultural encounter, "foreign" populations have been compelled to be the subjects and subalterns of Western empire, while, no less significantly, the west has come face to face with the "alien" and "exotic" culture of its "Other." (Robins 1991, 25, quoted in Hall 1992, 305)

Western societies themselves are being affected by the accumulated residue of non-Western values and social practices, partly because of the coercive globalization of Western institutions (McGrew 1992, 78). Perhaps this is due to the interconnectedness between material and nonmaterial forms of culture; objects cannot be moved across borders without transporting some associated ideas. But a prominent role is also played by the vast forced and unforced migration of peoples that defined the latter part of the twentieth century—sometimes as the result of global accumulation. "The movements of Western styles, images, commodities, and consumer identities outwards has been matched by a momentous movement of peoples from the peripheries to the centre" (Hall 1992, 306). Migrations have occurred to the United States from Latin America, the Caribbean, Southeast Asia, and the Far East; and into Europe from the Middle East, Africa, West Indies, Surinam, and Southeast Asia (307).

But hybridity does not just affect local forms of identification, but also affects global formations. Some commentators note that a world civilization is emerging as a result of "a dynamic form of global 'syncretization'" (McGrew 1992, 78, quoting Perlmutter 1991, 911). John Boli, John Meyer, and other world-polity theorists have reached a similar conclusion.

Hall concludes that globalization allows new forms of identification to emerge, which represent neither an embrace of homogenization (assimilationism) nor a return to former roots (nationalism; fundamentalism). Instead, they are "poised *in transition*," a position that draws "on different cultural traditions at the same time" (Hall 1992, 310). Tradition needs not be contrasted only with modernity, but also with what Hall calls *translation*—or, cultures of hybridity:

> This describes those identity formations. . . . which are composed of peoples who have been *dispersed* forever from their homelands. Such people retain strong links with their places of origin and their traditions, but they are without the illusion of a return to the past. They are obliged to come to terms with the new cultures they inhabit, without simply assimilating to them and losing their identities completely. . .they are irrevocably the product of several interlocking histories and cultures. (Hall 1992, 310)

Such cultures of hybridity "are one of the distinctly novel types of identity produced in the era of late-modernity, and there are more and more examples of them to be discovered" (Hall 1992, 310). Hall limits his discussion to people of the new postcolonial diasporas, for instance, British Muslims—such as Salman Rushdie—who are secular *and* Islamic in cultural orientation. While hybridity "is a powerful creative source" that allows displaced people to adjust to late-modernity, it also has a shadow side. At the subjective level, hybridity could mean varying degrees of uncertainty, or even physical opposition, as Rushdie's case reveals (310).

Research on AICs demonstrates that the continuing integration of the world system through economic and cultural globalization causes hybrid forms of identification to emerge *within* national boundaries. Hybridity is not just a feature of permanently dispersed immigrant communities. Globalization creates the material conditions against which agents can construct hybridity as a means of defence—and offence, as the formation of an anticorporate globalization movement shows. In the latter case, the development of hybrid identifications enables activists to engage in transnational action anywhere on behalf of others with whom they identify. Hybridity becomes a cultural resource that enables an antisystemic movement to expand beyond national concerns.

In retrospect, Sundkler's image of a bridge proves more valuable than at first glance, although in a different way than he originally intended. A bridge joins two apparently distinct points between which it allows two-way traffic. At closer inspection, the banks on which the ends of the bridge rest belong to the same river. Instead of being a bridge *back* to tradition, which implies a flight from modernity, AICs provide a way of linking backwards and forwards at the same time. AICs are bridges that allow modernity to be represented in older cultural forms, while cloaking older forms of tradition in newer guises. AICs, as Kwark argues, represent a strategy for constructing a legitimising tradition that combines older and newer elements.

REFERENCES

Allen, John, P. Braham, and P. Lewis, eds. 1992. *Social and cultural forms of modernity*. Cambridge: Polity Press.

Bocock, Robert, and K. Thompson, eds. 1992. *Political and economic forms of modernity*. Cambridge: Polity Press.

Daneel, Marthinus L. 1987. *Quest for belonging: Introduction to a study of African Independent Churches*. Mambo Occasional Papers—Missio-Pastoral series No. 17. Gweru: Mambo Press.

Giddens, Anthony 1991. *The Consequences of Modernity*. Stanford: Stanford University Press.

Hall, Stuart, and B. Gieben, eds. 1992. *Formations of modernity*. Cambridge: Polity Press.

Hall, Stuart, David Held, and Andrew McGrew, eds. 1992. The question of cultural identity. In *Modernity and its futures*, 274–316. Cambridge: Polity Press.

______. 1992. The Question of Cultural Identity. In *Modernity and its futures*, ed. Hall, Stuart, David Held and Andrew McGrew, 274–316. Cambridge: Polity Press.

Held, David. 1992. Liberalism, Marxism, and democracy. In *Modernity and its futures*, ed. S. Hall, D. Held, and A. McGrew, 13–42. Cambridge: Polity Press.

McGrew, Andrew. 1992. A global society? In *Modernity and its futures*, ed. S. Hall, D. Held, and A. McGrew, 62–102. Cambridge: Polity Press.

Oosthuizen, G. C. 1987. The AICs and the modernisation process. *Africana Marburgensia* XX (1):59–81 and XX (2):5–17.

Oosthuizen, G. C., ed. 1986. *Religion alive: Studies in the new movements and indigenous churches in South Africa*. Johannesburg: Hodder and Stoughton.

Oosthuizen, G. C. and C. D. Clark. 1994. *The development activities of African Independent Churches*. Unpublished paper, University of Durban-Westville, Durban.

Perlmutter, H. V. 1991. On the rocky road to the first global civilization. *Human Relations* 44 (9): 902–906.

Robins, Kevin. 1991. Tradition and translation: National culture in its global context. In *Enterprise and heritage: Crosscurrents of national culture,* ed. J. Corner and S. Harvey, 21–44. London: Routledge.

Sundkler, Bengt G. M. 1948. *Bantu prophets in South Africa*. London: Oxford University Press.

______. 1961. *Bantu prophets in South Africa.* 2d ed. London: Oxford University Press.

Swingewood, Alan. 1998. *Cultural theory and the problem of modernity.* Houndmills: MacMillan Press.

PART I

A CONCEPTUAL PERSPECTIVE

1

Concepts and Theories in the Study of African Independent Churches

Dawid Venter

INTRODUCTION

The contributors to this book report on recent social science research that they conducted on African Independent Churches (AICs) in South Africa. These churches are more like a social movement than a single organized denomination. Many disparate groupings are usually treated as belonging together under the AIC umbrella. Due mostly to their desire not to be controlled by whites, that is, to be "independent," AICs have been a subject of scrutiny by South African state authorities at various times since the early part of the twentieth century. Subsequently, numerous South Africans and foreign individuals have studied them, so that by 1995, at least twenty-six institutions worldwide housed historical documents relating to AICs (Pretorius 1995).

All this activity may create the impression that a consensus has emerged about which terms and theories are most appropriate for studying AICs. And researchers do generally agree on when the movement first appeared (1884), who the central figures are (e.g., the Lekganyanes, the Shembes), which groupings can be included under the umbrella term and how they can be typified (as Ethiopian, Zionist, or Apostolic) (lists were compiled, for example, by Bengt Sundkler, Allan Anderson, and Martin West). There is also consensus about the abbreviation AIC. As for theory, Pato (1990, 24) notes that the study of AICs remains confined to description and classification rather than theorization and interpretation, despite being urged onwards by Glenda Kruss (1985) and David Chidester (1988).

But there is little agreement on whether the term indigenous, independent, initiated, or instituted best describes the movement as a whole. Indeed, Stephen Hayes (1992) contends that AICs seem to be regarded as part of the same group merely because they were so defined—first by South African colonial authorities, and later by scholars. Differences between some AICs are so great that the only factor they appear to share *is* the assumption by outsiders that they somehow belong to the same phenomenon (Hayes 2000). Hayes's comments echo those of Gideon Khabela regarding similarities between AICs of structure, worship, and organization (Khabela 1989, 30, who also quotes from Itumaleng Mosala and Buti Thlahale 1986 in this regard). Researchers have not reached consensus on which factors contributed most to the emergence of the movement. Even the threefold typification for AICs—Ethiopian, Apostolic, Zionist—is a bone of contention, as some scholars maintain that a fourth type should be recognized, namely Messianic (or Prophetic) AICs. Differences have been noted between congregations within the same type (such as Zionists), or within one church of that type (such as the Zion Christian Church) (Fay 1996).

The roots of these conceptual difficulties are located partly in the sheer number of small groups that make up the movement as a whole, perhaps more than six thousand. Those that share two or more Ethiopian-Apostolic-Zionist features make a clear-cut allocation of a particular church to one particular type tenuous. Hayes (1992) points out that some characteristics ascribed to Zionists are not only found among Ethiopians, but also among Methodists, Presbyterians, and Congregationalists. The major difference is that unlike the latter denominations, Ethiopians, Zionists, and Apostolics share a desire for independent control of their own religious structures. But independence, again, is a similarity that AICs and certain South African Pentecostal and Charismatic churches hold in common. Other complicating factors include the differing theoretical starting points and agendas of researchers, as well as the scarcity of reflexive contributions from within the movement itself, for whatever reason. Failure to resolve these difficulties will continue to delay the development of a substantive theory that could address the nature, form, and functions of AICs.

This chapter reviews the major conceptual and theoretical debates about the field of study, in order to alert readers to agreements and unresolved tensions among researchers—including those who contribute to this volume. Hopefully such an undertaking will help scholars to increase the reflexivity of their own reading and research on AICs. The first section provides an overview of central concepts, including generally used descriptive terms and typologies, followed by an empirical snapshot of AICs, including attention to socioeconomic indicators such as income and education. A third section divides the typical arguments for the emergence and rapid growth of AICs according to how they fit into two major social scientific theories, namely functionalism and materialism.

CENTRAL CONCEPTS IN THE STUDY OF AICs

In this section, I review the major terms used to distinguish AICs from other religious formations, and those used to group them into different broad types. The first subsection retraces the arguments about whether AICs should be classified as indigenous, independent, or initiated churches. In particular, I evaluate alternative proposals for resolving the issue, such as those put forward by Stephen Hayes (1992) and Robert Garner (1998). Next, I overview the literature on whether three or four types of AICs exist, focusing particularly on suggestions by Allan Anderson (1992), as well as Hennie Pretorius and Lizo Jafta (1997).

Indigenous, Independent, or Initiated Churches?

African *Independent* Churches in South Africa have also been described as African *Indigenous* Churches, and—most recently—African *Initiated* or *Instituted* Churches (see West 1975, Daneel 1987, Lamola 1988, Khabela 1989, Anderson 1995, Masuku 1996, and Pretorius and Jafta 1997 for more substantive discussions). By the time Sundkler produced his seminal work in 1948, the South African authorities had officially defined the religious movement as "Native Separatist Churches." But as "Native" had become pejorative for black South Africans, Sundkler amended this title to "Bantu Independent Churches" (Sundkler 1961, 18, Hayes 1992). Sundkler (1961), Turner (1979), and Daneel (1987) refer to "Independent" churches, as does Kiernan in chapter 2 of this book. The differences between these terms correspond to the particular perspective and emphasis that individual researchers bring to the debate on the nature, structure, beliefs, and rituals of the AICs.

Anderson (1997) explains that historical shifts in self-perception led some AICs (and researchers) to abandon some designations for others, and indicates which one he prefers:

> Later, many African churches founded by European missionaries saw themselves as "independent", and the term "African indigenous churches" was proposed. This term also became inadequate with the movement on the part of many mission-founded churches towards inculturation and to be seen as "indigenous". "African initiated churches" and "African instituted churches" are terms which avoid these difficulties by simply indicating that these many different kinds of churches were initiated by Africans, and not by Europeans.

In the absence of definitive resolutions as to what constitutes the correct term, researchers tend to use *indigenous, independent,* and *initiated* more or less interchangeably. In 1995, Pretorius wrote of *independent* churches, which he had exchanged for *initiated* by 1997 (with Jafta). Similarly, the Council of African *Independent* Churches, an AIC-founded umbrella organization established in South Africa in 1965, was later renamed the Council of African *Instituted* Churches (italics added). In addition, scholars tend to use the same threefold typology (Ethiopians, Zionists, Apostolics) when writing about AICs—even when they attempt to create alternative typologies. This is illustrated in the work of Anderson (1992), as well as of Pretorius and Jafta (1997).

While the uncertainty concerns the accuracy of one particular descriptor above others, Hayes (2000) proposes that we accept them all, understood as follows:

- African ***Independent*** Churches that "originated in Africa, and are not dependent on any religious groups outside Africa for funding, leadership or control."
- African ***Initiated*** Churches that "were started as a result of African initiative in African countries, but may be affiliated to wider bodies that include non-African members."
- African ***Indigenous*** Churches that "have and retain an African ethos, and whose theology has developed a distinctive local flavour."
- African ***Instituted*** Churches "whose establishment and growth have taken place on African soil."

We can evaluate how useful Hayes's definitions as complementary categories are against empirical evidence, using the Zion Christian Church (ZCC). Hayes (2003) indicates that he did not conceive the distinctions as mutually exclusive. The ZCC can serve as an example because it is not only one of the most well-known Zionist churches, but is also accepted as an AIC by all scholars, without exception. Hayes's preference for complementary notions should not prevent us from considering them as mutually exclusive classifying devices for identifying different types of churches in Africa. I will consider this option below when I discuss possible ways to resolve these conceptual tensions.

Engenas Lekganyane (c. 1885–1948), an African, founded the ZCC around 1925, and so the church can be viewed as *independent*, at least. But while certainly *initiated* by an African, the ZCC does not completely fit this category: no broader affiliations with organizations outside Africa exist. At the same time, the ZCC may definitely be classified as an *instituted* type of African church.

But whether we accept the ZCC as *indigenous* is more complicated. What evidence do we accept as indicating an "African ethos," or "a theology with a distinctive local flavour"? Evidence that seems contradictory makes allocation particularly difficult. Anderson (1992) for example, found that most ZCC respondents (73%) in his 1990–91survey had abandoned ancestral cult (slaughtering animals to honour ancestors) and did not consult diviners (85%). Yet 58% of ZCC members did report adherence to ancestral beliefs (i.e., accepted that ancestors do exist). Anderson concluded that "for most ZCC people the ancestors still play an important role" (1992, 104). So most ZCC members abandon some practices—but not others; while just over half still hold beliefs that could be regarded as African and "traditional." Does this make the ZCC *indigenous* or not? Similar questions can be raised about the hereditary practice associated with the successive Lekganyanes who come to occupy the position of ZCC leader. Sole leadership merges the traditional roles associated with the diviner, healer, and tribal leader.

Does the annual Easter pilgrimage by ZCC faithful to Moria, their sacred site, constitute "a theology with a distinctive local flavour" or not? Pilgrimage is, after all, not by any means a local phenomenon unique to the ZCC. Does the belief in the healing qualities of the ZCC brand of tea constitute a local theological flavour or not?

From this perspective, local responses to pressures towards a global identity can take many forms, and Africans can be both Western and African; both Christian and traditional. Through contact with Christianity and in pluralist township situations, Africans can adjust their cult and beliefs in several ways, ranging from strong beliefs and practise of cult to weak beliefs and little or no cult, or altered beliefs in which Christian ideas influence traditional ones. Religious identity involves both cult and beliefs, and the pluralist urban situation leads to changes in one or the other.

Despite their potential, Hayes's suggestions would need to be carefully operationalized and tested for reliability against empirical evidence. At present, the proposals do not seem to move us far enough beyond present conceptual difficulties, partly because they overlap too much.

An inherent problem in the notion of *African* Independent Churches is what constitutes "African." Researchers assume that "African" means "*black* African," and so they exclude churches founded by individuals born in Africa from, for example, European or Asian descent. This implicit racial understanding carries more weight in identifying AICs than interpreting "African" to mean "on the African continent" (compare Hayes 1992). As far as I am aware, none of the published research on AICs deals with religious movements initiated in Africa by individuals born in Africa but of European, Indian, or even mixed-race descent.

The difficulty in operationalizing AIC as a concept demonstrates the practical problems that researchers face when they have to determine whether a particular local assembly of African believers is, in fact, an

AIC. For example, Nicholas Bhengu (1909–85) founded what became the Assemblies of God movement in South Africa. Bhengu's congregations could be classified as Ethiopian-type AICs, or under the broader term 'African Pentecostal churches' (see fuller discussion of Anderson's use of the term on p.19). The difficulty in placing Bhengu's Assemblies is understandable. Bhengu had founded more than fifty autonomous congregations by 1959 (Millard 1999), and helped to indigenize the movement (Anderson 2001), yet he remained affiliated to the Assemblies of God, a Pentecostal denomination.

As a result of the problems that beset the present classification system, Garner (1998) prefers to emphasise two of the criteria generally used to classify AICs. The first is place of *origin*—"founded by an overseas mission or by indigenous South Africans?" The second criterion is *charisma*—"emphasis on Charismatic experience of faith, or on a routinized discourse featuring set ritual and liturgy?" To this, I would add *historical period*—founded between 1892 and the 1920s (Ethiopians), between 1910 and the 1940s (Zionists in the form of Zion City churches), or afterwards (Zionist-Apostolics)? But while the emergence of different types of African churches does correspond roughly to specific eras, as demonstrated by Glenda Kruss (1985) and Pretorius and Jafta (1997), there is also some overlap. Similarly, Garner's suggestions are by no means unproblematic; his term *indigenous,* for instance, contains the same conceptual (and political) difficulties as defining the middle initial of the AICs does.

The long-standing debate about the correct term has not been resolved, despite general agreement about using the abbreviation "AIC." National survey data (not always a reliable indicator of accurate classifications) still refers to "African *Independent* Churches"; for instance, in the Human Sciences Research Council's 1993 *Omnibus Survey*.

The uncertainty about how to typify this social and religious movement extends to debates about the number of categories that make up the often repeated Ethiopian-Apostolic-Zionist typology, a subject we return to now.

Three or Four Types of AICs?

South African AICs are commonly grouped into Ethiopian, Apostolic, and Zionist types of churches. Bengt Sundkler (1961, 53) was the first to distinguish between so-called Ethiopian and Zionist AICs. Daneel (1971, 285) found a similar distinction between "Spirit-type" and "Ethiopian-type" churches in Zimbabwe (compare Turner 1979). Each type can be subdivided into smaller categories, as illustrated in table 1.1.

For instance, Pretorius and Jafta (1997, 211) recognize Zion City and Zion-Apostolic as subtypes of Zionist churches. The Zionist typology derives from the titles that the churches use to refer to themselves, which tend to have Zionist, Apostolic, Ethiopian, or some combined name. The Zion Apostolic Faith Mission of Edward Motaung, and the Zion Apostolic Church of Elias Mahlangu, provide examples of Zionist-Apostolic combinations. While not all Zionist or Apostolic churches identify themselves by these titles, most share Pentecostal roots and styles (Anderson 1995, 283). Similarly, the Tembu Church (founded in 1882) was the earliest church that can be classified as Ethiopian, yet obviously did not have "Ethiopian" in its title. The first to call itself such was the "Ethiopian Church" (*Ibandla lase Tiyopia* in Zulu), founded in 1892 (Pretorius and Jafta 1997, 214).

The Ethiopian, Apostolic, and Zionist distinctions point to ontological, historical and doctrinal differences between the types, as follows:

- Ethiopian churches were the first to emerge in South Africa towards the end of the nineteenth century, and exhibited antiracist and Pan-Africanist tendencies,[1] while retaining the organization and doctrines of the white-dominated Protestant churches from whom they broke away—but now under black (African) leadership, as part of the Ethiopian emphasis on exclusive black institutions. Present-day examples in South Africa include the Ethiopian Order and the American Methodist Episcopalian Church.

- Zionist churches emerged during the early twentieth century, are Pentecostal in worship, emphasise healing and immersive baptism, and wear distinctive uniforms. Present-day examples include the Zion Christian Church.

- (Zionist-)Apostolic churches lay claim to Apostolic succession, in which the authority of leaders is seen to derive directly from Christ's twelve apostles. Women tend to play a greater role, often as prophetess, and some have even founded churches—for example, Christina Nku of the St. John's Apostolic Faith Mission. (For discussion, see Sundkler 1961, 38–59; West 1975, 190; Pretorius and Jafta 1997, and Garner 1998).

The Ethiopian-Apostolic-Zionist distinction is also not without difficulties, among both AICs and those who study them. For example, themselves so (Daneel 1987, 39–41). Contrary to Pretorius and Jafta (1997), Khabela (1989, 29) allocates Zion-city types to what others call "Messianic"-type AICs, a designation whose accuracy he doubts. Anderson (1997) concluded that Sundkler's Ethiopian-Zionist duality "now seems inadequate." By contrast, Pato (1990) finds differences between Zionists and other black Christians, most notably with regard to rituals associated with the dead after burial (e.g., *ukubuyisa*, recognizing the deceased).

As a result, some scholars have advanced alternative typologies and

Table 1.1:

African Independent Churches in Census 1996 and 2001[a]

Church	*Affiliates*	*% of Total Population*	*% of All Christians*
ZCC	3,854,898	9.5	12.8
	(4,971,931)	(11.09)	(13.91)
Other Zionist	2,136,728	5.3	7.1
	(1,887,147)	(4.21)	(5.28)
Engenas ZCC	12,905		
Nazaretha	454,765	1.1	1.5
	(248,825)	(0.56)	(0.70)
Other Nazarite	22,526	0.1	0.1
Other Apostolic	3,077 789	7.6	10.2
	(5,627,320)	(12.56)	(12.56)
St. John Apostolic	217,601	0.5	0.7
Other African Apostolic	12,702		
Ethiopian	474,258	1.2	1.6
	(1,150,102)	(2.57)	(2.57)
Ethnic	35,529	0.1	0.1
Other AIC	229,037	0.6	0.8
	(656,644)	(1.47)	(1.84)
Other Baptist	139,777	0.3	0.5
Total AICs	10,668,515	26.3	35.3
	(14,541,969)	(32.45)	(36.84)
Total South African Christians	30,058,742		74.1
	(35,750,641)		(79.77)
Total South African Population	40,583,639	100	
	(44,819,774)		

Sources: Hendriks 1999, 64; StatsSA 2004.

Note: a. The current state of Census 2001 data does not permit as detailed a breakdown, and are presented here in parentheses.for comparison.

categories, while others have merged the terms Zionist and Apostolic.

For Daneel (1987) the alternative is "spirit-type" churches, under which he collects both Apostolics and Zionists. Kruss (1985) suggests that Zionist-Apostolic refers to a specific type of AIC, as I do in chapters 7 and 8. Her comment implies that she would not consider conflating the two designations. Garner demonstrates in chapter 4 that Apostolics and Zionists can be treated as distinct, as both overlap and differences between them remain.

Allan Anderson has promoted "African pentecostal churches" and "African pentecostal-type churches" as an alternative to the Apostolic-Zionist typology. By "African pentecostal churches," he means "Christian churches in Africa which emphasise . . . the working of the Holy Spirit." He includes "African pentecostal churches of 'Northern' origin," as well as Zionists and Apostolics under the term (Anderson 1995, 283). But for Zionists and Apostolics, Anderson (284) introduces the term "African pentecostal-type churches." He, in fact, subdivides "African pentecostal churches" into Pentecostal Mission Churches, Independent Churches, and Pentecostal-type (indigenous) churches.

Anderson suggests that *independent* and *indigenous* churches are similar in that they are controlled by Africans—and so they differ from what he calls "Mission Churches"—churches historically initiated by white missionaries. Pentecostal churches and Ethiopian-type churches share organisation, culture, and style of worship with their respective "Mission Churches." But Pentecostal-types include aspects of "African culture,"[2] as African Pentecostalism has translated African religious expressions into Christian worship (Anderson 1992, 74). Anderson's point is that AICs in Southern Africa—"including the so-called 'Zionist' and 'Apostolic' churches"—are related to the global Pentecostal movement (Anderson 1995, 284). In this he is right, as modern Pentecostalism had its roots in a black church on Azusa Street, Los Angeles in the United States. Paradoxically, South African Pentecostalism had white roots: locally, in the person of Dutch Reformed Church missionary Pieter L. le Roux (who later founded the Apostolic Faith Mission); and internationally, in John Alexander Dowie's Christian Catholic Church at Zion City, Illinois, rooted in the Holiness movement. Le Roux had read Dowie's *Leaves of Healing* pamphlets, which emphasised divine healing and baptism by immersion. After correspondence with Dowie's church, Daniel Bryant was sent to South Africa to act as official overseer from 1904 to 1908.

Ultimately, Anderson's alternative typology multiplies terms that are semantically too closely related. The similarity between "African Pentecostal Churches" (all African pentecostal churches) and "African-pentecostal-type churches" (Zionists, Apostolics, and other Pentecostal AICs) can be confusing. Anderson (1995) is sensitive to the charge that his conceptual strategy "colonizes" Zionist-Apostolics on behalf of Pentecostals. He rejects the argument that he overstresses similarities in a way that suppresses discontinuities and differences between Pentecostals and Zionist-Apostolics. Yet critics could argue that "African-pentecostal-type" appears to subsume differences between Zionist and Apostolic churches. Anderson recognizes with Tinyiko Maluleke (1994) that continuity between AICs and mission churches deserves as much attention as discontinuity. He attempts to resolve the difficulties inherent in Sundkler's terms by linking Zionists and Apostolics to a wider faith tradition, thus emphasising continuity with Pentecostalism. Yet his strategy of excluding Ethiopians and including non-AIC churches that are independent makes defining "AIC" even more problematic. The question of how to advance beyond Sundkler's distinctions—apart from acknowledging a debt to Pentecostalism—remains unanswered by the "African-pentecostal-type" formulation. This assessment does not detract from the overall contribution that Anderson's commendable empirical work, ongoing theorization, attention to insider perspectives, and sensitivity to sociohistorical context make to the study of AICs.

Some scholars argue that another category, 'Messianic' AICs, should be added to the Ethiopian-Apostolic-Zionist distinction. Kiernan, in chapter 2 of this volume, like Garner in chapter 4, concurs. They believe that 'Messianic' would best describe churches like those of the Shembes (the Nazarites) and Lekganyanes (the Zion Christian Church), which differ in some ways from other AICs. Anderson (1993) includes Frederick Modise's International Pentecost Holiness Church in Zuurbekom, near Johannesburg, under the Messianic label. Elsewhere, Garner (1998) noted that Messianic churches show "more routinized worship and concentrated leadership than the typically diffuse Zionist churches, but with an emphasis on healing and dance that separates them from the Ethiopian category."

The Ethiopian-Apostolic-Zionist distinctions that are applied in Southern Africa prove difficult to maintain in comparisons of similar movements across Africa. For this reason, some scholars prefer to subsume AICs under "new [African] religious movements," as Benetta Jules-Rosette (1989) does, while others distinguish between independent and spirit churches. Jules-Rosette estimates that more than three hundred such new forms of African religion have emerged since the turn of the century. New African Religious Movements can also be subdivided into three more generic terms: (a) indigenous or independent movements, characterised by the formation of own doctrines (the equivalent of Zionists); (b) separatist movements, which break away from existing religious structures (the equivalent of Ethiopians); and (c) neotraditional movements, which attempt to revive older traditional religious practices (Jules-Rosette 1989, 148). Southern African scholars seem to use AICs in a way that combines the first two of Jules-Rosette's types.

POSSIBLE WAYS TO RESOLVE CONCEPTUAL TENSIONS

Below I first examine some possible ways to resolve the difficulties in classifying AICs (as *Independent, Indigenous, Initiated,* or *Instituted*) and typifying them (as Ethiopian, Zionist, or Apostolic). That the conceptual tensions can still potentially be resolved implies that neither classifications nor typologies need be abandoned completely, but rather should be treated more rigorously.

Classifying AICs

The first possible response to the review of conceptual pitfalls is a conservationist defence of the validity of "African Independent Churches." From this position, the conceptual confusion surrounding the term is negligible and ameliorated by the long history of research on AICs. Scholars know what they are studying, even if they disagree on what it should be called. In addition, members of AICs have used the very term to describe themselves. AIC leaders have referred to *Independent* Churches; as Paul Makhubu did in the title for his 1988 book, and as Thompson Mpongwana Adonis, archbishop of the Reformed Church of Christ in the Transkei reportedly did in a 1999 interview (Isaac 1999). Similar conservationist defences could be mounted for variants such as *Instituted.*

A second possible response is a radical revisionist rejection of "African Independent Churches" as an empty term that fails to correspond to any actual social phenomenon. Such a revisionist stance could continue along either a postmodernist or a more ethnographic track, both proceeding from the perception that Western outsiders imposed the term on a variety of "others." The lack of conceptual consensus among researchers, added to the diversity of those who were unwillingly or unknowingly grouped together in this way, would serve to substantiate the argument. The integrity of scholarship on the topic over the last five and a half decades could be dissolved as based on an unsupportable premise. Assumptions and findings could be discarded or radically revised. The rejection of *AIC* would imply that groupings previously regarded as part of the same broad religious formation can now be treated as unrelated. By extension, similar responses may arise in relation to the Ethiopian-Zionist-Apostolic-Messianic typification, which could be discarded or revised in line with self-descriptions supplied by insiders.

Alternative collective terms would depend for ultimate validity on correspondence with insider descriptions of who they are and how they relate to one another. For example, "churches of the Spirit" (from the Xhosa *iinkonzo zoMoya,* also understood as "spiritual churches") is one such self-ascription, as Pretorius and Jafta (1997, 211) remind us. The overall effect of a revisionist position in relation to typology would be an atomistic approach to research. Isabel Mukonyora (2001) demonstrates this tendency when she rejects the broader "Zionist" term as "misleading," a conclusion West (1975, 17) foresaw. In her work on the Masowe Apostles of Zimbabwes, she reintroduces "their own vernacular name [Wilderness Church] to articulate the main ideas of the movement" (Mukonyora 2001).

A third possibility is a moderate empiricist response that retains the term *AIC,* but insists that it be operationalized and tested against empirical evidence—so combining the intentions of the conservationist and revisionist positions. The empiricist stance would be moderate in the sense that what is rejected is not metaphysical conceptualization itself. Instead, definitions of AICs are questioned, which is unsatisfactory because researchers do not rigorously test, apply, and adjust them against evidence arising from empirical research. Inattention to the implications of cases that do not fit the term adds to the present confusion. The empiricist project may lead to the revisionist position described above. In keeping with a theme in this book, scholars could find that the pluralistic logic of modernity (as promoted by colonial and apartheid regimes) have so impacted the religious field in South Africa as to render *AIC* inapplicable to the present. While it may accurately have described a nascent movement at a particular time, the term can no longer accurately describe the current proliferation of religious forms among Africans.

But a moderate empiricist response could lead to alternative outcomes, as Hayes's proposals imply at least three other possible approaches, which I sketch below in broad strokes. While all of them retain certain features of Hayes's definitions, the last two completely disregard his original intentions. I find Hayes's suggestions attractive as they assume that social reality is best described (or triangulated, in research methodology terms) from a plurality of viewpoints. I show that these possibilities can be taken as three steps through which a new understanding of how to apply *AIC* can be synthesized.

First, *AIC* can potentially be operationalized in terms of Hayes's definitions by revising them so that each one identifies a particular AIC denomination. Notions that currently overlap in Hayes's definitions would be eliminated, and then modified, to yield a single, mutually exclusive indicator for each one. *Independent* could refer solely to churches that are independent from religious groups outside Africa; *Initiated* to churches founded by Africans; *Indigenous* to churches with distinctive African beliefs and practices; and *Instituted* to churches located in Africa. Researchers could test these indicators during fieldwork or data analysis for their facility in distinguishing between denominations.

Second, the modified *Independent-Indigenous-Initiated-Instituted* designations can be applied as a list of minimum indicators that *together* define an AIC. All AICs value independence; and—depending on one's definition of *indigenous*—all exhibit some African characteristics, too.

Following Hayes (2000) and Makhubu (1988), a minimum definition can be constructed as follows: An African Independent Church (AIC) is a grouping established for religious purposes associated with Christianity in Africa by Africans for Africans, which remains independent of groupings outside Africa for funding, leadership or control—even should it affiliate to bodies that include non-Africans. AICs may exhibit distinctively African social structures, symbols, rituals, practices, beliefs, and liturgy.

Note that the minima comprise African *initiative* and *independence* from non-African control. *Indigenousness* is an optional indicator. *Instituted* can be omitted, as it is assumed in the designation *African* Independent Churches; or it can be retained if all terms are taken to refer to only one descriptor.

Researchers would still have to operationalize the major elements of the minimum definition, and then test it against a representative sample of empirical evidence from AICs to evaluate robustness. The formulation could then be altered, and the process of testing and adjusting it could continue. Concepts that would need operationalization include *African, church, religious purposes, associated with Christianity, African symbols, African social structures, African rituals, African practices, African theology,* and *African liturgy*. *Independent* is already operationalized by three indicators: "not funded by non-Africans," "not led by non-Africans," and "not controlled by non-Africans," but "led" and "controlled" would need elaboration. Given the research tradition that supports its use, the racial meaning of "African"—"*black* African"—would have to be included as an indicator of what constitutes an African Independent Church.

The minimum definition approach would still require us to decide which designation to use to define the "I" in *AIC*. Hayes's fourfold proposal raises the question whether the *Instituted* or *Initiated* designations are as helpful to researchers as *Indigenous* and *Independent*. As discussed above, *Instituted*—indicating geographic location—is already assumed by the other terms, and so seems less significant. *Instituted* could even be redefined for studying churches founded by African immigrants outside Africa, for example, in Europe or North America.[3] Gerrie ter Haar (2000) calls these churches African International Churches, and suggests that they represent a new type of AIC. *Initiated* (founded by Africans) seems less important than *Independent* (not reliant on non-Africans), as the early history of Zionism demonstrates. A black African did not initiate Zionism, as Kiernan confirms in chapter 2. But, of course, one could argue that since then, all initiatives to establish Zionist churches were taken by Africans.

For example, Daniel Nkonyane continued the work of Le Roux, and is credited with introducing innovations such as the wearing of robes into Zionism. We could ask whether the minimum definition could not subsume *Initiated* under *Independent*. But *Initiated* can mean "initially founded by an African but no longer under African control," or even "initially founded by non-Africans but since then under African control." The importance of independence in both the histories of Ethiopianism and Zionism suggests that it should be more significant than other designations. The issues surrounding *Indigenous* have already been dealt with, and I will not reiterate them here.

If the four variants are arranged in a hierarchy according to their importance in defining *the* characteristic feature and the whole range of AICs, then *Independent* seems logically to emerge at the top.

A third possibility for identifying AICs would be to construct a classifying device as represented in figure 1.1, which retains all four modified designations. While more than one of these descriptors could be present in any church, each would regarded as receiving a different emphasis. The revised *Independent-Indigenous-Initiated-Instituted* designations could be used as orienting points with which to triangulate the Ethiopian-Zionist-Apostolic classifications. In Ethiopian churches, for example, independence seems more prominent, and so could be a primary feature. Wider affiliation to non-African bodies could be a secondary characteristic, and indigenousness a tertiary attribute. While Ethiopian congregations appear not to endorse African cultic practices and beliefs publicly, individual Ethiopian members do retain them to varying degrees—even if only privately (as demonstrated in West 1975; Anderson 1992; and Garner in this volume). Independence here seems more important than indigenousness. Among Zionists, indigenousness may be primary, independence secondary, and wider, non-African affiliation excluded.

TYPIFYING AN AIC

In chapter 3, Garner admirably answers the question about possible indicators that a researcher can use to classify a particular AIC group as Ethiopian, Zionist, Apostolic, or Messianic. He not only provides a good example of how to operationalize the Ethiopian-Zionist-Apostolic types, but also explains why these types continue to be useful for empirical researchers. The caution sounded by Kiernan in chapter 2 needs to be heeded: many AIC congregations exhibit more than one type's characteristic, as Garner's work in chapter 4 confirms. The Ethiopian-Zionist-Apostolic-Messianic typification is well established, but should be treated as having porous membranes rather than rigid walls. The Messianic category seems more problematic, as leaders such as Isaiah

Figure 1.1:

Classifying device for AICs

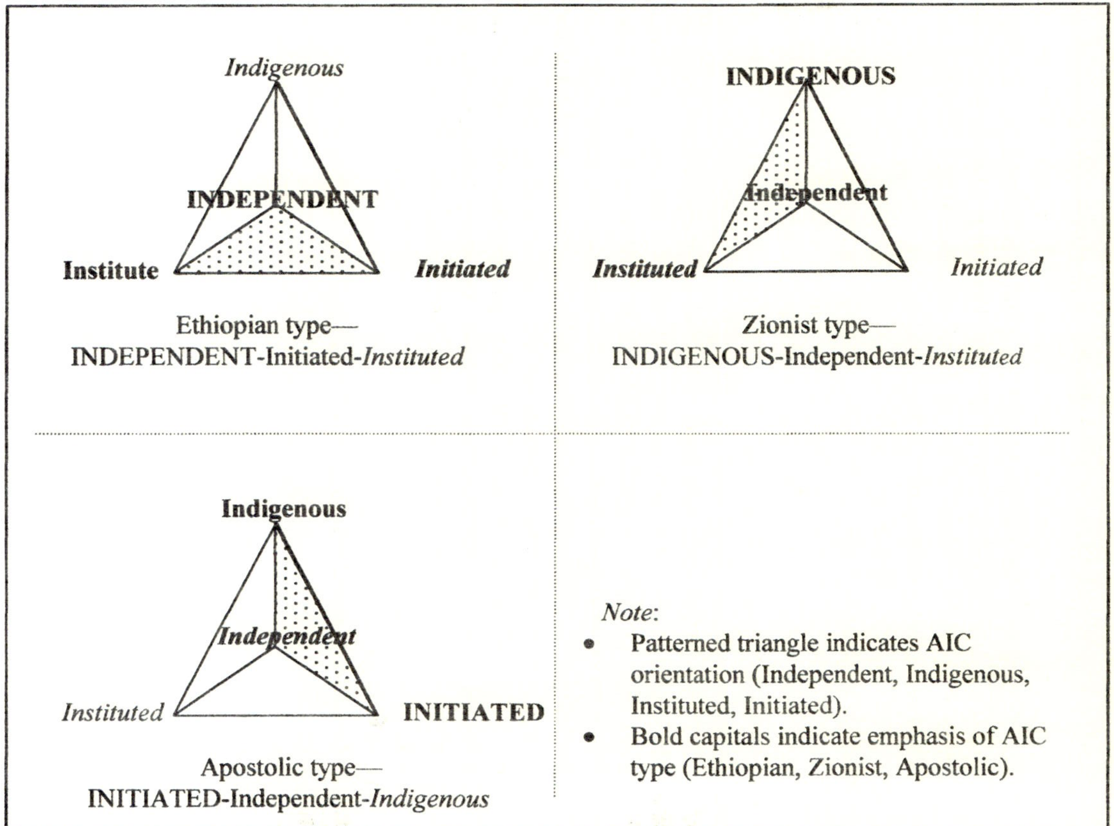

Shembe did not encourage this perception, which followers seem to have attached posthumously (compare Khabela 1989, 29).

EMPIRICAL PROFILES OF AFRICAN INDEPENDENT CHURCHES

AICs are perceived to be among the fastest growing religions in Africa, and form the largest single religious grouping in South Africa. AICs are more numerous in South Africa than anywhere else on the continent (Daneel 1987, 43). South Africa's more than six thousand AIC denominations are found mostly in the central and northern parts,[4] that is, the Free State and former Transvaal areas (Zaaiman 1994, 572). Khabela (1989, 32) claims that by 1989 there were more than nine hundred AICs in Soweto alone. Regrettably, commentators seldom provide the base on which they calculate the number of AIC denominations.

Estimates of AIC affiliation in South Africa rose from 9.6% of all blacks in 1940 to 20% in 1960; to 37%[5] in 1991—perhaps even to 47% (Daneel 1987, 25; Hendriks 1995; Anderson 1995, 287). By 1991 almost one out of every three blacks belonged to the AICs (Chidester 1992, 114; Zaaiman 1994, 570; StatsSA 2004). The 2001 census estimates the number of AIC affiliates to be about 14.54 million, including 37.75% of all black South Africans (StatsSA 2004). This phenomenon is not limited to South Africa alone: by 1989, AIC members comprised about 15% of the Christian population of Sub-Saharan Africa (Jules-Rosette 1989, 149).

Although AICs in West and South Africa are known to draw large numbers of adherents from the historic mission churches, this is not the case for Shona adherents in Zimbabwe, of whom about 60% had never been full members of any other church—although some had attended and received instruction from the mission churches (Daneel 1987, 98–99). Anderson found in a survey conducted between 1990 and 1991 in Soshanguve that between 26% of Pentecostal-type church members and 36% of Ethiopian-type church members had not belonged to any church before joining AICs. By contrast, 35% of Pentecostal-type church members and 39% of Ethiopian-type church members had belonged to a mission church before joining the AICs (Anderson 1992, 77).

There are several reasons for the continued growth of South African AICs. Some attract members because of their acceptance and promotion of traditional beliefs and ways of life, by contrast to the dismissive attitudes towards these matters within the mainline churches (compare West 1975). Numerical growth within the AICs seems linked to urbanisation, which has not yet levelled off in South Africa. AICs appear to function as a bridge between the rural-urban and Western-African continuums. In this sense, the growth of AICs like the Zion Christian

Table 1.2:

Estimated Mean Monthly Income by Selected Religion and Denomination 1993

Religion/Denomination	*Rand per Month*
Judaism	4873.53
Dutch Reformed Church	4253.31
Hervormde Kerk	3425.00
Hinduism	2711.41
Islam	2227.50
Afrikaans Protestant Church	2260.71
Anglican Church	2139.42
Full Gospel Church	2067.16
Methodist Church	1443.55
Presbyterian Church	1390.00
Assemblies of God	1246.55
Traditional African Beliefs	943.75
Ethiopian Independent Churches	897.06
Uniting Reformed Church	820.25
Apostolic Independent Churches	741.30
Zionist Christian Churches	690.45

Source: Human Sciences Research Council Omnibus Survey 1993. Used by permission of the sociology departments of Huguenot College and the University of Pretoria.

Church is related to urbanisation—in direct contrast to the notion that urbanisation contributes to secularization (compare Brown 1992, 47).

Researchers frequently point out that AIC affiliates come from the poorest sectors of society.[6] Of all AIC categories in table 1.2, "Other African independent churches" (i.e., excluding the Zion Christian Church, Ethiopians, and Apostolics) had the lowest income and education levels. Almost 64% of all nominal "other" AIC members belonged to households earning less than R600 per month, while 64.2%

had a "Std. 3 or less" education. An estimated 50.3% of ZCC members were part of households earning less than R600 per month, while 59.7% had Std. 3 or lower qualification (Human Sciences Research Council 1993). Put differently, 11.03% of all South Africans who earn less than R600 per month claimed to belong to the ZCC, as did 12.9% of all South Africans who had Std. 3 or less (Human Sciences Research Council 1993).

Zionists comprise approximately 80% of the AICs, and the Zion Christian Church is the largest Zionist denomination. In the 2001 census, 11.09% of all South Africans claimed to belong to the ZCC (over 4.9 million people; StatsSA, 2001). Sotho-speakers form the largest single language group within the ZCC at 46.4%; similarly, Anderson (1992, 63) notes that in Soshanguve, 51.5% of ZCC members were Northern Sotho. Researchers attribute the growth of the ZCC to several reasons, most similar to those advanced for Pentecostal churches, others peculiar to Africa. The growth of the ZCC seems related to the continued urbanisation of South Africa's black population. Like other Zionist churches, the ZCC appears to facilitate movement along the rural-urban and Western-African continuums. The growth of the ZCC contrasts directly with the notion that urbanisation contributes to secularization (compare Brown 1992, 47).

Obviously, these national figures for personal income are not always reflected in local situations. For instance, in Heidelberg in the Western Cape, the largest percentage of people with incomes below R500 (36.6%) belongs to the Anglican Church (Datadesk 1996). And in Stellenbosch, the largest percentage of people with incomes below R500 (24.9%) belongs to the old Dutch Reformed Mission Church (Datadesk 1996).

AIC affiliates score highly in surveys measuring religious participation as well as religious membership and preference. In the 1995 World Values Study, for instance, 70.3% of Zionists surveyed indicated that they attended religious services at least once a week. The same figure was 54% for Catholics, 63.6% for Protestants, 69.5% for Muslims, and 76% for "Other Christians." Zionist religious participation thus runs counter to the trend that regular participation tends to score lower than nominal affiliation in surveys.

South Africa's major black ethnic groups are distributed evenly among the AICs. Of those who claim AIC affiliation, 36% were Swati- and Ndebele-speakers. Xhosa-speakers comprise the largest single language group within the Ethiopian churches at 39.4%. Within the Apostolic churches, (Northern) Sotho-speakers form the largest group (37.4%). Of those in the "Other Independent churches" category, 42.8% were Zulu-speakers (Human Sciences Research Council 1993).

TYPICAL ARGUMENTS FOR THE EMERGENCE OF SOUTH AFRICAN AICs

The emergence of AICs within Africa as a whole can be periodized in terms of three peaks: the 1880s, 1914–25, and 1930 to the present (compare Jules-Rosette 1989, 147–48). Daneel (1987, 45, 53) argues that the Ethiopian AICs were strongest between 1890 and 1920, and started declining from the 1930s.

In South Africa, Zionist churches emerged between 1917 and 1927, and were at first localised in the northern provinces (De Wet 1994, 152). The growth of Zionists occurred from 1920 on (Daneel 1987, 38, 40, 45). From the 1930s on, AICs became the fastest growing sector in the religious market. In Zimbabwe the Shona Zionists grew fastest during this period (55). In South Africa, the southern, Xhosa-speaking regions (Ciskei and Transkei) proved more resistant—although "a few Zionist churches . . . occurred in the Transkei from about the 1930s" (De Wet 1994, 152).

Between 1939 and 1955, the number of AICs doubled (from 600 to 1,286 respectively) (Anderson 1992, 58). By the 1950s, Zionist and Ethiopian AICs "were powerful forces" in KwaZulu-Natal and Transvaal[7] (De Wet 1994, 152). Their growth accelerated after 1955, doubling in five years to 2,200 in 1960, and slowing down between 1960 and 1970 (Daneel 1987, 38, 40, 45), increasing to "only" three thousand in 1970 (Anderson 1992, 58). From 1960 to 1980, AICs gained more followers in the southern areas, so that 2–5% of the Ciskei and 10–15% of the Transkei population had become members, of whom 71% were Zionist-Apostolic (De Wet 1994, 153). The 2001 census data shows an estimated 12.19% of Eastern Cape population (including the Transkei and Ciskei) affiliated to Zionist-type churches.

Among the better-known arguments for why AICs emerged are those of Bengt Sundkler (1961) and David Barrett (1968), which have been adequately summarised by Daneel (1987), Da Silva (1993), Pretorius (1995), and critiqued by Kruss (1985). The reasons vary from individual motivations to institutional innovation, and tend to focus on intra- and intersocietal factors.

The various explanations for the emergence of AICs fit loosely into three important perspectives in the social sciences, namely functionalism, historical materialism (and so conflict theory), and Max Weber's contributions. In chapter 4, Robert Garner (1998) summarises these three approaches somewhat differently, but we can still recognise each one's place in his description:

- *Materialist treatments* (including *conflict theory*) view religion primarily as the product of economic realities, and tend to interpret AICs "in terms of the phases of capitalist development in South Africa." The overall emphasis in this approach is on social change driven by class conflict.

- *Functionalist approaches* understand religion to help people to adapt in various ways to particular social and economic realities. The overall emphasis in this approach is on social change, and on cultural factors.

- *Idealist perspectives* regard religion as operating independently of social and economic realities, although it is affected by—and affects—them. Some scholars argue that Max Weber's work fits into the idealist perspective.

Of course, as Garner points out in chapter 4, various combinations of the materialist and functionalist perspectives are possible. As chapters 4 and 5 by Garner in this volume demonstrate the idealist perspective well, I will only review the functionalist and materialist/conflict approaches here. Garner also revisits these theories from a different perspective in chapter 9 (see "Past Explanations for the Rise of the AICs").

Functionalist Explanations for the Emergence of AICs

In general terms, functionalism emphasises that institutions function to maintain social stability. For example, using the description provided by Jim Kiernan (1990), we could consider Zulu Zionists who live in KwaMashu, near Durban, from a functionalist perspective. We could then interpret their beliefs as creating expectations of mutual financial care, and of the need to maintain high moral standards. Functionalist explanations would draw attention to how Zionism provides a transitional buffer between the rural areas and the city, which allows Zulu Zionists to reject some of the traditions associated with the rural areas. One such a prohibition would be against drinking traditionally brewed beer with other Zulu men—a practice associated with rituals that demonstrate respect for the ancestors. At the same time, Zionists are able to maintain and adjust *certain* of their traditional beliefs to life in an urban setting. In short, Zionism helps affiliates adapt to a changing environment in which it provides spiritual, moral, and economic resources for survival without disrupting the existing social order.

With reference to why AICs emerge, Garner (1998) suggests that functionalists think they did so:

> as an attempt to create an alternative community of hope and meaning in the context of severe poverty, especially in urban areas, with the object of adapting to capitalism. There is a very positive assessment in some of the literature of the economic potential of these AICs, portraying them as a new form of civil society in the townships, on the basis of their support networks and voluntary associations.

The more frequently cited functionalist reasons for the emergence of AICs—even if phrased in cultural, political, and economic terms—

typically pinpoint the impact of a capitalist economy, a colonial political structure, and an alien religious belief system on African societies. Other commonly cited factors include (a) disappointment with Christianity; (b) translation of the Bible into different indigenous languages; (c) denominational divisions and a failure to meet local needs; (d) a desire for physical healing; and (e) a desire for community (Jules-Rosette 1989, 148).

Below I discuss the more typical functionalist arguments for the emergence and growth in the number of AICs in more detail, as presented by various major scholars:

1. AICs emerged due to prolonged *contact between nonindigenous and African belief systems* (embedded in, for example, Western cultural systems) and cultures. "Nonindigenous belief systems" means religions like Christianity and Islam, while "indigenous cultures" refer to the ways of living and understanding of people who date their presence in Africa to precolonial periods. Yet, contact and social change by themselves cannot be the only major causal factors. The extent, persistence, intensification, "interference by the out-group," and level of tolerance towards change play a role (Daneel 1987, 79).

2. According to a second perspective, AICs emerged as *cultural responses to secularization.* Jules-Rosette (1989, 156–57) argues that the multiplication of New African Religious Movements—of which AICs are one form—are cultural responses to secularization, which take one of four forms:

    - *neotraditionalism,* in which references to an idealised past are used to reestablish an authoritative tradition (such as African Traditional Religion);

    - *revitalisation,* in which new religious concepts are used to renew older traditional ones (e.g., AICs, fitting ancestors into new cosmology alongside God). This represents a cultural attempt to resacralize "dominant traditional symbols" through preserving "customary notions of community and conventional expressive symbols";

    - *syncretism,* in which old and new concepts are combined; or

    - *millenarism,* in which an ideal future is posited, with new definitions of the sacred and a new social order. Millenarism represents a cultural attempt to redefine social and political values.

New African Religious Movements represent Africanised forms of religious identity—not Westernized forms of African religions. They involve the adjustment of Western religious systems, or the addition of new doctrinal systems to Western ones. Jules-Rosette's discussion counters the usual view of AICs as altering African values and forms of social organisation to reflect Western forms. Instead, she argues that AICs represent the adaptation of Western forms to the African context. As an ultimate outcome, new forms of identities are emerging, which combine African and Western elements. They contribute towards "new forms of cultural expression, such as discourse and dress" (Jules-Rosette 1989, 159). Similarly, Lamin Sanneh (1994) argues that the translation of the scriptures in Western Africa lead to indigenous languages being held in a high regard in African churches, which contributed to the development of resistance to colonialism. Jules-Rosette regards secularization as a result of modernization, which is also a spin-off from globalization.

Jules-Rosette (1989, 159) argues that where AICs engage in fundamentalist scriptural interpretations, this "serves to develop a new fabric of ideas through which individuals attempt to create alternative types of social relationships." According to Sanneh, Christianity—through translation of the scripture into indigenous languages—opened up new possibilities for Africans to define themselves. Pride in indigenous languages bolstered nationalist movements in their struggle against colonialism. An African content is given to doctrine and leadership structures—for example, in Nigeria in the Native Baptist Church movement from 1888 onwards, and in the Aladura revival in Yorubaland between 1928 and 1930 (Sanneh 1994). African religious identities in West Africa have changed in different ways through contact with Islam and Christianity.

According to Jules-Rosette (1989), developments in African religions in fact affirm African robustness in resisting, creating, and adapting to changing environments. From this perspective, AICs represent the emergence of a new African identity, which spans traditional and modern cultural practices. The innovation of AICs lies in "unique forms of social and political organization" and in the development of their own doctrines (Jules-Rosette 1989, 149). AICs in Zaire (Kimbanguism) and the Ivory Coast (Harrist Church) have supported political movements. In South Africa, the members of most Zionist churches individually supported the African National Congress (ANC), according to a preelection poll.

3. AICs emerged as a *reaction to mission.* David Barrett (1968) suggested a general theory, based on reaction to mission as a primary cause, after his wide-ranging systematic study of 336 "tribal" units. His thesis is that "independency is a societal reaction to mission arising out of a tribal *zeitgeist* or climate of opinion in which Christian missions were believed to be illegitimately mounting an attack against African traditional society and in particular its basic unit, the family" (Barrett 1968, 74). According to Barrett, national, "tribal," and mission factors all play a role. National correlates with schism occur in societies that had a large number of Protestant missionaries, a relatively high ratio of whites to blacks, higher standards of living for whites than blacks, and

a high percentage of literates. "Tribal" correlates include polygamous tribes with ancestor worship, where missionaries have been working for a long period, and the Bible has been translated into an indigenous language (mission correlates) (Daneel 1987, 73–75).

4. The *social structure of particular ethnic groupings favours the formation of AICs*. Among the Swati, the "custom of a kinship group to secede and become independent on the death of the head of the family is projected directly onto the structure of the church" (Daneel 1987, 69, 86–88). Similar patterns occurred in southern Malawi and for the Luo of Kenya. Schism is also far more common among Protestant denominations than in the Roman Catholic Church, although not exclusively so, as breakaways in Zambia and Zaire in the 1950s and 1960s show (Daneel 1987, 88).

5. *Passive resistance to white political domination and cultural control of colonial church structures*. In South Africa, the resistance of Africans to colonial economies and belief systems were highly successful until the destruction of their political systems through warfare (compare Kiernan 1995; Chidester 1992; De Wet 1994). The breakaway from white-dominated mainline denominations around the turn of this century indicates a mixed source of rejection of racism and assertion of Africanist identity.

6. The growth of AICs relates to the *continuing urbanisation* of rural South Africans, bridging rural-urban contexts and Western-African forms of self-representation. I discussed the link in the previous section. More independent churches emerged in the urban areas of the Reef "than in any other urban area in the whole of Africa"; obviously due to migratory labor—this despite AICs being essentially a rural phenomenon, with urban congregations usually established only subsequently (Daneel 1987, 102–103).

7. The emergence of an increasing number of AICs relates to the eventual *relaxation of legislation*. Claassen (1995, 32) has shown how by 1945 "not a single Zionist church had received government recognition." More accommodating recent legislation has made it easier to register these churches than was the case before (Oosthuizen 1994).

8. The number of AICs grow because the *level of intimacy and care* offered by Zionist churches—financial and otherwise—cannot be matched by larger mainline congregations (compare Kiernan 1990a).

Limitations and Advantages of Functionalist Explanations

Glenda Kruss (1985) has strongly criticized the theoretical assumptions and contents of many of the arguments above from a historical-materialist (Marxist) perspective. She categorises Sundkler, Barrett, Oosthuizen, West, and Daneel as operating from a hidden functionalist perspective. By this, she means that they emphasise cultural aspects (values, beliefs, and worldviews) and emphasize function in a way that does not pay attention to the historical and material forces at work. Khabela (1989, 31), in a different context, argued similarly that an emphasis on (indigenous) culture that is not yoked to a liberation ethos is as "powerless" as an emphasis on power without attention to culture.

Functionalists analyse AICs in terms of social change, which they perceive happens at the level of ideas as a reaction to external forces, within existing structures, and in terms of a clash between cultures or identities (Kruss 1985, 44). The functionalist approach, Kruss believes, tends to view African and Western cultures (e.g., particular practices or beliefs) and modes of production (e.g., preindustrial agrarian) in a static way as fixed and diametrically opposed (simple vs. complex; traditional vs. modern) (Kruss 1985, 39; 72). She argues further that functionalism is a bourgeois enterprise based on the capitalist mode of production (44).

Functionalist interpretation of AIC affiliation does allow for a focus on individual religious motivations of those who start or join AICs. For example, Daneel contests that AICs flourish because they present a vigorous, indigenous, and "symbolically intelligible" alternative religion that does not reject all traditions out of hand. This recalls Cox's comment about the growth of Pentecostal-charismatic churches: that they grow because they offer a comforting emphasis on a miracle-working God who can deal with people here and now (Cox 1995).

But from a world system perspective, the most significant limitation of the functionalist arguments is that they restrict causative factors to cultural, economic, and political change at the level of individual *societies* (e.g., South Africa) or—more rarely—of a particular region (West Africa). Although functionalist explanations touch upon global trends (e.g., capitalism, colonialism), the expansion and dynamics of such institutions as part of a world system are not considered. The potential to portray capitalism as a global system remains unfulfilled. Instead, the interaction between the local features of the economic system and local institutions are considered. Yet a number of concepts in functionalist interpretations could usefully be expanded to consider possible connections with globalization. These include acculturative factors, cultural and social disintegration, religious competition within the same area, the structure of tribal organisation, industrialization, urbanization, rising secularism, and rapid social change (compare Daneel 1987, 69–88).

Pretorius (1995) touches on similar issues to those that I raise. He faulted functionalism for tending to encourage an ahistorical approach (as does Pato 1990) and commended the strengths of historical materialism to AIC researchers. Pretorius called researchers to adopt a global perspective that compares AICs to similar movements across the world, and to search for linkages between international events and the emergence of AICs.

Historical-Materialist Explanations for the Emergence of AICs

Kruss (1985, 74) proposes that the different forms of AICs emerged during two phases of social formation, built around specific classes.

Ethiopian churches arose during the *first phase* of transition (from before 1870 to the late 1930s) from a colonial trade-based (mercantile) relation of exchange to an industrial capitalist system, which contradicted the precapitalist African social formations (Kruss 1985, 73–74). Most Ethiopian churches were founded between 1884 and 1900, and arguably were most influential from 1872 to 1928 (80). Ethiopian leaders were often from the African elite and from wealthy farmers, well educated, professionals, and craftsmen (81). They were well connected with the old preindustrial political structures (95, 98, 101). Their families tended to be landowners, and so they formed part of an emerging black bourgeoisie. Ethiopian leaders believed that political equality was possible if they assimilated European values through the education system, and so they accepted the culture and religion of the Western colonists. When they were disappointed by white racism, these leaders broke away from the mission churches to form part of an Africanist movement. Ethiopians saw their task as generating parallel systems of politics, education, and commerce to those of the colonists; and their followers shared their class aspirations (97, 108). This also explains why they did not alter the church structures that they inherited from the mission churches. The Ethiopian project was overtaken by the extension of capitalist production over the country, resulting in the loss of land on which the African middle class had depended, and the increasing destruction of agrarian systems of production (113).

The struggle to retain land contributed to the emergence of *Zionist*-type churches during the first thirty years of the twentieth century, particularly between 1917 and 1920. These Zionists emphasised occupation and control of land, and comprised people who became alienated from the means of production. The formation of these churches should be viewed as a struggle to resist being dispossessed of land (Kruss 1985, 74). Membership consisted of semieducated black peasants, who emphasised establishing a self-supporting religious community on their own land (125, 137). Church structures imitated the tributary mode of production, with leaders set up as "theological versions of the pre-capitalist ruling class" who were to provide for their followers' every material and spiritual need (138). This early form of Zionism was essentially a rural phenomenon, from where it migrated to the cities (129). Both the ZCC and the Church of Nazarites (*Ibandla AmaNazaretha*) of Isaiah Shembe (1870–1935) were founded during this period. In the Eastern Cape, early

Zionism assumed a millenarian character (e.g., Mgijima's Israelites), as opposed to its "chiefly" character in the old Transvaal and KwaZulu-Natal (122).

The *Zionist-Apostolic* churches emerged during the *second phase* of the dominance of the capitalist mode of production from the 1940s to the present, along with the impoverished black working class (Kruss 1985, 73, 152). Before the Second World War, the absence of a large proportion of the white working class led to a rapid increase of the black industrial labor force, while the black labor force on the mines, comprised essentially of landless people from "Reserves," also grew steadily (154). Along with industrialisation came urbanisation and proletarianization, creating a sizeable but impoverished urban black working class between 1939 and 1952 (155). Struggles for economic and political improvement took a more organised form in urban and rural areas (158). Between 1932 and 1960, AICs increased by 56%, with Zionist-Apostolic titles becoming noticeably prevalent after 1945 (159, 165). A struggle emerged during 1951–58 between larger rural and smaller urban AIC congregations for control, partly through the need for official permission (until 1963) to get land (161–62).

In short, Kruss (1985, 173) argues that AICs cannot be understood as bridging two worlds, two cultures, or the urban and the rural; as both "worlds" have been drawn into a single complex socioeconomic system. Kruss's alternative to functionalist interpretations is to analyse each AIC in terms of a particular historical social formation in the context of colonial conquest. She takes her cue from Marx's notion that "The mode of production of material life conditions the social, political, and intellectual life process in general. It is not the consciousness of men [sic] that determines their being, but on the contrary, their social being that determines their consciousness" (Kruss 1985, 68, quoting from Marx's *Preface to a Contribution to the Critique of Political Economy*, p. 20).

Limitations and Advantages of Materialist Explanations

Materialist explanations tend to disregard the significance of cultural considerations, probably because they interpret culture as dependent on material realities. At the same time, Kruss's arguments did not fulfil their potential for interpreting capitalism and class systems in terms of the operation of a global economic system. In her defence, the implications of Wallerstein's interpretations had not yet percolated into the South African academic world when she wrote. As I strive in chapters 7 and 8 to synthesize materialist and functionalist arguments in understanding AICs, I will refrain from elaborating further here. Garner's critical evaluation of materialism and functionalism at points in his chapters will have to suffice.

CONCLUSION

This chapter introduced some of the major concepts and theories used to study AICs, as well as some of the basic dilemmas that arise when researchers apply them. The work of each contributor to this volume demonstrates both the struggle to operationalize key concepts and possible ways to resolve them. I argued that the *Independent-Indigenous* designations require further definition and operationalization, preferably by selecting indicators from existing ethnographic studies that highlight the self-understanding of insiders. Only once the terminology has been thus standardized can research on AICs respond to the challenge from those like Pato (1990) and move beyond the present descriptive formats towards establishing a comprehensive theory.

Because *Independent* seems to be more useful an umbrella term with which to accommodate *Initiated, Indigenous,* and *Instituted* than the others, contributors to this volume have agreed that *AIC* will refer to African *Independent* Churches. The four generally accepted Apostolic-Zionist-Ethiopian-Prophet types are included in the term. As a very broad concept, we can then conflate Anderson's separate "indigenous Pentecostal-type churches" (PT) and "Ethiopian-types" (ET) under AIC.

My suggestions for an identification device and for further operationalization of disputed terms obviously await elaboration, rejection, or falsification, and by no means necessarily resolve all difficulties. Clearly, in the manner of grounded theory, categories are needed that depend more on empirical evidence of the perceptions and experiences of AIC participants themselves than on the judgement of researchers, as Anderson (1995) suggested. Unless this is done, researchers will remain vulnerable to the challenges by Mosala (1985) and Kruss (1985) that their work reflects their own interests along with the class base on which the dominance of their interpretative paradigms rest.

NOTES

1. Some commentators argue that the Ethiopian separatist tendency had not only contributed to the ideal of unifying all black South Africans in a United National Church of Africa by the 1920s (Lamola 1988, 11, referring to Sundkler 1961, 50), but had also fuelled the creation in 1959 of the Pan-Africanist Congress (Lamola 1988, 12; Khabela 1989, 32).

2. The notion of a singular African culture is obviously problematic, not only due to the continued debate about the meaning of the term, but also given the variety of ethnic and racial groups that inhabit the various subregions of the continent. Regardless, there are Africans who do insist that commonalities can be found among all black groups, such as a group from the Church of the Lord (Aladura) who, during a World Council of Churches

consultation with African independent churches in Nigeria in 1996, defined "African culture" as including: "(a) Traditional African worship of God; (b) African traditional rites (planting festivals); (c) Chieftaincy appointments; (d) Traditional African costumes; (e) Medicinal herbs; (f) Marriages (dowries); (g) Child naming ceremonies; (h) Burial ceremonies" (URL: http://www.pctii.org/wcc/group96.html).

3. The study of AICs founded outside Africa is relatively new. Researchers include Afe Adogame (2001), Gerrie ter Haar (1998, 2000), and Benjamin Simon (2001). In 1999, the Millenial Conference of the Partnership of African Christian Communities in Europe was held at Westminster College, Cambridge in England. The Primate of The Church of the Lord (Aladura), Worldwide, His Eminence, Most Rev. Dr. Rufus Ositelu spoke on "The Role of an African Instituted Church in the Mission's Debate" (URL: http://www.aladura.de/artikel.htm).

4. Regional religious differences are fairly well marked among South African Christians: most reformed people live in the southern parts of South Africa (the former Cape Province and Ciskei), while most Catholics live in the east (Kwazulu Natal).

5. The optional nature of the question on religion in state census forms, coupled with an apparent reluctance on the part of blacks to indicate their affiliation with an indigenous belief system, means that estimates regarding AICs should be treated with caution.

6. The only contradictory evidence comes from a Daneel survey, which showed that Shona Zionists were better off than affiliates of either mission churches or of African Traditional Religion (Daneel 1987).

7. Old names are used because some of the data comes from an era before name changes were effected for provinces. As I lack access to the original data sources, recalculation on the basis of newly drawn provinces is not possible

REFERENCES

Adogame, Afe. 2001. *Betwixt identity and security: African New Religious Movements (ANRMs) and the politics of religious networking in Europe.* (URL: http://www.cesnur.org/2001/london2001/adogame.htm).

Anderson, Allan. 2001. Pentecostals and apartheid in South Africa during ninety years. *Cyberjournal for Pentecostal-Charismatic Research* 9.

———. 1997. *Pluriformity and contextuality in African Initiated Churches.* Paper read at a conference on Christianity in the African Diaspora, University of Leeds, September. (URL: http://artsweb.bham.ac.uk/aanderson/Publications/pluriformity_and_contextuality_i.htm).

———. 1995. Challenges and prospects for research into African Initiated Churches in Southern Africa. *Missionalia* 23 (3): 283–94.

———. 1993. H. Frederick Modise and the International Pentecost Church: A modern African Messianic Movement? *Missionalia* 21 (1): 26–39.

———. 1992. *Bazalwane: African Pentecostals in South Africa.* Pretoria: Unisa.

Barrett, David. 1968. *Schism and Renewal in Africa.* Nairobi: Oxford University Press.

Brown, C. G. 1992. A revisionist approach to religious change. In *Religion and modernization: sociologists and historians debate the secularization thesis*, ed. Steve Bruce, 31-58. Oxford: Clarendon Press.

Chidester, David. 1992. *Religions of South Africa.* London: Routledge.

———. 1988. Religion alive/religious studies unborn?. *Journal for the Study of Religion* 1 (2): 83–93.

Claassen, J. W. 1995. Independents made dependents: African Independent Churches and government recognition. *Journal of Theology for Southern Africa* 91: 15-34.

Cox, Harvey. 1995. *Fire from heaven. The rise of Pentecostal spirituality and the reshaping of religion in the 21st century.* Reading MA: Addison-Wesley Publishing Co.

Daneel, Marthinus L. 1987. *Quest for belonging: Introduction to a study of African Independent Churches.* Mambo Occasional Papers—Missio-Pastoral series No. 17. Gweru: Mambo Press.

———. 1971. *Old and new in Southern Shona independent churches.* Vol. I. The Hague: Mouton.

Da Silva, J. A. 1993. African Independent Churches: origin and development. *Anthropos* 88: 393-402.

Datadesk. 1996. *Survey of Heidelberg.* Stellenbosch: University of Stellenbosch.

De Wet, J. 1994. Social change, resistance and worldview of a community in the Transkei. In *Afro-Christianity at the Grassroots*, ed. G. C. Oosthuizen, M. C. Kitshoff and S. W. D. Dube, 137-164. Leiden: E. J. Brill.

Fay, Derick. 1996. Review of Piet Naudé: The Zionist Christian Church in South Africa: A case-study in oral theology. *H-Africa, H-Net Reviews*, July. (URL: http://www.h-net.msu.edu/reviews/showrev.cgi?path=1483 4878944524).

Garner, Robert C. 1998. *Religion and economics in a South African township.* Ph.D. Dissertation, University of Cambridge.

Hayes, Stephen. 2003. Personal communication.

———. 2000. More on AICs. URL: http://www.geocities.com/missionalia/ aic1.htm.

———. 1992. The African Independent Churches: Judgement through terminology? *Mi*ssionalia 20 (2): 139–46.

Hendriks, Jurgens. 1995. South African Denominational Growth and Decline 1911-1991. *Journal of Theology for Southern Africa* 91: 35-58.

———. 1999. Religion in South Africa: Census 1996. In *South African Christian Handbook 1999/2000*, ed. Marjorie Froise, ch. 4. Welkom [South Africa]: Christian Info.

Human Sciences Research Council. 1993. *Omnibus Survey.* Pretoria: Human Science Research Council.

Isaac, Jean. 1999. A South African AIC leader's vision. *Messenger* LXVI. (URL: http://www.aimmintl.org/Messenger99.htm).

Jules-Rosette, Benetta. 1989. The sacred in African new religions. In *The changing face of religion*, ed. James A. Beckford and Thomas Luckmann, 147–62. London: Sage.

Khabela, M. Gideon. 1989. The socio-cultural dynamics of the struggle for liberation and the coherence of Black faith. *Journal of Black Theology in South Africa* 3 (1): 23–38.

Kiernan, James P. 1990. *The Production and Management of Therapeutic Power in Zionist Churches within a Zulu City*. Lewiston, New York: Edwin Mellen Press.

———. 1995. The African Independent Churches. In *Living Faiths in South Africa*, ed. Martin Prozesky and John W. DeGruchy, 116–128. Cape Town: David Philip.

Kruss, Glenda. 1985. *Religion, class and culture: Indigenous churches in South Africa, with special reference to Zionist-Apostolics*. MA thesis, University of Cape Town.

Lamola, Malesela John. 1988. Towards a Black church—A historical investigation of the African Independent Churches as a model. *Journal of Black Theology in South Africa* 2 (1): 5–14.

Makhubu, Paul. 1988. *Who are the Independent Churches?* Braamfontein: Skotaville.

Maluleke, Tinyiko S. 1994. Review of Anderson, Allan, 1993. *TUMELO: The faith of African Pentecostals in South Africa.* Pretoria: University of South Africa. *Missionalia* 21: 61–62.

Masuku, T. 1996. African Initiated Churches: Christian partners or antagonists? *Missionalia* 24 (3): 441–455.

Millard, Joan A. 1999. *Malihambe—Let the word spread.* Pretoria: Unisa Press.

Mosala, Itumaleng. 1985. African Independent Churches: A study in socio-theological protest. In *Resistance and hope: South African essays in honour of Beyers Naudé*, ed. Charles Villa-Vicencio and John DeGruchy, 103–111. Grand Rapids: Eerdmans.

Mosala, Itumaleng, and Buti Thlahale. 1986. *The unquestionable right to be free*. Maryknoll, NY: Orbis.

Mukonyora, Isabel. 2001. Review of Bengt Sundkler and Christopher Steed: The history of the church in Africa. *H-S Africa, H-Net Reviews,* May. (URL: http://www.h-net.msu.edu/reviews/showrev.cgi?path=21359905 51518).

Oosthuizen, G. C. 1994. The South African New Age movement and the African Indigenous Church movement—a comparison. In *Afro-Christianity at the Grassroots*, ed. G. C. Oosthuizen, M. C. Kitschoff and S. W. D. Dube, 231-245. Leiden: E. J. Brill.

Pato, Luke 1990. The African Independent Churches: A socio-cultural approach. *Journal of Theology for Southern Africa* 72: 24–35.

Pretorius, Hennie L. 1995. *Historiography and historical sources regarding African Indigenous Churches in South Africa.* Lewiston, NY: Edwin Mellen.

Pretorius, Hennie L., and Lizo Jafta. 1997. 'A branch springs out'—African Initiated Churches. In *Christianity in South Africa: A political, social and cultural history*, ed. Richard Elphick and Rodney Davenport, 211–

26. Cape Town: David Philip.

Sanneh, Lamin. 1994. Translatability in Islam and in Christianity. In *Religion in Africa: experience and expression,* ed. Wouter E. A. Van Beek, D.L. Thomson and T.D. Blakely, 23-45. London: James Currey.

Simon, Benjamin. 2001. *Christian pluralism and the quest for identity in African Initiated Churches in Germany.* (URL: http://www.cesnur.org/2001/london2001/simon.htm).

StatsSA. 2004. *Census 2001 by province, gender, religion recode (derived) and population group.* Statistics South Africa. (URL: http://www.statssa.gov.za/SpecialProjects/Census2001/Census/Dialog/varval.asp?ma=Religionbyprovince&ti=Table%3A+Census+2001+by+province%2C+gender%2C+religion+recode+%28derived%29+and++population+group%2E+&path=../Database/Census%202001/Provincial%20Level/Persons/&lang=).

Sundkler, Bengt. 1961. *Bantu prophets in South Africa.* 2d ed. London: Oxford University Press.

Ter Haar, Gerrie. 2000. *World religions and community religions—Where does Africa fit in?* Occasional paper, Centre of African Studies, University of Copenhagen. (URL: http://216.239.53.100/search?q=cache:-X-X1AtQq68C:www.teol.ku.dk/cas/NYHOMEPAGE/mapper/Occasional%2520Papers/Occ_paper_Haar%2520(Word).doc+%22African+independent+churches%22+%2Beurope+%2Bter+haar&hl=en&ie=UTF-8).

———. 1998. *Halfway to paradise: African Christians in Europe.* Cardiff: Cardiff Academic Press.

Turner, Harold W. 1979. *Religious innovation in Africa.* Boston: G. K. Hall.

Wallis, R. and Bruce, Steve 1992. Secularisation: the orthodox model. In *Religion and modernization: sociologists and historians debate the secularization thesis,* ed. Steve Bruce, 8-31. Oxford: Clarendon Press.

World Values Study. 1995. Dataset used in the Department of Sociology, University of Stellenbosch, South Africa.

West, Martin. 1975. *Bishops and prophets in a black city: African Independent Churches in Soweto, Johannesburg.* Cape Town: David Philip.

Zaaiman, Johann. 1994. Kerk en geloofsaffiliasie in Suid-Afrika [Church and religious affiliation in South Africa]. *Nederduits Gereformeerde Teologiese Tydskrif* 35 (4): 565–74.

2

African Independent Churches and Modernity

Jim Kiernan

INTRODUCTION

In this chapter, I argue that the emergence of African Independent Churches (AICs) epitomises responses of the African population to the strains and stresses of modernity. Their reactions to modernity vary from closing the hatches to vigorous opposition or partial acceptance—primarily because AICs differ in origin and character. My argument serves as a caution against the easy supposition that South Africa was confronted with modernity only after the demise of apartheid. While it is true that the country may well have been spared the full force of modern influences as long as the *lager* mentality persisted as a barrier, this cushioning effect has been more noticeable in the political and economic spheres than in the religious domain. Despite the strictures of apartheid, the religious strains among the African population, which are manifested in the AICs, have flourished unabated. Not only that, but they have engendered a wide spectrum of diversity in church organisation, religious belief, ritual observance, and moral behaviour.

In one sense, the ferment of religious transformation exhibited by the AICs is a direct reflection of the freedom of expression that is symptomatic of the modern age. This claim must appear anomalous in the context of a state that devoted the considerable force of its bureaucratic and communicative machinery to the repression of freedom of speech. But by the 1920s, when they were officially exonerated of complicity in the Bambata Rebellion of 1906, the AICs had adopted an attitude of political quiescence, which they still retain and which rendered them innocuous, if not quite invisible, in the eyes of the government. In short, the AICs evaded state controls precisely because they engaged Africans in the exploration of novel religious combinations and nothing more. The doyen of AIC studies, Bengt Sundkler, had depicted them as safety valves for the release of pent-up energies. Expressed in 1948, this authoritative statement probably served as a recommendation to the government to tolerate the eccentricities of the AICs and resulted in their being given a licence to follow their own devices without let or hindrance. If there was a locus of religious opposition to political oppression, it was confined to the mainline churches of earlier mission provenance.

My purpose in what follows is to sound a twofold caution—against conceptualising AICs as a singular monolithic movement; and against assuming that modernity is a recent intrusion into the lives of black South Africans. The argument unfolds through three sections. First, I supply a brief historical overview of the emergence of four forms of the AICs as African responses to modernity. While all types remain in comparative focus throughout, I emphasise Zionists as the largest AIC grouping. Next, I trace the growth of Zionists in urban areas that not only in themselves represent modernity, but also bring various aspects of modernity to bear on migrant laborers. I conclude with a discussion of the future of the Zionists and the other AICs.

MODERNITY AND THE EMERGENCE OF AICs

AICs derive from a number of quite disparate sources, and their historical development has been one of increasing diversification—which I suggest is one of the distinctive trends of modernity: the liberalisation of religious expression. This feature of modernity has clearly been rampant over the past ninety years in the AICs, which crystallize the religious experimentation and invention that has thrived among the African population without any noticeable restraint.

Independent Churches as Appropriations of Modernity

To speak of the African Independent Churches (AICs) as if in some sense they constituted a single coherent and undifferentiated entity is a mistake. The field encompassed by the AICs is simply too broad and variegated to be comprehended under a single label, no matter how descriptively convenient or desirable that label might seem to be. So great is this diversity, today spread over an estimated four thousand churches, that it defies systematic ordering.

Nevertheless, some attempt at clarification is essential in order to discern different tendencies and to avoid gross simplification. This clarification can best be sought in the early emergence of these churches around the turn of the century, where we can more easily detect different manifestations of the striving for independence and different responses to the adoption of Christianity in Southern Africa. While four distinct developments may be noted, bear in mind that individual churches may not fall neatly into one or other category of emergence, but may straddle more than one.

The first and earliest manifestation may be described as *the tribal incorporation of Christianity.* The establishment of the Tembu Church by the Wesleyan, Nehemiah Tile, in 1882 is the perfect example of a pattern that others, in different parts of the country, speedily adopted (Sundkler 1961, 384). Although these tribal churches were all short-lived, what they had in common was an earnest attempt to capture mission Christianity, to absorb it into and subordinate it to existing traditional structures.

In a sense, the emergence of these tribal or "national" churches represented a more offensive form of a widespread resistance by the traditional order to one of the major prongs of imperial modernity, that is, Christian missions. Inevitably, the traditional order had to give way without being entirely erased; but even as the missionary denominations expanded among Africans, they were arrested by a second wave of independence, all the more telling because this erupted within the denominations themselves. The Methodists and Congregationalists were particularly shaken, though none was left unscathed (see Sundkler 1961, 39ff.).

The second wave of independence took the form of *a rebellion by the black clergy*—which really signified the appropriation of Christian equality. That all were equal in the sight of God was a precept more honoured in the breach than the observance. If African ministers failed to win recognition as the equals of their European counterparts within the denomination, they could appropriate equality by setting themselves up as leaders of independent black denominations of the same religious persuasion.

Equality, one of the foremost icons of modernity, was pressed into the service of African redress and was concretised in the secession of viable black religious bodies, organisationally separate from their parent churches. And it is no coincidence that the secessionary tendency arose in the emergent modern city of Johannesburg, which was being shaped by the mining industry and its consumption of migrant labor, irrespective of tribal or ethnic distinctions.

However, this polyglot city-in-the-making also produced a trend that ran counter to the secessionary tendency, one that found expression in another strong feature of the modern era, namely nationalism. A black Wesleyan offshoot departed from precedent; instead of the standard "African Wesleyan Church," an "Ethiopian" Church emerged. Since Ethiopia was a biblical metaphor for Africa as a whole, the title was a means of pitching the church's appeal across tribal and linguistic differences. As an emotionally-laden symbol for Africa and Africans, Ethiopian became a rallying cry for the formation of a truly African national church. Although this remained for long a nationalist ideal, its realisation could not prevail against more powerful pressures towards secession. Once the ploy of secession had been released from its missionary cage, there was no way of restraining it. A strategy used by a black subordinate to claim equality with his white superior could also be brought into play to wrest equality of status from a black superior. And so it was, again and again; and still there is no end in sight.

A third wave of black religious independence was gathering much less conspicuously in the remote countryside, in the shape of *a revolt on the part of a rural underclass* deprived of ancestral lands.

Later known as Zionism, the movement began at Wakkerstroom on the Transvaal-Natal border as a straight American import from Chicago that harnessed the power of the Holy Spirit to ritual healing (Comaroff 1985, 177–84). Though originally sponsored by a Dutch reformed missionary, Pieter L. Le Roux, his Zulu converts soon appropriated and refined the movement. The resultant appearance of the Zion Apostolic Church in 1908 was the root from which today's legions of African "Zionist" churches grew. Quite unlike the rebellion of a discontented African elite, which gave birth to the denominational offshoots, this development took shape among the poor and the dispossessed, virtually enslaved as agricultural laborers and harshly dominated by Boer landlords. Zionism provided them with an independent identity and offered them a renewal of self-respect. At the same time, it catered for their most pressing needs, namely, economic security, physical well-being and social welfare.

As expressed by the Chicago founder of Zionism, John Alexander Dowie, this form of religious observance aimed at the delivery of "salvation, healing and holy living" (Mahon 1986, 170)—a charter for self-improvement. One of the more obvious effects on the Wakkerstroom converts was that Zionism inspired them to accumulate the means of buying their own tract of land across the border in Natal on which they could settle.

Whereas the urban schismatics were motivated by a burning desire for equality of status, these early Zionists were clearly fired by a more fundamental thirst for freedom. Despite the eventual success of the antislavery campaign of the modern era, vestiges of the institution of slavery survived in the Boer republics until the turn of the century. Only in the aftermath of the British victory in the Anglo-Boer war was relief at least envisioned by African labor tenants, though no sweeping changes took place. Because Zionists possessed a unity of purpose and a collective cohesion, they were able to ride the tide of prevailing sentiment to the practical realisation of some measure of freedom from economic oppression. No more than the denominational dissidents were the Zionists able to escape the hydra of secession—though this was less debilitating to the Zionist movement as a whole than to the thinning ranks of the "Ethiopians."

The appeal of Zionist healing to impoverished Africans was to produce a phenomenal rate of growth, particularly from the 1940s onwards. With the increase of labor migration to the burgeoning industrial centres, Zionism travelled the migrant routes and became entrenched in the urban African population. While the movement continued to expand at both ends of the migrant journey, its congregations offered a caring community that particularly appealed to the homeless urban worker as a haven and a refuge from social disorder. Secessions were a feature of growth, for more Zionists meant more opportunities for leadership and this meant more churches. Besides, the central commitments to a communal healing service and to the sharing of burdens meant that Zionism functioned more effectively in small-scale units than in mass rallies.

However, the rate of growth and of corresponding secession, in the absence of a coordinating mechanism to regulate conformity, resulted in the introduction of modifications to the original model. Expansion has bred a bewildering array of diversification in belief, rules, behaviour, and healing techniques. Relatively few churches consciously adhere to the orthodoxy of foundation and most have departed from it, many considerably, by incorporating more and more elements of traditional African religion or of eccentric religious invention. Zionism no longer exhibits a single recognisable pattern, no more than do the AICs as a whole.

Independent Churches as Rejection of Modernity

The fourth form of AIC was *founded by a prophet-messiah* as a firm reaction against modern conditions. Although such churches share some common ground with Zionism, as both give prominence to the healing function, they differ considerably in other major respects. This type of church first emerged after Zionism was founded.

The promise of prophetic or messianic deliverance from the evils of the modern world is a distinctive characteristic of this form of AIC, and the best examples of this today are Shembe's Nazareth Baptist Church and the Zion Christian Church of Lekganyane. That they are better known by their founders' names rather than by their official designations is quite significant. In their youth, these men acquired some experience by belonging either to a "Zionist" or "Ethiopian" church, but were led by visionary compulsion to claim extraordinary prophetic powers and to house their growing body of followers within the institution of a church of their own. The strength of their appeal, mainly to those steeped in African tradition, lay in the charismatic force of their personalities and the wonders of their miraculous healing. Aside from the reaction against modern conditions, such churches represented a defensive retreat into familiar customary observance, and a conscious rejuvenation of African religious beliefs. Yet, at the heart of this conservative emphasis was the captive power of Christianity, distilled from the pages of the Old Testament and acknowledged as the source of healing. In effect, these churches display a tendency to indigenize Christianity, not unlike the short-lived intent of the tribal church, and much like what is happening on the fringes of the Zionist movement.

The antimodernity trend is also expressed in the deification of the founder, at least in some of these churches. Unlike the Zionists, whose healing powers are widely distributed and dispersed among members, here healing is the sole preserve of the prophet-founder and is dispensed spectacularly at mass rallies. Such highly charged large-scale public performances lend themselves to claims of miraculous cures. Though the prophet himself may not make excessive claims on his own behalf and readily attributes his healing to divine intervention, he cannot prevent the more credulous of his followers from conflating the medium and the source. Though more pronounced after his death, his healing takes on legendary, even mythical proportions, and he is equated with divinity, thus emerging in popular consciousness as a black or African messiah. The concentration of all spiritual powers in a single charismatic person is paralleled by an equal centralisation of the indicators of economic success in the form of fixed and movable assets.

Although the churches of singular prophets are not immune to secession, this remains limited in incidence and the main core of the church is large enough to discount the loss should a fragment hive off. Secession becomes an issue only when succession does—when the leader dies. Because of the concentration of spiritual and economic resources in one person's hands, the contest is primarily between his siblings and sons to take his place and the prize is inheritance as much as succession. However bitter the rivalry, the principal concern is with outright control of an undivided church, rather than with carving out a second preserve of independent leadership. Should the failed contender with least support sullenly decide to decamp with his followers, this is not the desirable outcome for either party. In other churches, succession is usually the explicit aim of a serious dispute; but here it is reluctantly accepted as a last resort. In consequence, few damaging ruptures are recorded.

In any event, leadership in these churches is dynastic, continuing in the same family for three generations to date and this is a means of securing the delivery of mystical benefits in the church. As the original purveyor of spiritual blessings and healing power, the founder is believed to continue to make these favours available through his chosen descendants, in much the same manner as the ancestor in African religion looks after the spiritual and material welfare of his progeny. And this belief serves to bolster the messianic status of the prophet among the rank and file.

MODERNITY AND THE GROWTH OF URBAN ZIONISM

Cities as Transmitters of Modernity

The draconian measures of the apartheid state failed to arrest the free play of other significant features of modernity, the most prominent and visible of these being the city. As the nuclei from which the most potent influences of modernity radiate, the large urban industrial centres, or metropolitan cities, generate employment, promote labor migrancy and, in times of economic recession, create and house an army of unemployed. Attempts to stunt the growth of industrial cities like Johannesburg and Durban by implementing policies of influx control signally failed to contain the steady urbanisation of the African population. The transition from countryside to city exposed Africans, like others across the globe, to the influences of modernity.

As the seat of scientific rationalism, the city represents a mode of ordering reality according to scientific principles, which yields technological advances in movement and communication. In this way, the city is subject to a process of secularization. Since the publication of *The Secular City* (Cox 1965), much has been written debating the compatibility—or otherwise—of religion with this tide of secularization. Christianity has generally adapted quite tolerably to the secular milieu; the question is, how have the AICs coped?

Cities compress people together in dense settlement, so much so that the "crowd" is accepted as a social image of the city. What characterises the crowd, however, is its constitution by strangers. The city throws one into the company of strangers, on packed trains and crowded streets, in restricted work space and compact neighbourhoods. These associations, combining physical closeness with social distance, are unavoidable. To the extent that they curtail choice and therefore the possibility of control, they can carry overtones of threat and danger. Urban crime reinforces this experience of strangeness. In South Africa, until very recently, urban Africans could not choose their place of residence or be selective about the neighbourhood in which they settled. This option—however limited—was open to most urban dwellers elsewhere.

The urban context can also engender individual isolation, even alienation. The city induces a feeling of being alone and adrift in a sea of strangers without a life belt of social support. This is particularly experienced by the migrant worker; nowhere more starkly than in the single-sex hostels of South Africa's industrial heartland. If prevalent, this condition of anomie implies the collapse of normative structures, the absence of a community dimension, and a disruption of normal family life. On the other hand, the consciousness of being on one's own directs the individual to the necessity of self-realisation and to the single-minded pursuit of self-interest.

Yet despite their forbidding and inhospitable appearances, cities also reveal great zest and energy. This positive aspect arises—paradoxically—from the anonymity of the crowd and the self-drive of the individual. A city's diversity and mobility, lack of conservative structures and suffocating conformity, can produce great vitality, creativity and variety of artistic and cultural expression. Even in the darkest days of apartheid, the congested townships around Johannesburg bred a vibrant pulsating popular culture that was a passionate celebration of a prolific diversity. From this point of view, the city has a profoundly liberating influence. City life is both accelerating and exhilarating.

Finally, we may note the effect of the modern city on identity. The effervescence and disorientating ephemerality of urban life rests on the heterogeneity of its social composition. The contrast between city and countryside is between a society that is highly differentiated and one which is much more homogeneous.

Migrants submitting to urbanisation are divested of the singular all-encompassing identity of belonging to a well-defined social group among similar groups. Instead, they are caught up in several separate identities emerging from their attachment to a variety of quasi groups, categories, classes, and networks of association. These multiple and fragmented identities are dispersed and diffused over a wide range of diverse interests and activities. By the same token, of course, identity is expanded and enlarged, presenting new options and opportunities, and at the extreme becomes a realm of pure possibility. But identity remains elusive, situationally shifting, and constantly open to redefinition. An open divided self replaces a closed, compact, and centralised identity. Consequently, the challenge confronting the city dweller is one of attempting to put back together the scattered pieces of the jigsaw of his/her social being, and urban culture becomes a struggle to restore and reassert a central identity.

A pertinent question that emerges particularly strongly in urban settings is how to impose a degree of manageability on who one is, when identity appears to be slipping out of one's control. Short of reorganising identity by subjection to the sheer force of a strong personality, the options are those of joining a voluntary association—at best only a partial solution. The alternative is to submit oneself to the rigours of a total institution, which stamps a group impress on the disparate parts of the individual's identity. And, as often as not, this more radical resolution of the crisis of identity posed by the city takes a religious form.

If I have somewhat labored the several influences of modernity at large in the city—the ubiquity of strangers, individual isolation and self-interest, secularization, cultural innovation, and the multiplication of identity—it is because I am at pains to discredit any claim that the shutters of apartheid screened the burgeoning African population of our cities from the impulses of modernity. For more than half a century, not only have urban dwellers been vulnerable to the forces of modernity, but also because of much oscillation of migrant labor over the same period, these modern influences have radiated and have had an impact far beyond the confines of the industrial city. Furthermore, I want to demonstrate that the AICs, or at least a large proportion of them, have provided a strong antidote to these modern strains.

Zionism as Response to Modernizing Urban Influences

Zionists represent a more interesting case than do Ethiopians or the prophet churches, not only because of their numerical strength, but because they have undergone a full transformation to modernity. They have made a long and difficult transition from the quasi-feudal relations of the Transvaal countryside, along migrant paths, to a settled urban existence. Although they remain a strong presence in rural areas, their most spectacular gains in recent years continue to be registered in the major cities. Zionists form the dominant strand of the AICs today, and probably represent some 20% in the 30% of the African population that claims affiliation to an AIC.

The now languishing denominations of mission extraction had been weaned during the infancy of Johannesburg before it assumed the proportions of a metropolitan city. However, being faithful reproductions of their parent churches, they have been unable to offer anything distinctive—beyond a nebulous African identity and the upholding of African self-respect—to the confrontation with modernity. The earlier nationalist aspirations of the Ethiopian tearaways weakened in the face of a steadily diminishing recruitment from their churches of origin, Christian denominations. It would seem that, far from resisting the process of modernity, these African denominations have in large measure succumbed to or come to terms with it.

The prophet churches, on the other hand, have consciously turned their backs on the modern world in an attempt to reinvigorate the traditional order. However, this ostrich-like rejection may be self-deceiving, for it cannot secure immunity from the reach of modernity; yet clearly indicates a resolute unwillingness to enter into any meaningful engagement with it. This dominant attitude is not without ambivalence;

witness the conspicuous presence in an election year of the leaders of the three major political parties at the annual gathering of the Zion Christian Church.

There is clearly a strong correlation between Zionist strength and modern urban conditions. Zionism presents a robust riposte to the modernity of the city.[1] Pushing against the tide of secularization, Zionism insists on the efficacy of mystical healing. Despite some pragmatic concessions to modern medicine,[2] Zionists entertain little doubt that the healing power of the Holy Spirit and/or ancestors is both superior and far more accessible.

The enforced confinement with strangers that is associated with urban settings creates relations of tension and competition, long recognised in African cultures as the ideal breeding ground of sorcery—the belief that a rival can mobilise mystical force to harm you. Zionists not only acknowledge this widely held fear, but also claim to possess the means in their healing ministry of offering relief from and protection against sorcery. This provides an effective mechanism for managing urban strangers by a form of remote control. Zionists also avoid the company of strangers as much as possible without being offensive. This might appear to exacerbate the isolation of the individual in urban life.

In their close-knit congregational communities, Zionists have the perfect response to the structural atomism of city existence. The congregation constitutes a refuge in which men and women can create a social order distinct from the surrounding "chaos." A definite system of leadership, rules, and discipline serve to shape the congregation; but what gives it substance as a community is the firm expectation of sharing and mutual support. In a time of need, a member can confidently rely on the community to rally to the relief of his/her problem, and to pool whatever resources are at hand, both spiritual and material, to ease his/her burden. In this kind of caring welfare association, no Zionist need ever feel alone or adrift.

While Zionism is clearly a negation of modernist isolation, the concomitant modernist feature of self-interest is paradoxically not rejected but actively encouraged. Zionism preaches an ethic of self-help and self-improvement through dedication to temperance, hard work, and thrift. However, this drive towards self-realisation is firmly tethered to community goals. It is the engine room that generates the small surpluses that become community parcels to be distributed as largesse on occasions of individual crisis. Those who better themselves to the point of consistently giving more are rewarded by the congregation with tangible forms of recognition, namely rank and office. None of this works perfectly or like clockwork, but the principles of reciprocity that bind the congregation into a community are never in dispute, and by and large, they operate to the benefit of all.

Zionists neatly circumvent the splintering of identity associated with modernity by their communal emphasis. Belonging to a Zionist congregation is a full-time undertaking, although membership can on occasion be marginal, whether incoming or outgoing. The congregation has the character of being virtually a total institution that seeks to command all aspects of a member's life so as to effect an all-encompassing identity. The congregation engages all of one's loyalties and interests; it morally supervises all actions and omissions, and caters for almost all needs. In addition, the congregation forms an enclosed exclusive social unit that frowns on the cultivation of external relations. There is not much scope for multiple alternative identities to that of Zionist. And the frequency of Zionist meetings, several a week, simply leaves no room for other conflicting identities. Finally, that identity is reinforced by the ridicule that other Christians almost uniformly heap on Zionists. Being a Zionist is therefore an all-or-nothing choice of commitment. In all probability, only the prophet churches can create something like this assured sense of selfhood.

Zionist churches cope with the cultural flair of the city by unambiguously turning their backs on this feature of modernity. They have their own Christian culture, which they cultivate to the exclusion of all else. One symptom of this has been the resolute refusal to participate or take an interest in political developments. In addition, the violence recently associated with political rivalry has not recommended politics to an essentially peace-loving people. Nevertheless, there have been some isolated instances of Zionist groups pledging allegiance to warring political parties. Such instances are highly exceptional, and can perhaps be expected, granted the range of variation spanned by Zionists as a whole. Evidence suggests that these aberrations have not been out of conviction, but rather enforced by circumstances or strategically adopted for protective reasons. At the other extreme, Zionists rule out of bounds all harmless recreational pursuits, such as playing football, on the grounds that they deflect time and energy from their own religious concerns. In this is reflected an uncompromising rejection of the leisure-based excitement of the city.

Nonetheless, there are some indications that the culture of modernity may now be making surreptitious inroads into Zionist lives. When I began my research at the end of the 1960s, there were few radios among them. Today, television sets[3] are owned by the relatively more affluent Zionists, such as the congregational ministers, to whose homes members of the congregation come to watch programmes—usually sports. For the moment, the ministers may exercise some control over what followers see and hear, but this may change as second-hand sets become more affordable and available to members at large.

MODERNITY AND THE FUTURE OF ZIONISM

The argument that the African population is acquainted with modernity can now be extended into a hypothesis, by supposing that the buffeting winds of change are about to approach gale force as we settle into a more open and democratic society. How will the dismantling of apartheid and the consequent liberalisation of the economy, of social and political structures, attended by reconciliation, tolerance, and greater freedom of speech and association, affect the AICs? The culture of mass consumerism, backed by international capitalism, which will flow through the electronic media, must surely bring a wave of new secular perspectives to bear on established orthodoxies. Will the AICs survive such an onslaught?

Note that only the denominational separatists have at any time hankered after a more liberal social and political dispensation and the degree of freedom and equality that accrues from it. Much of their *raison d'etre* has fallen away with the winning of these freedoms and, being better educated on the whole, their members are well placed to take advantage of these freedoms and opportunities for self-advancement and thus to become compliant with the emergent secular order. Walter Johnson's 1977 study of the Black American Episcopal Church (AME) in Zambia may be a source of further instruction. In a divided colonial society in which black people were subservient, the AME thrived on promoting African self-respect. But, with the advent of freedom and Zambian independence, the church lost much of its appeal and became "a dying institution." Its remaining function was to ease the transition of people from the countryside into the novelty of an urban way of life. In a sense, the church had become a partner in secularization. It is difficult not to envisage the same inclination on the part of all those churches, loosely termed "Ethiopian." If they do not seek amalgamation with their parent bodies, they face extinction.

The historical reaction to secular encroachment—that is, avoidance for prophet churches and consistent resistance among Zionists—is unlikely to change. Neither type of church has shown any interest in hastening the removal of barriers to the liberalisation of social and political structures; and both have opted for the creation of alternative social orders. As prime example, Zionism demonstrates that adherents are vitally concerned with the attainment of security rather than with the securing of broader societal freedoms. To this end, they construct small pockets of orderly and peaceful existence over which they can exercise control—not least by subscribing to a strict behavioural code. Within this created order they can generate mechanisms that provide mutual protection from the vicissitudes of secular life, in the form of economic support and ritual therapy.

The key to this emphasis on security and well-being is that Zionists, like the prophet churches, recruit from the ranks of the poor, particularly the impoverished urban working class. It would be utopian to believe that the liberalisation of the economy will engulf the poor in an unprecedented wave of prosperity. The poor will, therefore, remain a fixture on the urban map and the churches of healing will be one of their few recourses in their quest for security, protection, and health. Widespread poverty is not the only prop of the healing churches. If sorcery were eliminated, the appeal exercised by Zionists would be severely damaged, though it would hardly make a dent in the miraculous qualities of the great prophet leaders. There is little likelihood, however, that sorcery will dissipate under the enlightenment of secular rationalism. It will keep pace with the growth of African cities and provide ample evidence of the persistence of the prerational. This is because sorcery is an African device for explaining and managing the stresses and strains arising from the propinquity of strangers, itself an inescapable feature of the modern city. To that extent, sorcery is a symptom of the pressures of modernity. The greater the drift from the countryside and the more people are compressed in crowded cities, all of which can be anticipated, the more will sorcery surface as a social sore demanding mystical treatment. To a lesser extent, much the same can be said of the prerational belief in ancestors. Although it has a less consistent influence than sorcery on Zionist healing, it is a means of invoking and rallying close supportive relationships between kin. The city has made some inroads into this belief, depriving it of its broader basis in a coresident descent group, but a network of scattered kin, particularly of primary family relations, can be activated in the ritual invocation of a close ancestor, to serve as a safety net for survival in a city of strangers. Zionists, on the whole, do not need to draw on this device quite so much, since their religious communities supply a ready substitute.

It would be naive to suggest that healing churches will be completely unaffected by the changes introduced by an accelerating modernity. Neither the march of modernity, nor the toll it takes on resistance movements, nor their defensive adjustments to it, can be glibly predicted. If gradual shifts and changes do occur, they can only be assessed in retrospect. We know, for instance, that Zionist youth are increasingly exposed to education, subjected to the siren calls of secular fulfilment relayed through advertising and television, and jostled towards party political allegiance. It would seem safe to conclude that, because of these combined pressures, the youth will become disaffected in large numbers, thus pulling the plug on the future of their churches. But this would be misleading, because we also know that the Zionist churches have sustained considerable loss of young people over the years and have managed to survive it quite handsomely. Besides, the prospect of unbridled secularism may stiffen the resolve of the youth that remain.

To bring this to some firmer conclusion, it seems to be that the one realistic prediction that can be entertained is that neither the Zionists nor the prophet churches will yield much ground to the advance of modernity. Resting on some greater degree of certainty is the proposition that, encased in their small, close-knit and well-ordered communities, Zionists are particularly well equipped to stand firm against the invasive secularization of the modern and postmodern age.

NOTES

1. For a further treatment of urban Zionists, see West 1975 and Kiernan 1990.
2. For instance, recognising the need for a signed death certificate in order to proceed with burial.
3. Television was introduced to South Africa in 1974.

REFERENCES

Comaroff, Jean. 1985. *Body of power, spirit of resistance: The culture and history of a South African people.* Chicago and London: The University of Chicago Press.

Cox, Harvey. 1965. *The secular city.* London: SCM Press.

Johnson, Walter R. 1977. *Worship and freedom. A Black American Church in Zambia.* London: International African Institute.

Kiernan, James P. 1990. *The production and management of therapeutic power in Zionist churches within a Zulu city.* Lewiston, NY: Edwin Mellen Press.

Mahon, E. H. 1986. The formation of the Christian Catholic Church in Zion and its earliest contacts with South Africa. In *Religion alive—Studies in the new movements and indigenous churches in Southern Africa,* ed. G. C. Oosthuizen, 167–75. Johannesburg: Hodder and Stoughton.

Sundkler, Bengt. 1961. *Bantu prophets in South Africa.* 2d ed. London: Oxford University Press.

West, Martin. 1975. *Bishops and prophets in a black city.* Cape Town: David Philip.

PART II

A COMMUNITY PERSPECTIVE

3

Combining Ethnographic and Survey Methods for a Local, Comparative Study of African Independent Churches

Robert Garner

INTRODUCTION

When researchers set out on the journey of discovering the African Indigenous Churches (AICs), they immediately face a familiar choice between a quantitative and a qualitative route. The advantages—and disadvantages—that inhere in these methodological options led me to use both in a two-phase strategy for conducting research on three types of churches in Edendale township in KwaZulu-Natal, South Africa (Garner 1998). A third motive for doing so was provided by the twin aims of my research—to assess the impact of church membership on social and economic life, and to clarify the diversity of religious habits across the African indigenous, mainline, and Pentecostal churches.

My purpose in this chapter is to explain why I decided on a two-phase research strategy to test my hypotheses, which I developed from an analysis of economic and sociological theory. I will describe the steps taken at each stage of the fieldwork, such as the training of field-workers, as well as the difficulties encountered in implementing the strategy. During the course of my discussion, I will point out some of the complexities of definition in research on the AICs. This chapter introduces many of the empirical results—of my survey and of interviews conducted—that inform my analysis in chapter 4.

METHODOLOGIES USED TO STUDY AICs IN SOUTH AFRICA

Brief Critique of Some Methodologies

Table 3.1 summarises some of the research conducted on AICs in

Table 3.1:

A Summary of Methodologies and Theoretical Approaches in Previous Studies

Theoretical Paradigm	*Secondary Methods*	*Primarily Ethnographic Method*	*Primarily Survey Method*
Materialist	Chidester (1992) Kruss (1985) Mosala (1985)	*Gifford (1991)* Mosala (1989)	
Materialist/ Functionalist	Comaroffs (1991, 1992) Petersen (1996) Venter (1998)	Comaroff (1985) *Gifford (1998)* Mafeje (1975) Thomas (1994) West (1975)	West (1975)
Functionalist	Barrett (1968) Oosthuizen (various)	*Dubb (1976)* Kiernan (various) Mohr (1993) Sundkler (various)	Bekker et al. (1992) *Dubb (1976)* Oosthuizen (1987)
Idealist/ Theological	*Cox (1996)*	Makhubu (1988) Naudé (1995) Ngada (1995) Sundkler (various)	*Anderson (1992)*

Note: This (highly selective) table only includes works that add to the knowledge of AICs and black Pentecostals in South Africa. Studies that emphasize Pentecostalism are italicized.

South Africa, and illustrates the variety of methodological and theoretical approaches brought to bear.

In a survey article, Tinyiko Maluleke draws attention to the fact that most of this research has been undertaken by whites. He does not applaud this state of affairs:

This is the reason why White researchers have self-consciously had to deal with the question: what am I, as a White person, part of the oppressor group, doing amongst Black people? What right do I have to be here. Will I cope with being here? Will I understand what happens here? (Maluleke 1996, 43).

He does concede that a lifelong commitment to the people studied might mitigate the disadvantages and the impertinence, with which the White researcher embarks on such a project; but, in his view, few have demonstrated such a commitment.

Another criticism of research on AICs is that it is too partisan, often conducted by people with a theological position to vindicate (Chidester 1989, 27). Certainly, missionaries or missiologists, who have been concerned to reach a specifically theological evaluation of AICs, have conducted a number of studies. But the many works by social anthropologists, such as Martin West and Jim Kiernan, do not fall into this category. In any case, the possibility of intellectual neutrality (methodological atheism) in social research is increasingly discounted.

My own position needs to be clarified. As a white Englishman, there was never any doubt that the subjects of my study would consider me an outsider. I am also an Evangelical Christian. Hence I fall foul, potentially, of both Maluleke's and Chidester's criticisms. I would counter that both factors had a positive flip side. My obvious "otherness" as *umlungu* (white), and my limited command of *isiZulu*, certainly meant that I missed much that a Zulu researcher would have noted. But this was compensated for by the fact that people were usually interested to meet me, and willing to spend time with me for their own amusement. My familiarity with theology and church practice in several traditions, and in some cases my Evangelical experience of faith, were invaluable in the understanding and interpretation of some events and discussions, and gained me access and openness that would have been denied to a more agnostic researcher. This is particularly true of the Pentecostal churches in my study, with their pervasive dualism and scepticism of those who are not "born again."

COMBINED RESEARCH STRATEGY AS ALTERNATIVE

At an early stage of my planning I decided that it would be necessary to conduct primary research. This was, first, because socio-economic concerns feature only marginally in the studies that exist, and when they do, they are not framed in the categories developed from the theoretical approach I had adopted. Second, very little primary research exists on Pentecostal or Mainline churches. Third, much of the work based on secondary sources (especially census data) fails to capture the nuances of belief and worship, or the significance of religious intensity. Finally, it may rely too heavily on the official statements of church leaders, rather than lay members—this is certainly true of research on Mainline Christianity.

But what form should this primary research take? A review of the literature left me torn between the rival attractions of survey and ethnographic approaches. Without doubt, the ethnographic work produced in Latin America and in Africa on Pentecostals and on the "grassroots" Base Communities which incarnate Liberation Theology provides the richest and most interesting accounts. However, there is a tendency in these accounts to rely on anecdote, and so there are frequently doubts as to the generalizability ("reliability") of their conclusions. They may become highly subjective interpretations. This is especially true of the most attractive accounts, such as those of the Comaroffs, whose fecund imaginations extrapolate creatively from the banal.

Survey research also has limitations. It is questionable whether the kind of information that can be thus gathered will ever reflect the subtlety of the complex relationship between religious affiliation and economic behaviour. Nevertheless, I initially hoped to explore certain social and economic *attitudes*, as well as basic household data, in this way. However, after a period of preliminary research—during which I visited about 30 churches and conducted 50 questionnaire-based interviews—I was forced to accept that the survey, even when translated into Zulu and administered by Zulu speakers, could be trusted (would have "validity") only for factual—rather than evaluative—information. For issues that required more detailed probing, I would use in-depth interviews, and also attend as many religious events and services as possible.

Hence, the adoption of a two-phase strategy. Over a nine-month period, I used a questionnaire for a large-scale survey, and followed this with in-depth interviews and ethnographic study of selected congregations. During this time, I lived in Edendale, a step that immeasurably enhanced my exposure to the environment and people that I wished to study, and the facility of implementing my strategy. The various stages are summarised in table 3.2.

In the following sections, I describe the area in which I conducted the study and outline the physical, social, and theological factors that shaped

Table 3.2:

Fieldwork Timetable

Preliminary	October to December 1996	Church visits, questionnaires
Phase 1	March to May 1997	Survey
Phase 2	June to November 1997	Ethnography

the questionnaire, the sampling strategy, and the implementation of the survey.

USING A QUESTIONNAIRE SURVEY ON AICs

Locating the Study

Edendale is a township at the southwestern edge of Pietermaritzburg, the old provincial capital of KwaZulu-Natal. Located in the beautiful valley of the Msunduzi River, and flanked by rolling hills, the township is socially diverse. There is plenty of poverty: more than one adult in three is unemployed, 30% of households live below the extreme poverty line, 40–50% live in mud-built dwellings, 60% have no sanitation (in each case, not dissimilar to the aggregate data for black South Africa). Yet there is a small core of high-income households, and Edendale boasts some fine houses and the occasional Mercedes. In 1997, only three years after South Africa's first democratic elections, genuine improvements in infrastructure were already evident, notably in the almost universal provision of electricity. Bustling, diverse, often violent, it is in many ways a socioeconomic microcosm of black South Africa. Indeed, it was the fascinating juxtaposition of such economic and theological variety that first persuaded me to undertake my research in South Africa.

The area I chose for detailed study, which covered the most populous parts of Edendale, was a 2 km. by 4 km. strip straddling the highway through the township. The population of this area is perhaps eighty thousand. Edendale was a suitable context for the research because of its size (large enough to encompass real diversity, small enough for me to get to know it pretty well), and also because of its cultural homogeneity (as the survey confirmed, it is almost completely Zulu).

Deciding on a Unit of Study and Constructing a Questionnaire

The unit of study was primarily the individual respondent and secondarily the household. Individuals were asked a series of questions concerning the practices of the church they attended, and their own religious habits (i.e., frequency of church attendance, prayer life, bible reading, reasons for joining or leaving a particular church). There were also questions about basic personal data (age, sex, occupation, household and personal income, education). The 334 individuals interviewed comprised the "small" sample referred to later.

I also wanted to use the survey to find out about the religious habits of the household. I realised that women, many of whom are housewives, or unemployed, would answer most of the questionnaires. So, a section of the questionnaire was devoted to other adult household members, but was confined to categories where the respondent would be able to give accurate information (age, sex, occupation, church membership and attendance, if any; but not educational level, prayer and Bible reading habits, or reasons for attending a particular church). In this way, data was gathered on 1,003 adult inhabitants of Edendale—the "large" sample.

The questionnaire contained very few open questions. Most of the answers required would be brief and factual, and many would be limited to a multiple choice between four or five alternatives. Many of the questions, especially those relating to the practices of each church and its members, were modelled on Anderson's survey of Soshanguve (1992). My intention was to provide comparative data to that research.

The questionnaire aimed to identify the theological type attended by each respondent. In the case of the AICs, this is a particular challenge, due to the great proliferation of churches, their frequently extraordinary—and misleading—names, and the impossibility of checking out each church with a visit. The questionnaire asked whether the church attended by the respondent made use, in its public worship, of certain practices (a positive response being associated with Zionism). These practices were: baptism by immersion; the office of prophet; the office of bishop; the use of drums; dancing; healing in church meetings; the use of accessories—ropes and the like—in healing; casting out demons; and speaking in tongues.

I then compiled a "Zionist Index," which was merely a sum of the answers to these questions. A church with a high score would be more likely to be Zionist. However, some of the practices might be common to other types of churches. Mainline churches and non-Zionist AICs usually have bishops, for example. Pentecostal churches baptise by immersion, heal people and speak in tongues, but do not usually have bishops, use accessories for healing, or African drums in worship. Apostolic churches eschew some of the trappings of Zionism—the use of drums, and accessories in healing. In my categorisation, a church would count as Zionist-Apostolic if it included the word "Zion" or "Apostolic" in its name, or registered a medium to high score on the "Zionist Index." I placed other AICs, which mostly demonstrated a smaller number of "Zionist" tendencies, or whose character I could establish from other research, in a "non-Zionist AIC." This corresponds to the "Ethiopian" category in Sundkler's classic typology, except that it includes the Shembe church that Sundkler originally thought "Zionist."

The questionnaire also explored the religious and social habits of church members. Following Anderson (1992), my questions followed the form: "Do members of your church . . . ," rather than "Do you . . ." The latter format might have discouraged honest responses; and it seemed probable that many would answer the former question with their own practice, anyway, under the cover of anonymity. These questions focused on two areas. First, their involvement with traditional African culture: Did they offer animal sacrifices; consult with their ancestors;[1] consult with diviners (*izaNgoma*); consult with traditional healers (*iziNyanga*)? Responses to these questions were summed into an "African Index." The second focus was lifestyle—questions on smoking, drinking, tithing.

The questionnaire then asked about the personal religious habits of the respondent. How often did they attend church, pray on their own, and read the Bible. Responses to these three questions were then summed into a "Religious Intensity Index."

Finally, the questionnaire gathered basic socioeconomic data on both the respondent and other members of that household.

Administering the Questionnaire

Most interviews were completed during daylight, for reasons of personal safety. Edendale was one of the most violent townships in South Africa in the late 1980s and early 1990s. By 1997, the situation was qualitatively different, but remained volatile, and locals still considered some areas "no-go" zones after dark. While I encouraged the field-workers to work on weekends, limiting them to this would have delayed completion of the survey considerably; so much of the work was done during the week. This inevitably meant that a preponderance of the respondents were women, and people not working. As one of my objectives was to discover information about churches, the first imbalance did not concern me—a South African woman is much more likely to be well acquainted with her church than her male counterpart. The occupational imbalance did concern me; but I hoped that a representative picture of the population would emerge from the "large" sample, which included all adult household members.

Training Field-Workers

To prepare and administer the questionnaire, I employed six field-workers, all graduate students at the local university. Meeting twice a week over four weeks, I took these field-workers through a four-week programme to train them for the specific requirements of the survey (see table 3.3, see next page). I briefed them on the general aims and objectives of my research, the type of data that I wanted to gather, and the gaps that I felt existed in other research. I did not, however, discuss with them the nascent hypotheses that I had formed.

Table 3.3:

Timetable for Training Field-Workers

Week one	Introduction to my research, its objectives and methodology	Translation of questionnaire into Zulu, by field-workers, in pairs; translation back into English
Week two	Discussion of sensitive questions: e.g., ancestor worship, political affiliation	Review of first translation attempts
Week three	Pilot interviews in Edendale using Zulu translation	Review of second translation
Week four	Discussion of problems encountered in pilot interviews	Explanation of sampling method, household selection. Schedule for real interviews

This period also served as an opportunity to translate the draft questionnaire into Zulu and to identify questions that were ambiguous or that respondents would be unlikely to answer truthfully or fully. One example was political affiliation: I would have been interested to know if this related to religious affiliation. However, I had discovered in my preliminary study that political affiliation was a highly charged question: for many in Edendale, over the previous decade, it had been quite literally a matter of life and death. I decided it was not ethical to ask people to share information that could, however remote the possibility, place them in any kind of danger or cause them serious anxiety, and this decision was reinforced by the outbreak of political violence in Dambuza, a part of Edendale, during Phase 1.

To obtain a good translation, I divided the draft questionnaire into two parts, and split the six field-workers into pairs. I then gave each person a copy, in English, of one-half of the questionnaire, and asked them to translate it into Zulu. When this was completed, I asked the members of each pair to take away with them the Zulu translation prepared by their "other half," and to translate it back into English. At the following session, we reviewed these English versions, and noted where they differed from my English original. We then discussed these differences, and worked together on a collegiate Zulu draft. Over the following weeks, further changes were made, correcting mistakes and ironing out lingering misunderstandings. The Zulu version was formatted so that each interview fitted onto the two sides of a single sheet of A4-sized paper (21 cm by 29.7 cm)—a small detail that greatly simplified data management and reduced costs.

A further aspect of this training period was to pilot the Zulu questionnaires and to provide practice for the field-workers. To do this, I took each field-worker to some part of Edendale (usually just outside the 2 km. by 4 km. grid) to spend three hours conducting questionnaires. After this, I discussed with them the problems they had encountered and the questions that people were unwilling to answer.

In the final training session, the sampling process was explained using the map I had obtained of the area. I also explained the procedure for choosing the houses that they had to visit, and the numbering system.

On reflection, it would have been worthwhile to spend longer on this preparation and training. Despite all attempts to iron out ambiguities, some misunderstandings came to light after the real interviews had been conducted. Two field-workers had not followed my numbering process, although this was not of great consequence other than from the perspective of my own administration. More seriously, one of the workers misunderstood one of the church attendance categories, and it was necessary to send this worker back to all the households concerned to clarify their data. This was costly, time-consuming, and inconvenient. All of the field-workers made some mistakes or omissions in their interviews, although the incidence of this was thankfully small. Most questions were answered for around 99% of the sample.

Field-workers were paid by the hour rather than per interview, in an attempt to prevent them rushing the respondents. Each kept a printed time sheet that included the time spent locating each household and returning to households where they could not originally conduct an interview. The average time per interview was forty-five minutes. I also paid them a quality related bonus at the end of the survey.

The Sampling and Selection Process

I knew that my limited resources would only allow me to conduct three to four hundred interviews. Under pressure of time as well as money, I wanted to conduct the whole survey during the month of April 1997. I decided to use a combination of cluster and random samplings in an attempt to ensure even coverage of the diverse conditions that coexist in Edendale, socially (from well-appointed brick houses to single-room shacks built of mud or corrugated iron) and geographically (from concentrated periurban areas to open fields and steep hillsides).

No sample frame of the population of Edendale exists. Only a minority of the homes have telephones or water, and while the provision of electricity is remarkably widespread, it is far from complete. For this reason, the records of these utilities could not be used to create a frame.

The area has recently passed from the municipal authority of the Province of KwaZulu-Natal to that of the Transitional Local Council (TLC) of Pietermaritzburg. Records of land tenure exist, but are frequently at variance with the situation "on the ground"; informal and semiformal housing has flourished without respect for official boundaries.

In the absence of a sample frame, I obtained a detailed map,[2] which, based on aerial photographs taken in 1995, showed almost all of the dwellings in the area concerned. Although this map proved to be extremely accurate, even down to the shape of the houses and their outbuildings, I decided not to create a sample frame by numbering all of the houses in the selected area, for three reasons. First, some informal dwellings had sprung up since 1995, and a few houses had been demolished. Second, it could not be assumed that one dwelling would be equivalent to one household: there was no way of telling from the photograph the difference between a garage, an empty storeroom, and a family dwelling. And, frequently, more than one household would live in a single building. Third, it would have taken much longer to number the houses than to adopt the spatial cluster method that I eventually used—as it would also have taken much longer to visit and interview four hundred randomly selected households than five households at each of eighty cluster points. A similar selection process and sample size was used by Bekker et al. (1992).

I decided to choose, randomly, eighty points on this map, and to interview one individual from each of the five households closest to that point. To choose the points, I laid a grid of two hundred "squares," each 200 metres by 200 metres, across the map of Edendale, covering the study area of 2 km. by 4 km. Each of these squares was then divided into twenty-five "mini-squares" (each 40 metres by 40 metres). This gave me a total of five thousand mini-squares; from 0.0 to 199.25. Using a list of random numbers, I selected eighty of these mini-squares. These numbers were taken from appendix A in H. R. Bernard (1994). I entered the list at random, chose eighty numbers between 0 and 199 (using the last three digits of successive columns of five-digit numbers). For each of these "squares" I then randomly chose a number between one and twenty-five (using the last two digits of another series of columns) to choose the "mini-square."

On two occasions, a mini-square was chosen twice, and for these two duplicates, the next mini-square up was taken. Another more frequent occurrence was that the mini-square would fall on land that contained fewer than five households, or was in nonresidential use. On these occasions, I selected the five households closest to the centre of the mini-square, even if they were outside the mini-square itself, provided that they did not fall more than 100 metres from the centre of that mini-square. Hence, some mini-squares produced fewer than five completed questionnaires, and some produced none at all.

To identify selected households, I visited each mini-square with the field-worker allocated to that area. Using the map, it was possible to pinpoint each building, and to ascertain which of these were inhabited by more than one household. The field-workers, who also had copies of the map for their areas, noted the selected houses and made the necessary return trips until this survey was completed.

Unfortunately, a major revision of this strategy was necessitated by events in March and April 1997. I have already alluded to the violent recent history of Edendale. The bloody battle for supremacy of the valley between the mostly urban African National Congress (ANC) and the mostly rural Inkatha Freedom Party was decided in favour of the ANC in 1991, and all of the areas in my study were ANC-controlled. A political feud within the ANC had been developing in the latter months of 1996, revolving around the Dambuza branch of the organisation. In early 1997, this feud broke out into violence, with random shooting sprees between groups of armed youths in the area where the territories of the rival factions met. Eventually, in early April, when daily shootings and frequent deaths threatened to undermine the everyday life of Dambuza completely, troops were sent in to patrol the streets. This brought an end to the shooting, by day at least. However, Dambuza was cast under a pall of suspicion and mistrust.

Approximately twenty of the eighty mini-squares chosen fell within Dambuza. I was extremely reluctant to abandon these mini-squares, and at the outset of the survey, at the beginning of April, the field-workers and I decided that we would begin with other parts of Edendale, and come back to Dambuza later in the month. In the second half of April, one of the field-workers, who was an ANC member and very familiar with the area, agreed to conduct some interviews in the part of Dambuza under the sway of his "faction." However, he encountered a great deal of suspicion and little cooperation from the people he tried to interview. After this attempt to preserve the original strategy, I capitulated.

To replace the thirteen mini-squares lost in this way, I obtained a map of an area adjacent to the original 2 km. by 4 km. area, which was reasonably similar, both in size and in social constitution, to the area lost. I applied the same selection technique to this area, and field-workers completed the necessary interviews early in May 1997.

Analysing the Responses

I immediately coded and recorded the 334 completed interviews and loaded the results onto an Excel spreadsheet database. This made it possible to sort and analyse the data by various criteria.

This analysis produced a number of surprises, and suggested various insights and connections relating to my hypotheses that had not previously occurred to me. The process of sifting through the data, and thus becoming familiar with the social and theological landscape of Edendale, equipped me for the next stage, the ethnographic study.

CONDUCTING AN ETHNOGRAPHIC STUDY WITH IN-DEPTH INTERVIEWS

Selection of Churches

The survey showed that the two dominant types of churches in Edendale were the mainline churches and the AICs, especially those designated Zionist-Apostolic (table 3.4).

Table 3.4:

Membership of Church Types in Edendale[a]

Mission Churches	*%*	*African Independent Churches*	*%*
Mainline	46.6 (37.5)		
		Non-Zionist AIC	7.4 (10.4)
		Zionist-Apostolic AIC[b]	24.9 (32.4)
Pentecostal	3.6 (6.0)	Pentecostal AIC	0.7 (2.9)
All Mission Churches	50.2 (43.5)	All AICs	33.0 (45.7)

Notes:

a. The figures in parentheses represent the findings of Anderson's survey (1992, 62), the closest proxy that exists in the literature.

b. The Zionist-Apostolic category includes the Zion Christian Church (ZCC).

The "market share" of mainline churches was, at 46.6%, well above the national average for blacks of 32% in the 1996 Census. The share of Pentecostal churches, at about 4%, was lower than anticipated, well below the 8.9% Anderson had found in Soshanguve, or the 8%–10% for blacks in the 1996 Census.

I decided to study two churches from the Zionist-Apostolic category—one Zionist in the traditional sense, another Apostolic—and to treat these, in the later analysis, as representatives of different "types." Based on the survey responses, I explored the possibility of establishing a taxonomy to distinguish between "Apostolic" and "Zionist" churches. This would have enabled me to distribute the 24.9% of respondents between the two subcategories. However, this was simply impossible: reported practices and characteristics overlapped too extensively. Yet, despite the fuzzy boundary between the two, differences between churches at opposite poles of the Zionist-Apostolic continuum are both striking and substantive, as chapter 4 demonstrates. This distinctiveness is illustrated by the fact that some members of Apostolic churches refer to themselves as *amaZiyoni* (Zionists); whereas others prefer the term *abaSindiswa* (saved), the self-designation of Pentecostals.

The largest church in this category at the national level is the Zion Christian Church (ZCC) of South Africa, with more than 4,97 million claimed adherents (2001 census). Periodic national surveys by the Human Sciences Research Council confirm its considerable reach: the (1996) survey found that 10.1% of all respondents belong to the ZCC, the (1997) survey 6.3%. Anderson found 10.3% in his survey of Soshanguve, and Census 2001 indicates 11.09%. However, the ZCC is strongest in the northern provinces of South Africa (Gauteng, Limpopo, Mpumalanga, Free State, North West), where 64.02% of affiliates reside. Far fewer adherents come from KwaZulu Natal; about 24% (2001 census). In my survey, exactly 3% of the sample claimed to belong to the ZCC, and I later discovered that many of these in fact belonged to the local Zion Congregational Church, which is also called "ZCC" by Edendale residents. During my eight months there, only twice did I see the green felt badge and silver star that all members of the "real" ZCC wear.

The Zionist-Apostolic Church with most members in the survey was the Twelve Apostles Church in Christ (TACC), with 3.4% of the sample. After a few visits, it was evident that the TACC was not Zionist in the classical mould, but rather Apostolic. Some close neighbours of mine in Edendale belonged to a more traditional Zionist congregation, the Golden Christian Society of Zion in South Africa (GCSZ). I divided my research time and interviews for the Zionist-Apostolic category equally between these two churches.

In addition, I interviewed members of mainline and Pentecostal churches, as well as a "No Church" control group, as table 3.5 shows.

Instruments and Unit of Study

The main unit of study was the individual church member. From each of the chosen theological types I attempted to interview twenty people. I

Table 3.5:

Meetings Attended and Respondents Interviewed During Phase 2

	Mainline		*Pentecostal*		*Apostolic*		*Zionist*		*No Church*		*Total*
Meetings attended		12		14		9		5			40
Meetings of same church type		9		7				5			21
Occupation by gender	M	F	M	F	M	F	M	F	M	F	
Unemployed	2	2	1	2		1	2	3	2	2	17
Low Skill	1	2	2	2	2		1	1	2	2	15
Medium Skill	1	1	2	3	2	1			2	2	14
High Skill	3	2	1	2		1	1		1	2	13
Entrepreneur		1	1		1				1		4
Student	1	2	2	1	2			1	2	2	13
Minister	1		1								2
Total	9	10	10	10	7	3	4	5	10	10	78

chose these as follows: ten men, and ten women. Of each sex, two unemployed, two low-skill workers, two medium-skill workers, two high-skill workers, and two students. For each church, I enlisted the help of the minister and other senior members to identify the people I would interview.

Predictably, this neat outline was not strictly adhered to. As Kant so pertinently observed, out of the crooked timber of humanity, no straight thing was ever made, and few social researchers would take issue with the philosopher on this point. Sometimes the congregation simply did not contain people of the categories required; sometimes people were unidentifiable, unobtainable, or just unwilling to be interviewed. People also occasionally fell between my occupational categories. Some security guards, whom I would usually have categorised as low-skill workers, had received on-the-job training in, say, driving skills or the use of firearms, which would push them into my medium-skill category. One young woman, unemployed at our first meeting, had a medium-skill job soon after. Those who were unemployed all engaged in some kind of informal economic activity—sewing dresses, selling beer or vegetables, helping to build mud houses; but when did these informal activities constitute a low-skill job, or even entrepreneurialism? Nevertheless, with the exception of the Zionist church,[3] the general shape of my research design was maintained. Hence, the approximate numerical symmetry of table 3.5 in terms of both gender and occupation.

Group Discussions

In addition to these interviews, I wanted to conduct group discussions with young people from each church on sexuality and AIDS. This was only possible for two of the theological types. For the other types, and the control "No Church" category, it was not possible to convene a group discussion, but I talked with a number of young men and women individually, using the scenarios, to ascertain both their views and their assessment of typical behaviour among their peer group. These discussions, which were conducted in English and Zulu, also used scenarios to stimulate debate and draw out people's views.

CONCLUDING REMARKS: DATA, VALIDITY, RELIABILITY

The two phases of research, and the time spent living in Edendale, produced three formal data sets and much complementary material of an ethnographic type: dozens of informal interviews with Edendale residents, church leaders, and development workers; observations of more than sixty church services, prayer meetings, and healing rituals; and the group discussions on sexual behaviour.

Table 3.6:

Data Collected During Fieldwork

Research Phase	*Name of Data Set*	*n*	*% female*	*Selection Process*	*Type of Information*
Phase 1	Large Sample	1,003	59	Random Cluster	Quantitative: basic personal data and church attendance of all adults in household
Phase 1	Small Sample	334	68	Random Cluster	Quantitative: more detailed personal data and church characteristics of respondent
Phase 2	Interview Sample	78	49	Stratified (by sex, church, occupation)	Quantitative: detailed personal data of respondent Qualitative: opinions and reflections on scenarios
Phase 2	Group Discussions	2	n/a	Church Youth Group	Qualitative: opinions and reflections on scenarios

Before proceeding to an analysis of some of these data in the following chapter, some consideration must be given to their quality. In particular, we must consider the validity of the data (do they measure what they claim?); reliability (do they represent the population from which the sample is drawn?); and the soundness of the epistemological basis of this inquiry (what do we actually learn from the data?).

The validity of the quantitative data probably rises as the sample size falls (see table 3.6). The large sample relied on secondhand information, albeit of a basic nature, when the respondent was asked about the occupation, age, sex, and church attendance of other adults in the household. The unexpected preponderance of women and of the mainline churches in this sample must prompt a certain caution. Nevertheless, the selection procedure was sound and the field-workers competent, so I believe these data are, broadly, both valid and reliable. In the small sample, the same respondents were asked more detailed questions, but only about themselves, and only of a factual (rather than evaluative) nature. This data set merits a high level of confidence in terms of both validity and reliability.

In Phase 2, the researcher, not the field-workers, conducted the interviews and discussions, with an interpreter where necessary (roughly one interview in three). The quantitative data gathered in this way—detailed information about life history, education, income, occupation, and church attendance—have a high validity. The deliberate stratification of the sample does affect their reliability.

The qualitative data collected during these interviews was of various kinds. Some questions were completely "open," for example, "What do you think is good or bad about Zulu culture?" and "How would you stop the spread of AIDS in South Africa?" But many of the questions gave the respondent a range of possible answers, for instance, "Which language is it more important for children to know—English, Zulu, or both equally?" Although it was not always presented in this form to the respondent, I immediately coded some answers into an ordinal scale that, for example, measured the degree of support for the redistribution of wealth. More frequently, possible answers were suggested in a range of discrete or nominal possibilities. This happened in the scenarios, when respondents had to make choices between rival claims on savings, such as educational costs, payment of bride price, or ritual sacrifice. And even questions to which answers could be ordinally ranked also invited further discussion and elaboration.

Because the thrust of the inquiry was comparative—assessing the impact of different theological types—the comparability of these qualitative responses is important. To ensure this, as far as possible, all interviews used the same written schedule, the same wording, and the same alternatives. The respondent always had a copy of the questions in English or Zulu, as they preferred. All of the interviews that required translation used the same translator, a young Zulu woman from Edendale with impeccable and colloquial English, who worked from the same written schedule of questions and scenarios in Zulu. The group discussions also worked from a written sheet, which contained scenarios and a set of questions, and of which each member of the group had a copy.

Nevertheless, there are dangers attendant on any process of evaluative data collection. There could be a tendency to see nascent hypotheses confirmed, to lead respondents by a smile, a shrug, a strategic "really?" in the conversation. And, the researcher could be tempted to fish for certain responses with follow-up questions under the guise of clarification. Alternatively, a sudden feeling could dawn that perhaps you have completely misunderstood an answer you thought was leading to familiar terrain.

It is impossible to deny the subjectivity of this pursuit of capricious knowledge, of quicksilver truth. And this presumes that the answers given *contain* the truth. All that one can claim with certainty about a given response is that it was given as a response. Does it really convey what the respondent thought, or meant? As the poverty and insecurity of the respondent rises, so does the risk that respondents give the answer they think you want. For the wealthy or educated, does the response represent a justification, or an ideal that bears little resemblance to reality? This is a genuine risk, given the religious and value-laden quality of the questions asked, such as "How much money do you give to your church?" and "Do people in your church have premarital sex?" Finally, respondents may genuinely believe their answers to be true, but may construct or deconstruct the real and the imagined.

There seems to be no satisfactory answer to these objections. The researcher who continues to believe in the value of ethnography, observation, and subjective evaluation can only persist in making measured claims with a sense of epistemological humility. Because of these factors, the deliberate stratification of respondents, and the small size of the sample, the qualitative data from Phase 2 cannot do more than *suggest* conclusions that might hold more generally. Such data is perhaps most effectively used in support of data that are more objective.

NOTES

1. Choosing the right word here was the object of lengthy consideration. The verb *ukuxhumana*, to consult, or communicate with, was chosen instead of *ukukhonza*, to worship or reverence. Even in *ukuxhumana* there is some ambiguity over whether the ancestors (*amaDlozi*) are considered to have power to influence events and outcomes (and must therefore be propitiated), or whether they function more like saints in Catholic hagiopraxis, as intercessors between the believer and God.

2. The map was generously provided, at no cost, by Tarboton, Holder, Ross and Partners, surveyors in Pietermaritzburg. Their invaluable assistance is gratefully acknowledged.

3. None of the GCSZ members had jobs above low skill status. I supplemented this category with two other Zionists I had met: a man in a high skill job, and a female student.

REFERENCES

Anderson, Allan H. 1992. *Bazalwane: African Pentecostalism in South Africa.*

Pretoria: University of South Africa.

Barrett, David. 1968. *Schism and renewal in Africa*. Nairobi: Oxford University Press.

Bekker, Simon B., Catherine R. Cross, J. P. Evans, and G. C. Oosthuizen. 1992. *Rise up and walk: Development and the African Independent Churches in Durban*. Unpublished report, Centre for Social and Development Studies, University of Natal, Durban.

Bernard, H. R. 1994. *Research methods in anthropology: Qualitative and quantitative approaches*. London: Sage Publications.

Chidester, David. 1992. *Religions of South Africa*. London: Routledge.

———. 1989. Worldview analysis of African Indigenous Churches. *Journal for the Study of Religion* 2: 15–29.

Comaroff, Jean. 1985. *Body of power, spirit of resistance*. Chicago: Chicago University Press.

Comaroff, Jean, and John L. Comaroff. 1992. *Ethnography and the historical imagination*. Boulder: Westview Press.

———. 1991. *Of revelation and revolution: Christianity, colonialism and consciousness in South Africa*. Chicago: Chicago University Press.

Cox, Harvey. 1996. *Fire from heaven: The rise of Pentecostal spirituality and the reshaping of religion in the twenty first century*. London: Cassell.

Dubb, A. A. 1976. *Community of the saved: An African revivalist church in the East Cape*. Johannesburg: University of Witwatersrand Press.

Garner, Robert C. 1998. *Religion and economics in a South African township*. Ph.D. Dissertation, University of Cambridge.

Gifford, Paul. 1998. *African Christianity: Its public role*. London: Hurst.

———. 1991. *The new crusaders: Christianity and the New Right in Southern Africa*. London: Pluto Press.

Human Sciences Research Council. 1997. *Omnibus survey* (February). Pretoria: Human Sciences Research Council.

———. 1996. *Omnibus survey* (July). Pretoria: Human Sciences Research Council.

Kiernan, James P. 1990. *The production and management of therapeutic power in a Zulu City*. Lampeter: Edwin Mellen Press.

Kruss, Glenda. 1985. *Religion, class and culture: Indigenous Churches in South Africa, with special reference to Zionist-Apostolics*. MA thesis, University of Cape Town.

Mafeje, Archie. 1975. Religion, class and ideology in South Africa. In *Religion and social change in Southern Africa,* ed. M. G. Whisson and Martin West, 164–84. Cape Town: David Philip.

Makhubu, P. 1988. *Who are the Independent Churches?* Braamfontein: Skotaville.

Maluleke, Tinyiko S. 1996. Theological interest in AICs and other grassroot communities in South Africa. *Journal of Black Theology in South Africa* 10 (1): 18–28.

Mohr, Matthias. 1993. *Negotiating the boundary: The response of KwaMashu*

Zionists to a volatile political climate. Ph.D. thesis, University of Natal, Durban.

Mosala, Itumaleng. 1989. *Race, class and gender as hermeneutical factors in the African Independent Churches' appropriation of the Bible: A final report to the Human Sciences Research Council.* Research Report. Pretoria: Human Sciences Research Council.

———. 1985. African Independent Churches: A study in socio-theological protest. In *Resistance and hope: South African essays in honour of Beyers Naudé,* ed. Charles Villa Vicencio and John W. DeGruchy, 103–11. Grand Rapids: Eerdmans.

Naudé, Piet. 1995. *The Zionist Christian Church in South Africa: A case study in oral theology.* New York: Edwin Mellen Press.

Ngada, Nduruso H. 1995. *Speaking for ourselves.* Braamfontein: Skotaville.

Oosthuizen, G. C. 1987. The AICs and the Modernisation Process. *Africana Marburgensia* XX (1): 59–81 and XX (2): 5–17.

Petersen, Robin M. 1996. *Time, resistance and reconstruction: A theology of the prophetic and the popular.* Ph.D. Dissertation, University of Chicago.

StatsSA. 2004. *Census 2001 by province, gender, religion recode (derived) and population group.* Statistics South Africa. (URL: http://www.statssa.gov.za/SpecialProjects/Census2001/Census/Dialog/varval.asp?ma=Religionbyprovince&ti=Table%3A+Census+2001+by+province%2C+gender%2C+religion+recode+%28derived%29+and++population+group%2E+&path=../Database/Census%202001/Provincial%20Level/Persons/&lang=)

Sundkler, Bengt G. M. 1948; 1961. *Bantu prophets in South Africa.* London: Oxford University Press.

Thomas, Linda E. 1994. African Indigenous Churches as a source of socio-political transformation in South Africa. *Africa Today* 41 (1): 39–56.

Venter, Dawid J. 1998. Globalisation and the emergence of African Initiated Churches. *Missionalia* 26 (3): 412–38.

West, Martin. 1975. *Bishops and prophets in a black city: African Independent Churches in Soweto, Johannesburg.* Cape Town: David Philip.

4

African Independent Churches and Economic Development in Edendale

Robert Garner

INTRODUCTION

African Independent Churches (AICs) are the churches of the poor—that is to say, most of their members are poor, and most of the poor are their members. Both national survey data and the evidence from Edendale (see chapter 4) confirm this truism. A distinct but related question concerns the *effect* of AIC membership on the socioeconomic circumstances of members. In this chapter, I provide an answer by comparing two different AICs: one Apostolic, one Zionist.[1]

RELIGION AND ECONOMICS IN SOUTH AFRICA

The relationship between religion and culture, and the forms of economic arrangement that facilitate development, are contested questions to which all possible answers are ideologically framed. Objective analysis in these matters is notoriously elusive, and this chapter does not claim to be immune from the inevitable biases. The assumption underlying the following discussion is that, for all its faults, a market economy is the best option for a developing country. I also assumed that the market would function best, and distribute prosperity most widely, if it operates in a social, intellectual, and ideological context that endorses its existence, its mechanisms, and its outcomes. This support need not be unqualified—capitalism requires an ongoing critique to avoid certain built-in tendencies, such as monopoly, and rampant self-interest. But the critique should not go so far as to question the efficacy of the paradigm itself. Given this centre-right view of economics, the question for religion and culture becomes: To what extent do they create this context, in society and in the minds of men and women, this soil within which the market can take root and blossom?

Keeping this economic perspective in mind, the discussion will be arranged around four areas in which religious affiliation might promote and facilitate capitalism: the legitimation of the market economy; the creation of trust and cooperation; lifestyle; and worldview. These categories were developed from an analysis of the function of religion as perceived by two central figures in the history of economic thought, Adam Smith and Max Weber.[2] Each category is of direct relevance to present-day South Africa. Although the political dispensation of the "New" South Africa has widespread legitimacy, the economic agenda is contested: there are competing philosophies at work within the African National Congress (ANC), and contradictory interests in the population. The following outline takes into account the social realities that are symptomatic of these "contradictions": the extraordinarily high crime rate; increasing tension between the ruling ANC and its traditional allies in the labor movement; the persistent problem of nonpayment for public and private services; and the collapse of civil society, especially in the townships, where unemployment and violence are endemic. Another highly pertinent issue is that of HIV/AIDS, and the role of religion both in preventing the spread of the epidemic and in coping with its effects (Garner 1999, 2000b).

Religion has the power to *legitimate* the values and formal institutions required by a capitalist economy (private property, competition, credit markets, freer trade, specialisation) and the inequality that always accompanies these. Strongly enforced, this legitimation can reduce levels of protest in the economy and increase awareness of the need to pay for private and public services. These would seem to be necessary for economic progress, given that the new government of South Africa has decided to adopt a market-based economy and a growth-led strategy for development—in contrast to one based on redistribution, as formerly advocated by the ANC. However, religion may also *delegitimate* the system and its values, and undermine the smooth working of the system by increasing levels of protest, encouraging civil resistance, and even (unintentionally) lending legitimacy to theft as a form of "redistribution."

Religious communities may create *trust*. The high level of violence in South Africa reflects the breakdown of trust between many factions in society. Religion can catalyse the formation of new social institutions based on trust, which may be associated with economic enterprises and other types of *cooperative behaviour*, such as community efforts to reduce crime and nonpayment. Religion is therefore a source of "civil society." However, these communities may embrace the redistributive ethic that is also part of the Christian articulation, and call into question the anonymity and social distance, which facilitate the contractual requirements of an exchange economy.

Religious beliefs and practices have an impact on the overlapping categories of *lifestyle* and *worldview*. Protestant Christianity in particular has been associated with the creation of the modern mind, the idea of progress, the rejection of premodern values, and with the promotion of literacy. These factors, which might loosely be termed modernization, are taken to be positive for economic development. Religion may also foster an entrepreneurial spirit, a belief in the moral worth of advance, and "work ethic" effects such as higher rates of saving and a propensity for honesty and hard work: these have direct economic benefits for the individual and may also contribute to aggregate growth. Religion can enforce personal moral values such as sobriety, prompt payment, and avoidance of criminal activity.

If religion does impinge significantly on these categories of thought and behaviour, then the specific role of the AICs, which contain a third of South African blacks and a quarter of all South Africans, deserves careful analysis. This chapter will undertake such an analysis.

THE AICs AND ECONOMICS

The Secondary Literature

First, there is the question of the legitimation of the capitalist economy. The role of the AICs in this is difficult to gauge. While commentators almost universally agree that these churches were *politically* mute during the liberation struggle, their position on the merits of capitalism has received less attention. The Ethiopian churches (non-Zionist AICs) originated among the African bourgeoisie a century ago, and have always attracted the middle classes (Kruss 1985; Brandel-Syrier 1983, 14; Chidester 1992, 114–22). Zionist churches are harder to characterise. The oldest and largest, such as the Zion Christian Church (ZCC), may advocate prosperity, and their leaders have achieved it. The conjunction of this prosperity with a membership comprising the "poorest of the poor" has not escaped the critical eye of radical scholars (Mosala 1989, 13).

However, the ZCC, with its nationwide membership and centralised leadership, is not typical of the broader Zionist-Apostolic genre. For most Zionist congregations (and those of the ZCC itself, away from the centre) the issue is survival, not prosperity (Kiernan 1990, 42), so that they tend to treat economic success with scepticism. Matthias Mohr's (1993) discussions with economically ambitious young Zionists in KwaMashu suggest that it is necessary to leave a Zionist church to really get ahead. Not only does membership take up vast amounts of time, but also material success is considered irrelevant, or even harmful to spiritual health. If Zionists are successful, and earn any "surplus" to subsistence needs, other members expect them to share the material benefits, not to accumulate (Kiernan 1990, 222). Comaroff (1985, 237) and Petersen (1996) go further, and argue that Zionism delegitimates the whole money economy and tries to dethrone important capitalist symbols, such as time and money, through ritual.

Does Zionism create trust and cooperation? The AICs, especially Zionists, approach the model of tightly knit ideological communities that is also observed in Pentecostalism and sectarian religion. As their numbers are so much larger than these minority religious movements, the AICs may therefore represent a genuine resource for creating pockets of trust. Like Pentecostals, Zionists spend a great deal of time together—the church is the focal point of the member's social life, as confirmed by frequency of attendance. Naudé (1995, vi) argues that "[t]he inherent moral and religious force of the ZCC is an indispensable factor in shaping a new society," presumably because religious association and interaction create a form of "civil society." Such association may spill over into forms of economic organisation: the prominence of mutual aid associations, savings clubs, and *Manyano* in Zionist churches is well documented (Bekker et al. 1992; Brandel-Syrier 1983; Oosthuizen 1986; West 1975). Oosthuizen and Clark (1994, 4), perhaps contentiously, argue that Zionist churches "are increasingly coming to interpret their spiritual role in terms of the material conditions facing their laity." They allegedly promote economic advance by encouraging small business development, boosting the crucial informal sector. In so doing, the benefits may transcend the boundaries of the Zionist community, although, if it were to occur, this would probably be accidental: there is a strong current of exclusiveness in Zionist theology and practice, as Kiernan (1974) and Mohr (1993) found in KwaMashu (a Durban township). Bekker et al. (1992) identify several factors that limit the capacity of AICs to perform a developmental role: they are too fragile and fissiparous; they lack skills and resources for effective communication and organisation. Crucially, the strength of association and support in AICs depends on the fact that they are small, surrogate family structures, focusing *de facto* on the needs of each other rather than of the community.

Two of the most respected scholars in the field of AIC research (Oosthuizen 1987; Turner 1980) have argued that a change of worldview—from traditional to modern—is necessary for economic development to take place in the African community. This change in worldview will then lead to various changes in lifestyle, consistent with development. They define the essential changes in similar terms: a shift from communalism to individualism; a change in the perception of nature from a dominating force to a resource that can be controlled and utilised; the perception of time as a definable and measurable commodity; and an emphasis on the rational rather than the magical. Both authors, with some qualifications, go on to assert that the AICs assist this transition. This claim is problematic: some research on AICs points in exactly the opposite direction. For example, Sundkler's notorious observation that the Zionist churches were a bridge by which members were brought back to the "nativistic" world they had left behind (1961, 55).[3] In chapter 2 of this book, Kiernan depicts Zionism as providing both an antidote to modernity and an adaptation of it. Hammond-Tooke (1998) argues that Zionists "opt out of modernity." Anderson (1992, 35) found very high levels of involvement in traditional practices (such as communicating with ancestors) among Zionists—although this was also very common in mainline churches, which are usually associated with a higher level of "development." Bekker et al. designate the value structure of their AIC respondents as "traditional." The connection between Zionism and lower educational attainment (or opportunity) is surely pertinent here, as pointed out in chapters 1 and 4 of this volume.

Finally, what observations have been made about economically significant lifestyle patterns in the AICs? The whole question of healing and its contribution to the welfare of members is hard to assess. Most commentators see it as a source of hope, and even of material benefit, for those who cannot afford modern medicine. But any evaluation would require an inquiry into the efficacy of AIC healing rituals, which is beyond our scope here. As for the "work ethic," many observers of AICs have remarked upon members' apparent propensity for hard work and the desire to get ahead. This may be especially true of leaders, for whom church office is itself an indicator of entrepreneurial skill (Sundkler 1976, 216, 258; Oosthuizen 1987a, 69). The legend of the model Zionist employee occasionally surfaces in the literature (Chidester 1992, 137; Kiernan 1991, 4), as does the theme of a "reconstituted social order" for those living in anomie. Thomas (1994) records the example of a depressed, unemployed young man, whose progressive integration into the structures and religious experience of a Zionist-Apostolic church transforms his persona and economic circumstances.

In summary, Zionism tends to be portrayed as an essentially negative form of false consciousness, a passive response to the ineluctable spread of capitalist structures through South Africa; and, in the case of the larger churches, perhaps a form of manipulation of the uneducated poor by their more powerful leaders. Others have seen it as a form of resistance, conscious or unconscious, to the crushing realities of capitalism, or as a form of adaptation. A few observers have seen Zionism as a proactive force, a rediscovery of important religious realities and holistic spirituality, a community of healing, and even of development, enabling cooperative behaviour and positive changes in lifestyle and worldview. Does the sense of mutual care express itself in economic structures, and do these ever extend beyond the church into the wider community? "Work ethic" effects are frequently attributed to Zionist-Apostolic church membership—is this supported by observable differences in economic behaviour? Do these churches assist in members' adaptation to modernity, or hold them in the grip of a premodern worldview?

Table 4.1 distils some of the above discussion, incorporating my own expectations into a set of hypotheses with which I approached the field research.

RESEARCH FINDINGS FROM EDENDALE

As the previous chapter describes, my exposure to the churches in Edendale led rapidly to the conclusion that Apostolic and Zionist forms of AIC were operating very differently. I chose two churches, at diametric ends of this spectrum (if it can be thus simplified), for ongoing study. The rest of this chapter compares these two churches, and their impact on members' economic lives in terms of the four categories of table 4.1. I will occasionally introduce the results of a wider comparative study, which included a mainline, a Pentecostal, and a "No-Church" group, to add clarification and perspective to the findings. An unfortunate corollary of the broader comparative objective, and of splitting the Zionist-Apostolic category, is a very small sample size: only ten Apostolics and nine Zionists were interviewed in the ethnographic phase of the research. However, these interviews were supplemented with careful observation of each congregation, and of other Zionist-Apostolic churches.

An Apostolic Church: The Twelve Apostles Church in Christ

This fascinating church, which has not to my knowledge previously been researched, can be placed at the Apostolic end of the Zionist-Apostolic continuum. The church is characterised by formality, discipline, and exclusivism. It also embodies a synthesis of Africa and Western discourse not culturally dissimilar to that of the mainline churches.

The characteristics of the TACC resemble the megachurches of the ZCC and of Shembe in a number of ways. The TACC also claims to have several hundred thousand members in South Africa and elsewhere. Like the ZCC and Shembe's church, the TACC fits into a separate "Messianic" category that bucks the classic Ethiopian-Zionist dichotomy (Kiernan not dated; Sundkler 1983). Such churches feature an exalted leadership—in which succession is usually hereditary, and which greatly attenuates the tendency towards schism—and succeed in accumulating

Table 4.1:

Hypotheses on the Role of Zionist-Apostolic AICs in Economic Development

	Overall Effect	*Mechanisms*
Legitimacy of the Capitalist Economy	Ambiguous	Leaders support accumulation. Members are preoccupied with the struggle for survival, suspicious of wealth.
Trust and Cooperation	Positive (weak)	Trust is created in AICs; but does it translate into concrete forms of economic cooperation or extend to the wider community?
Worldview	Negative	Persistence of traditional worldview; costs of cultural practices are high for the poor.
Lifestyle	Ambiguous	Positive effects on consumption and lifestyle patterns. Less emphasis on education.

considerable assets and land (Mosala 1989; Kruss 1985).

In South Africa, the TACC is split into provinces, and the provinces into regions. In and around Pietermaritzburg, part of KwaZulu-Natal Province, there are four regions, of which Edendale is one. The Edendale region is then subdivided into fourteen *amaBandla* (cell congregations), which are scattered throughout the valley. The *amaBandla* meet almost every day, for "Bible" study, choir practice, and coordinated evangelism. These meetings are generally segregated by gender. On the first Sunday of each month, a plenary regional meeting is held in a large rented hall. This meeting, which lasts all day, is attended by up to one thousand members. Its focal point is a communion service that lasts for about three hours. At least two-thirds of the membership is female, although the ratio at some meetings was closer to three females for every male.

Despite the predominance of women, their role in combined meetings is purely passive. They are expected to chime in with the prescribed responses during the sermon—which they do with remarkable unison. Although women dominate the singing, by virtue of numerical superiority, they do not initiate it as in many other AICs, or enjoy the freedom in worship of Pentecostal women.

The single deviation from this passivity is the role of the prophetess. At the plenary meetings, a silence follows the extended opening prayer. During the ensuing minutes, various women advance from their seats towards the stage on which the leaders (and their wives) are located. The prophetess becomes apparent by a gradually increasing wailing and weeping, which crescendo as she nears the stage. The last dozen paces may be travelled on her knees, while she cries out under the power of the spirit. When the utterance is complete, two or three women move to where she lies, now prostrate and whimpering, and assist or carry her back to her seat. This process is repeated for three or four women, whose inspirations overlap somewhat. Meanwhile, the male leaders peer down from their lofty position, taking in the content of the utterances; these, I was told, are predictions of some sort, but may only be decipherable by the leaders. Their prophecies are brought to an end by the regional elder, who says "Amen, amen" rather brusquely, as if to round them up.

Women are otherwise limited. Their only potential for leadership or teaching within the church is at "women only" meetings or in children's Sunday school. I did not attend any "women only" meetings, but I gather that strict hierarchical principles apply—the main speaker will always be the senior woman present—which means, in fact, the woman who is married to the most senior man. All women, however, can be active in evangelism or in pastoral activities.

More than once I heard speakers ask the congregation, rhetorically, why the TACC was so successful with men. In numerical terms, this claim is hardly justified; but the church commands a level of commitment from its men about which most other churches can only dream. This is no doubt due, in part, to the status accorded men in the TACC, which is pervaded by a sense of hierarchical patriarchy. There are seven levels of membership for men, each distinguished by a particular colour tie that must be worn at all church meetings. It is not possible for a man to advance beyond basic membership (yellow tie) unless he is married. A woman automatically possesses the same rank as her husband, which gives her a status and some authority among the women of the church, but not with any of the men. For the men, advancement is based on marriage, age, and performance, especially in terms of commitment to evangelism. Economics may also play a role; most of the men at the fourth level (maroon tie) or above are reasonably successful in business. These men were younger, more articulate, and better dressed than the elders (red tie) whom they out-ranked. The regional elder (white tie) is a man in his early forties, who owns a clothing shop in Pietermaritzburg. Hence, the church implicitly encourages both marriage and material advance.

TACC members are, on average, less wealthy than that of a mainline church; but they do not approach the poverty of typical Zionism. Most of the congregation are in medium-skill jobs, and there are many students.

For the plenary meetings, men wear Western-style suits and the women wear white dresses of Western cut. As a result, an atmosphere of smart neatness and order pervades the meetings. A slightly different impression is gained by attending the midweek meetings in poor and violent Dambuza, which are held in a mud-built room lit by a single electric bulb, where the huddled faithful brave the night to assemble on old wooden benches under a leaky roof.

Music is central to the life of the church. Members of the various choirs meet three times a week for practice. Up to an hour of congregational singing precedes the monthly communion service, which, in turn, is followed by a choir festival. Beside the stage, a large stand carries some of the trophies that the region has won in various competitions. Within each *iBandla* and region there are several choirs, whose memberships overlap: Combined Youth, Young Women ("Junior Testifying Sisters"), Young Men ("Evangelical Brothers"), Apostles' Choir, Male Voice, and so on. The programme for these meetings runs to sixty or seventy items, and lasts for roughly five hours. The music is spectacularly good, all performed without accompaniment or score, with a strong African flavour—deep bass voices sing a different tune from the melody; there is occasionally heavy foot-stamping or synchronised rhythmic movement. The effect is quite different from either Pentecostal or Zionist music; the closest proxy that I encountered in Edendale was at the Shembe Nazareth Church.

Participation in these choirs is a powerful incentive for church membership. Order and respect prevail at the meetings and there is little spontaneity, but the youth have the opportunity to engage in a "safe" social context, in which roles are clearly defined and their dignity upheld. They obviously enjoy it. It must be pleasing to be involved in something that is manifestly successful and costs virtually nothing: the only expenses are travel costs and costumes for attending competitions.

All meetings are characterised by extreme formality and mutual respect. On arrival at the local meeting (*iBandla*), each man will quietly shake hands with the other men, acknowledging them by their clan names (*isiBongo*)—not by their given names (*iGama*), which would be considered too familiar. This is repeated, to the singing of a chorus, at the end of the meeting. As they sing, all the men walk past all the women, shaking hands with each, until the line thus formed doubles back on itself; so that everyone has shaken hands with everyone else. The senior man present does almost all of the talking at any of the meetings, and the audience (fifty to sixty in an *iBandla*) listen in respectful silence. No man of a lower rank will speak unless invited to do so by the senior man. The leader will open the meeting and engage in extemporaneous prayer for up to fifteen minutes, during which time the congregation is silent—there are no approving "Amens," as there would be in a Pentecostal meeting.

These prayers are not ecstatic. This is followed by a Bible-based talk or sermon, although a well-known verse is always picked and the Bible itself is rarely opened. These talks are exhortations to familiar themes, not detailed expositions, and last for thirty minutes or more. One of the other senior men may then speak, for ten minutes at most. There are notices, and the meeting closes. In between each of these items, there is plenty of beautiful singing.

There is a strong sense of order, even control, in the meetings, and this distinguishes the church from Pentecostal and Zionist gatherings. There is a parallel in the way that the speaker will call for a response from the congregation—as a Pentecostal preacher might shout out "Hallelujah!" confident of the enthusiastic response, "Aaymen!" But the responses expected in the TACC are paternalistic. A favourite prompt, heard over and over, is "*Siyazwana?*" (Do we understand each other?), to which the clear response "*Yebo, Baba*" (Yes, father) echoes through the flock. Other common responses reflect the theological views of the church: "*Umoya oNgcwele*" (the Holy Spirit), "*Abaphostholi*" (the apostles). These responses, enunciated clearly and uniformly through the congregation, suggest manipulation to the critical observer. But perhaps the practice merely reflects an emphasis on order and dignity, epitomising the quality of *inhlonipo* (respect, discipline), which Zulus believe to be one of the cornerstones of their culture. There is no spontaneous prayer in the TACC, and although the gift of *glossolalia* (utterances in a language unknown to a speaker who is regarded as prompted by the Holy Spirit) is affirmed, I never heard it being used. There are no drums or any other musical instruments, and the only dancing at services is a gentle swaying—people do not leave their places. So, despite the emphasis on the Holy Spirit in the teaching of the church, it is far from charismatic in its religious experience.

Although the strict observance of rank may appear to inhibit expression, it is a source of status for the men, emphasised through the ever-present symbol of the coloured ties. Linked to this is the attraction of a social and ecclesiastical order, which clearly (and deliberately) recalls traditional Zulu society. The TACC provides the social reconstitution noted by functionalist scholars. At the individual level, the necessity of explaining the "gospel" of the church to outsiders, and the regular discussion and exhortation in small groups, render church life a source of confidence, clarity, and rationality.

Several of the distinctive teachings and practices of the church reveal its exclusivism. Foremost among these is the emphasis on Apostolic succession. They believe that their own leaders are in direct line with the twelve apostles of Jesus, and that the Holy Spirit can only be received by the laying on of hands of one of the TACC apostles. No one outside the church is considered to be saved, with the inevitable corollary of aggressive proselytism. The attitude of the church towards my presence illustrated this. When I attended communion services, they took for granted that I should not participate, although they knew that I claimed to be a Christian. At cell meetings, it was clear that the men were trying to convert me, and the regional leader joked publicly that they hoped to baptise me into the church before long. By contrast, I was asked to pray, read scripture, or give some kind of message at almost every church I attended in Edendale—but never at the TACC. One of the most articulate members I met was a former Methodist. I asked if he thought any Methodists had the Holy Spirit. "No, they don't," he answered. "What about John Wesley?" I queried. "No, not even him. He reminds me of John 3, Nicodemus. He was Israel's teacher, but didn't understand about the Holy Spirit." Receipt of the Holy Spirit is considered a necessary but not a sufficient condition for salvation: it is also necessary to "work for your soul." This is done by showing love to others, but primarily in spreading the church's "gospel."

In its exclusivity, its claim of Apostolic succession, and its synthesis of salvation by works and grace, the TACC exhibits remarkable parallels with historic Roman Catholicism.

A Zionist Church: The Golden Christian Society in Zion (GCSZ)

With its colourful robes and noisy exuberance, the GCSZ represents the Zionist pole. The congregation, which fluctuates between ten and twenty adults, is comprised of the poor—above all, poor women. Only one of its members was formally employed at the time of my research, the others exist in various states of unemployment and desperate informal activity. There is no church building: the meetings take place in the homes of members, usually the three-roomed mud house of the leader. The brevity of my description here is mitigated by the large literature that exists on more typical Zionist churches, as table 3.1 in chapter 3 shows.

In this church type, the Western observer discovers a format of worship that does not obviously replicate some familiar version of imported Christianity; although, of course, it is much more like Pentecostalism than anything else. As Ranger (1987) and others argue, the inception of the Zionist movement owes more to early twentieth-century Pentecostalism than to traditional African religion. In chapter 4, I refer again to the relationship between Pentecostalism and the AICs. There is no liturgy, no set prayer, less predictability in both content and length. The only musical instruments are African drums (goat skin stretched tight over an empty oil can or wooden frame), and the songs follow a simple rhythmic pattern that is closer to a chant than a melody. Usually no more than three phrases are used, repeated dozens of times as the congregation sways, claps, or processes in a circle around the room, drummer to the fore. Uniforms are worn by all the men and women, and also the children.

These descriptions illustrate the cultural and theological contrasts between the two churches, despite their coexistence in the broad Zionist-Apostolic type. I will now return to the economic categories introduced earlier, in order to assess the impact of the two churches in relation to the social and individual conditions conducive to capitalism.

The Legitimacy of the Market Economy

Of the four categories considered in the research, this was the most difficult to assess. Several aspects required exploration, as illustrated by the range of questions asked. These covered crime, payment for services, levels of taxation, the theological legitimacy of economic inequality and wealth, the relationship between individual and structural causes, and the respondent's own expectations of prosperity. The responses given by the members within different church types were varied, and patterns were less obvious than I had anticipated. Nevertheless, some tendencies did emerge.

The Apostolic respondents, while manifesting diversity, inclined towards a legitimation of wealth, the market, and individualism. The ten interviewees strongly endorsed the market economy and viewed personal wealth positively. However, there were frequent allusions to three responsibilities: to remain faithful to God, to look after the poor, and to exercise personal initiative with hard work. These were exemplified in responses such as: "I think I will be rich, if I work hard. It would be okay to have a lot of money, to help other people. There's nothing wrong with money." And, "God can help you if you also help yourself. He wants everyone to be rich, as long as they trust God."

This emphasis on self-help and personal responsibility coloured the discussions of poverty and crime. Although the TACC members conceded that apartheid had played a role in exacerbating crime, they were more likely to identify personal morality: "At first, apartheid was the cause, now people use it as a reason to do whatever they want. Now they can go to school, they can get jobs, so it's their fault."

The individualist focus emerged again in suggestions for countering crime in Edendale, which relied almost without exception on the possibility of personal transformation: "We go to many houses with our evangelism. If people join the church, they will stop stealing. They will know it is wrong." And, "The church can help in the community, we can preach to them so that they know what we know. None of our members carry guns, or steal wires.[4] But we have many people in the church who used to commit crime—even me."

This faith in conversion and changed lifestyle reflects the teaching and experience of the church members, and closely mirrored the views of the Pentecostal respondents.

Consistent with their broad legitimation, TACC members were opposed to forced redistribution of wealth in the new South Africa, although less strongly than the Pentecostals and Zionists. The only exception to the legitimating trend was in the market pricing of electricity, where TACC members expressed the weakest support. Despite this, the TACC provided an overall legitimation second only to that of Pentecostalism.

The very poor GCSZ members did not represent a controlled group, and their responses might have been expected to reveal a delegitimation of capitalism. They were, indeed, clearest in their opposition to economic inequality, with only one—very atypical—Zionist believing capitalism to be the appropriate economic system for South Africa. The same man, rich by Edendale standards, advanced a positive assessment of wealth. In contrast, the other Zionists looked to God not for riches, but for their basic needs: "God will help me to have food in the house, but not to have lots of houses and cars. The little I have now, it is from God."

Some saw wealth in very negative terms: "Yes, it would be bad to be a rich Christian—you don't have time to pray to God, or to join the church when they praise him." Yet these poor Zionists did not necessarily delegitimate the wealth of others, which was accepted as the gift of God. They rejected forced redistribution more strongly than any other group: "No—apartheid condemned us to poverty, but the government shouldn't take money from the whites, because they worked for it, used it wisely. The poor would misuse it—blacks are bad in spending money."

Some saw their own poverty as a sign of spiritual failure. I asked one unemployed woman if she felt God had let her down: "I believe God will bless me, allow me to live without anxiety. No, he hasn't let me down, perhaps I don't pray enough." When I pointed out to her that she had just returned from an all-night service, she added: "or maybe my prayers are bad."

So, Zionist discourse provides a legitimation for the beneficiaries of the market, although it does not encourage members to seek wealth for themselves. This accords with the findings of much previous scholarship, and lends weight to the materialist interpretation of Zionism as false consciousness. This explains the frustration with Zionism among radical theologians.

Trust and Cooperation

Among the Apostolic respondents, there was evidence of trust being created based on the theological bond that existed between members. This was even stronger than among the Pentecostal respondents—in keeping with the fact that the TACC, which does not recognise the existence of saved people beyond its own confines, is even more exclusive than Pentecostalism. Trust existed because of shared faith and spiritual experience, but there was also recognition that the close ties of membership—which surpass those of extended family—might overrule the obligation to repay. This emerged from the comment of a respondent who said: "I would trust a church member the most, because I see them, and I know what they believe." Another said: "He will bring the money back, because of the spirit of God in him—he can't preach the word of God and fail to pay me back." "The cousin would take advantage of a relative. And a church member, I would sympathise so much, I wouldn't force her to give it back."

Although the TACC, to my surprise, did not operate either a *stokvel* (a rotating credit scheme or savings association) or funeral club (a proxy life-assurance scheme), it did have an "emergency" fund, a resource made possible by the high levels of giving in the church, which exceeded those of any other church type. Hence, the tithing of members can be seen as an insurance premium against hardship. The level of personal saving of TACC members was also high (19% of net income, compared to the average for the sample of 15%), supplanting the role of the *stokvel.*

The TACC also provided examples of employment networking. It operated an informal system for young adults: when looking for a particular job, they were put in contact with church members engaged in such work, to give advice, and to keep an eye open for vacancies. One small-scale entrepreneur employed other TACC members, and some men who were considering membership, in his garage. He explained this in terms of demonstrating practical care for members, confidence in their honesty, and the constant priority of evangelism.

Among the Zionist respondents, the sense of "family" was strongest of all, and the putative loan was frequently considered in the light of a gift. Those who did expect repayment relied to some extent on theological kinship, although reference was also made to the sort of social mechanism cited more frequently by mainline respondents: "If I gave to a person in the church, it would be a gift, not a loan. I do trust them, because I see them most days, and they believe in something." Or, "People in my church would be more likely to pay it back. It is God's law. They would be committing crime not to pay it back."

There was some evidence of the GCSZ and other Zionist congregations in Edendale functioning as networks of care and mutual support. Membership of funeral clubs and *stokvels* was surprisingly low among GCSZ respondents—24% compared to roughly 30% in the other church types and 42% in the "No Church" category. The GCSZ exhibited no employment network. Indeed, such a notion would be fanciful given that only one member was formally employed, while the others eked out a precarious existence from irregular, informal work. Members helped each other by sharing their homes for indefinite periods, cooking joint meals, and caring for children while mothers were looking for work. The absence of cash-based schemes from this circle of reciprocation was a function of genuine poverty, not a sign of missing trust. Between some other Zionist churches in the valley, with a slightly higher average income, a rotating saving scheme was operating, with each church receiving a payout in turn. This facility could not function without the spiritual bond that strengthened personal and social links: theological articulation and ceremony was liberally bestowed on each act of giving that contributed towards this scheme.

Lifestyle and Worldview

Many important issues explored in the field research fell under this heading, but only a few can be considered here. With respect to lifestyle, the discussion examines the requirements of church membership and their effect on economically significant factors. My research showed that the impact of membership on more traditional "work ethic" categories, such as personal saving and consumption of alcohol, does vary between church types. The consumption of alcohol and tobacco is almost nonexistent among Pentecostals, rare among Zionist-Apostolics, but quite common among mainline and non-Zionist AIC members (Garner 1998).

Moving on to the question of worldview, I will focus on education and the priority given to it by respondents.

While religious habits *per se* would appear to be neutral in their economic effect, the extremely high levels of attendance in some Zionist-Apostolic churches might be deemed a negative influence. In the TACC, members meet almost every day, and spend fifteen to twenty hours per week on church-related activities, *excluding* personal devotions. Yet these activities are a form of recreation, centring around music, teaching, or prayer. Although time-consuming, they provide an arena for building social skills, creating networks of relationships, and for just having a good time. They do not supplant other productive activities, and are flexible when the demands of study or work are pressing. The church provides an alternative value and entertainment system from that offered elsewhere in the township, in which alcohol and sexual activity figure highly.

In the GCSZ, members also meet frequently. The commitment of time is similar, but more agglomerated: perhaps three meetings a week, each lasting for several hours. These services, which feature almost constant activity (singing, dancing, processions, sacrifices, healings, ecstatic prayer), can be physically exhausting: by early morning, after an hour or two of sleep, the weary worshipper trudges slowly off to work or home. Mohr (1993) found that ambitious young people who had grown up within Zionism might leave the church when the time demands of membership conflicted with education or work. However, most of the longer services are at weekends, and many Zionists do not have jobs to go to anyway, so that the negative impact on work performance may be minimal. Nevertheless, it is hard to see this pattern as having a positive effect on economic behaviour, by contrast with the polished, literate, and "rational" meetings of some other churches. Rationality is a problematic concept within religion; but even nonrational beliefs can be communicated and reinforced through quasi-rational, orderly forms of religious praxis. This is the case in much Pentecostalism, and in the TACC. Although there are undoubted psychological benefits to membership, I take issue with the view that AICs as a whole facilitate modernization (e.g., Oosthuizen 1986, vi).

To illustrate the importance of worldview, I will look at the conflict between modern and traditional values in relation to education, as illustrated in responses to the "Dumisani" scenario. This scenario asked interviewees to prioritise the choices faced by a young man, Dumisani. Faced with the competing claims of an anniversary sacrifice to remember his deceased father, *lobola* (bride-price) payments to hasten his marriage, and an accounting course to further his own career, how would Dumisani spend the savings from his annual pay? Each of these options was of similar cost. Table 4.2 shows what percentage of each church type considered that the ritual should be performed, and how many considered it a higher priority than further education. Respondents were also asked which language they would prefer their children to be fluent in—English or Zulu.

The relationship between modern and traditional worldviews is complex. Although my assumption is that the persistence of the traditional worldview is economically detrimental, the retention of traditional constructs may be substantive or symbolic. Only the former is economically damaging. As table 4.2 demonstrates, the observance of traditional practices persists in all theological types except Pentecostalism: between 60% and 83% of the non-Pentecostal respondents thought that Dumisani ought to perform the sacrifice that was due to the shade (*iDlozi*) of his dead father. What is the significance of this?

Members of the TACC hold an ambiguous position. Despite the denials of some leaders, the ancestor cult is alive and well: some respondents told me they had joined the church specifically in order to integrate the ancestors into their Christianity. But in contrast to Zionism, the ancestors, while tangibly present in the cosmology of TACC members, have less potential for malevolence, and do not inspire fear: "They won't give him bad luck [for postponing the rite]; they will understand," judged a young garage attendant. This shift, though subtle, may have great

Table 4.2:

The Priority of Modern Education versus Traditional Culture

	No Church	*Mainline*	*Pentecostal*	*Apostolic*	*Zionist*
	%	%	%	%	%
(n)	(20)	(19)	(20)	(10)	(9)
Dumisani Scenario:					
Should perform ritual sacrifice	60	83	0	60	78
Should perform sacrifice before education	15	47	0	0	78
Education first choice	50	47	70[a]	100	0
Language:[b]					
Preference for children to learn English over Zulu	55	60	63	53	55

Notes:

a. Thirty percent of the Pentecostal respondents considered the payment of *lobola*—to hasten his marriage—as Dumisani's first priority.

b. Ratings are composites of the breadth and depth of approval; 100% would imply that all interviewees in that church type unequivocally preferred English for their children.

significance for the economic choices faced in real life. While 60% of the TACC respondents thought that Dumisani should observe the rite, none of them placed it before his own education.

Is the persistence of ancestor reverence a hindrance to full incorporation into modernity, and hence a barrier to economic progress? It need not be: the tension between modern and traditional, Western and local, may be creative. Japan has flourished by adopting various economic tenets of Western thought, but without ever embracing its thoroughgoing individualism, or jettisoning its own culture. Similarly, South African blacks (at least, middle-class blacks) may succeed in holding together the two prime sources of their cultural formation: Western liberalism and (Zulu) traditionalism. The traditional defines their identity and social relationships; the Western mode governs their education and economic functions. The TACC achieves a synthesis of modern and traditional symbols, emphasising identity while marginalizing practices entailing damaging levels of nonproductive consumption.

A similar synthesis is found in mainline churches, where support for traditional practices may coexist with high levels of education and income, and where the synthesis receives a more thorough and elegant articulation. The research revealed that traditional practices receive a strong affirmation in the mainline churches, not very different from that of the AICs. Among better-off mainline Christians, this retention is symbolic rather than substantive: they would not satisfy the demands of the ancestor cult if these came into conflict with the necessities of modern life. Among their poorer fellow members, of whom there are many, the persistence of the traditional worldview is substantive, and therefore costly. The percentage of mainline Christians prioritising the sacrifice above Dumisani's education was surprisingly high (47%). Such a priority can be considered economically punitive, from the promodernization perspective.

The Zionism of the GCSZ functions even more negatively: ancestors occupy a prominent and powerful place in the Zionist pantheon, and their propitiation is a constant priority.[5] Seven of the nine interviewees saw the rite as a priority for Dumisani, and all of these placed it ahead of education. These respondents were more likely to cite the power of the ancestors to give bad luck if the rite was neglected, than to stress its importance as a cultural or symbolic practice. As an analysis of *lobola* illustrates, the economic consequences of persistent traditionalism are potentially crippling for those in real poverty. The median Zionist respondent recommended a bride-price equivalent to three years' earnings. In the other church types, the recommended amount was around four months' earnings. In this manifestation, the Zionist worldview offers little integration of modernity or adaptation to it, although, equally, it displays no conscious resistance to it.

Evidence of Economic Advance

Whatever the attitudes cited above, do any of the types help members to advance in socioeconomic status? Table 4.3 shows the occupational status of the respondents compared to that of their parents, and reveals that members of the Pentecostal and Apostolic-type churches have advanced furthest, while the Zionist members have actually regressed slightly. Critics may pose a number of objections to this analysis, with regard to both the small sample size and the methodology. I offer it as illustrative, rather than conclusive, evidence.

Of course, it cannot be assumed that church membership caused the

Table 4.3:

Status of Phase 2 Interviewees - Education, Income and Occupation

	No Church	*Mainline*	*Pentecostal*	*Apostolic*	*Zionist*
(n)	(20)	(19)	(20)	(10)	(9)
Average years of education	11 yrs	11 yrs	11 yrs	12 yrs	5 yrs
Average occupational status[a]	1.6	1.8	1.8	1.8	0.8
Average net income	R 1,333	R 2,344	R 1,809	R 1,817	R 826
Average occupational status of parents	1.3	1.6	0.9	0.9	0.9
Average rise (fall) *vis à vis* parents' status	0.3	0.2	0.9	0.9	(0.1)
% rising 1 level or more from parents' status	40	32	60	60	11

Note:

a. This is calculated by allocating the following values: Unemployed = 0; Low skill = 1; Medium skill = 2; High skill = 3. Students were given a value of 2.

upward mobility. Most TACC members join the church as adults: successful people may choose membership, rather than membership creating their success. Neither can it be assumed that Zionism causes stagnation—the economically unsuccessful may be drawn to it consciously or unconsciously. However, it is at least possible that the positive legitimation of the market, the creation of cooperative networks, and the creative synthesis of worldviews encountered in the TACC create conditions for economic advance in a fashion markedly absent in Zionism.

CONCLUSION

The main conclusion of this research is that the Zionist-Apostolic category is simply too diverse to be spoken of homogeneously, at least in common characteristics in worship style and theology, and this was demonstrated by the impossibility of distinguishing between Zionist and Apostolic churches from the survey responses; but the differences between churches at opposite ends of the spectrum are immediately apparent to an observer. Differences in religious ambience may be matched, as they were in the case of the two congregations studied in Edendale, by differences in economically significant attitudes and behaviour. We have seen this across the categories of legitimation, trust, lifestyle, and worldview.

In the esoteric TACC, the market economy and personal responsibility received a strong legitimation. The TACC manifests some traits of the broader Zionist-Apostolic category as well as Pentecostalism and certain non-Zionist AICs. The more typically Zionist GCSZ provided a legitimation that was both weaker and differently focused. For themselves, members of this type displayed less enthusiasm for wealth; but, despite their poverty, they rejected the notion of forced redistribution and harboured little resentment or jealousy towards the rich. It is possible to interpret these attitudes, with materialist scholars, as a form of false consciousness projected onto the underclass. But the leaders of most Zionist churches—as opposed to the "Messianic" megachurches—are themselves poor, and there are few direct ideological influences on them or their congregations. The functionalist reading of Zionism as a coping mechanism within extreme poverty is more persuasive.

In the low-trust environment of Edendale, violence and theft are rampant, civil society is weak, cooperation and entrepreneurial activity are rare. Community leaders and potential investors agree that higher levels of trust and cooperation are a prerequisite for social and economic progress. Against this bleak background, both of the churches studied created, to a limited extent, networks of trust. In Zionist-Apostolic AICs, the social mechanisms that create trust are supplemented by a theological dimension: trust increases in proportion to the strength of religious experience and the perception of transformative spiritual power. This was strongest in the TACC, with its ultraexclusive theology, but was also evident in the GCSZ. Both churches yielded examples of social and economic cooperation, although fewer than anticipated. Nevertheless, high levels of socialisation contribute to the nonpecuniary well-being of members. This trust *may* extend to other Zionist-Apostolics, and because of the popular reach of these churches, they could conceivably contribute to the creation of a new civil society, although this is not really happening in Edendale.

In the categories of lifestyle and worldview, the differences between the two AICs were considerable. If modernization is epitomised by values such as literacy, rationality, and control over natural and spiritual forces, then Zionist churches cannot with integrity be portrayed as forces, then Zionist churches cannot with integrity be portrayed as facilitating that process. This is certainly true for those churches that are similar to the GCSZ. Their reinforcement of highly consumptive aspects of Zulu culture, and resistance—whether construed as active or passive—to modernity (and its definitive categories such as money and time) hinder the attempts of the poor to raise themselves out of poverty. Zionism perceives no tension between the traditional worldview and Christianity: members are fully involved with the ancestor cult, entailing material and damaging expense for people who live on or below the poverty line, as most Zionists do. Although these churches discourage drinking and smoking, the actual impact on lifestyle is variable, and the expected effects on consumption are weak. But they do emphasise and display certain traditional values, such as ***uBuntu*** (community) and *inhlonipo* (respect), which promote a form of social integration. These qualities receive little recognition in the economic assessments of a capitalist worldview, but may be highly prized in alternative value systems. Further, the religious experience of Zionism is strong, and the nonpecuniary benefits of membership—social, spiritual, and psychological—must be given their due.

The Apostolic TACC demonstrated considerable power to influence members' lifestyles, in areas where it chose to focus its teaching agenda (notably in tithing, attendance, and commitment to evangelism). The traditional worldview is upheld in certain regards, but its demands are subordinated to economic expediency. The emphasis on education in this church was strong, against expectations, although biblical/literacy effects were weak. Again, the Zulu value of *inhlonipo*, and the rigorous discipline (both social and financial) associated with membership, assist in the reconstitution of members' lives. High levels of socialization, and self-esteem flowing from status and participation (for the men, especially) provide a useful platform for socioeconomic advance, even among the very poor. The synthesis of modern and traditional value systems, avoiding the cognitive dissonance of a clearer break, yet asserting the priority of economic rationality in many contexts, may prove to be both fruitful and sustainable as a context for the shaping of an African brand of capitalism.

NOTES

1. A broader account, including an analysis of Mainline and Pentecostal churches, can be found in Garner (1998; 2000a).

2. In terms of contemporary economic theory, the perspectives of this chapter can be identified with those of New Institutional Economics. See Garner (1998: Chapter 1).

3. While Sundkler later mollified this critical position (1976, 1983), he never completely reversed it.
4. The persistent theft of telephone and electricity cables has been a major barrier to economic development in Edendale, as elsewhere in South Africa.
5. Kiernan (var.) stresses the persistent threat of sorcery rather than the ancestor cult, but the two are related in the Zulu worldview.

REFERENCES

Anderson, Allan H. 1992. *Bazalwane: African Pentecostalism in South Africa.* Pretoria: University of South Africa.

Bekker, Simon B., Catherine R. Cross, J. P. Evans, and G. C. Oosthuizen. 1992. *Rise up and walk: Development and the African Independent Churches in Durban.* Unpublished report, Centre for Social and Development Studies, University of Natal, Durban.

Brandel-Syrier, Maria M. 1983. The role of women in African Independent Churches. *Missionalia* 11 (3): 13–18.

Chidester, David. 1992. *Religions of South Africa.* London: Routledge.

Comaroff, Jean. 1985. *Body of power, spirit of resistance.* Chicago: Chicago University Press.

Garner, Robert C. 2000a. Religion as a source of social change in the New South Africa. *Journal of Religion in Africa* 30 (3): 310–43.

———. 2000b. Safe sects? Dynamic religion and AIDS in South Africa. *Journal of Modern African Studies* 38 (1): 41–69.

———. 1999. Religion in the AIDS crisis—Irrelevance, adversary or ally? *AIDS Analysis Africa* 10 (2): 6–7.

———. 1998. *Religion and economics in a South African township.* Ph.D. Dissertation, University of Cambridge.

Hammond-Tooke, W. D. 1998. African renaissance and African religion: The South African case. *Aambeeld* 26 (2) (URL: http://www.general.rau.ac.za /aambeeld/november1998/african%20religion.html).

Kiernan, James P. 1991. The healing community and the future of the urban working class. In *The contribution of South African religions to the coming South Africa.* Conference papers, University of Natal, Pietermaritzburg.

———. 1990. *The production and management of therapeutic power in a Zulu city.* Lampeter: Edwin Mellen Press.

———. 1974. Where Zionists draw the line: A study of religious exclusiveness in an African township. *African Studies* 33 (2): 79–90.

———. Not Dated. *Modernity and the African Independent Churches—Adaptations of an indigenous Christianity.* Unpublished paper.

Kruss, Glenda. 1985. *Religion, class and culture: Indigenous Churches in South Africa, with special reference to Zionist-Apostolics.* MA thesis,

Africa, with special reference to Zionist-Apostolics. MA thesis, University of Cape Town.

Mohr, Matthias. 1993. *Negotiating the boundary: The response of KwaMashu Zionists to a volatile political climate*. Ph.D. thesis, University of Natal, Durban.

Mosala, Itumaleng. 1989. *Race, class and gender as hermeneutical factors in the African Independent Churches' appropriation of the Bible: A final report to the Human Sciences Research Council*. Research Report. Pretoria: Human Sciences Research Council.

Naudé, Piet. 1995. *The Zionist Christian Church in South Africa: A case study in oral theology*. New York: Edwin Mellen Press.

Oosthuizen, G. C. 1987a. The AICs and the modernisation process. *Africana Marburgensia* XX (1): 59–81.

———. 1987b. The AICs and the modernisation process. *Africana Marburgensia* XX (2): 5–17.

Oosthuizen, G. C., ed. 1986. *Religion alive: Studies in the new movements and Indigenous Churches in South Africa*. Johannesburg: Hodder & Stoughton.

Oosthuizen, G. C., and C. D. Clark. 1994. *The development activities of African Independent Churches*. Unpublished paper, University of Durban-Westville, Durban.

Petersen, Robin M. 1996. *Time, resistance and reconstruction: A theology of the prophetic and the popular*. Ph.D. Dissertation, University of Chicago.

Ranger, Terence. 1987. Religion, development, and African Christian identity." In *Religion, development, and African identity*, ed. K. H. Petersen, 29–57. Uppsala: Scandinavian Institute of African Studies.

Sundkler, Bengt G. M. 1983. The challenge of the Independent Churches" *Missionalia* 11 (3): 3–6.

———. 1976. *Zulu Zion and some Swazi Zionists*. London: Oxford University Press.

———. 1948 [1961]. *Bantu prophets in South Africa*. London: Oxford University Press.

Thomas, Linda E. 1994. African Indigenous Churches as a source of socio-political transformation in South Africa. *Africa Today* 41 (1): 39–56.

Turner, Harold W. 1980. African Independent Churches and economic development. *World Development* 8: 523–33.

West, Martin. 1975. *Bishops and prophets in a black city: African Independent Churches in Soweto*. Johannesburg, Cape Town: David Philip.

PART III

A NATIONAL PERSPECTIVE

5

A Methodology for a National Comparative Study of African Independent Churches

Lawrencia Kwark

INTRODUCTION

In the sociology of religion, as in other sociological subdisciplines, methodology is an important consideration. Methodology concerns ways of producing and analysing data that, in turn, are used to test hypotheses and sociological theories. Without this systematic way of producing and testing sociological knowledge, the pretension of sociology to be a social *science* cannot be upheld, since sociologists could then not verify their results. Yet, despite sociology's efforts to be a science of society, sociological methodologies cannot be based on the same rules as their counterparts in the natural sciences. To study human behaviour is fundamentally different from studying the natural world. For, unlike the subject matter of physics or chemistry, humans possess consciousness. The sociological study of human behaviour requires a different type of methodology.

In any sociological study, the first methodological issue is often whether to choose a quantitative or qualitative avenue of enquiry - a choice that presents peculiar challenges for the sociological study of religious phenomena. This will become clearer if we consider the debates between those sociologists of religion who can be described as substantialists and those who can be seen as functionalists. While substantialists attempt to understand religion on its own terms, functionalists essentially perceive religion as something to be explained away.

Because religion has been so central to both human consciousness and social organisation, the study of religious phenomena formed a central concern for sociology from its very birth as a discipline. From the start, scholars accepted that a sociological researcher should have a *scientific* attitude towards the religious subject under scrutiny. This became the prerequisite not only in practice but also in theory for sociologists interested in studying religious phenomena as *sociological* phenomena.

Yet, while the scientific attitude was often seen as embracing detachment, objectivity, and professional and ethical neutrality towards the object of study, the sociological analysis of religion in its cognitive, evaluative, and affective thrust in effect opposed religion. This oppositional posture became very much intertwined in the concepts and theory of the sociology of religions as an ideological thrust *against* religion. European scholars such as Auguste Comte, Herbert Spencer, and L. T. Hobhouse devoted much of their sociological thrust to a search to replace religion by education or industrial development. This insight seems to have been largely ignored by sociologists in the United States, where the practical positivism of Comte was consonant with American pragmatism. Consequently, in the United States, sociology was often used as a propaganda for the social gospel, while religious voluntarism was perceived as evidence of a commitment to social good in the sociological sense.

METHODOLOGICAL ATHEISM AND THE STUDY OF RELIGIONS

The demand for a critical and dissenting attitude towards religion was labelled "methodological atheism" by Peter Berger. This posture was embraced as the appropriate attitude for sociologists who wanted to study religion as a key issue in understanding social and human consciousness. Emile Durkheim (1858–1917), Karl Marx (1818–83), and Max Weber (1864–1920) were among the most famous exemplars of methodological atheism in Europe. Weber was preoccupied with the sociology of religion in his work because he wanted to explain the very source of the value systems that determined the social organisation of his time. In particular, Weber's concern at the turn of the twentieth century was with the development of Western rationality, as illustrated by the economic development of German capitalism (Weber 1905).

But the pioneer of this intellectual tradition in the sociology of religions was Emile Durkheim (1912), who explained how religion had fulfilled certain functions in primitive aboriginal Australian societies. Durkheim's work is often considered the theoretical basis for the study of religion from a functionalist perspective.

THE SCIENTIFIC ATTITUDE, RELIGIOUS PHENOMENA, AND SOCIOLOGY

Durkheim believed that the scientific study of society should be confined to collecting information and data about phenomena that can be objectively observed and classified as "social facts." He argued that belief systems, customs, and social institutions are the facts of the social world, and exist as the external phenomena of society. Social facts should be considered as external "things" in the same way as objects and events are thought to exist in the natural world of science. Durkheim believed that these "things" can be directly observed and objectively measured with scientific methodology of sociology. In Durkheim's view, society is not simply an aggregate of individuals, but consists of members that are governed by social rules. Collective belief systems, values, and customary laws are social facts that have an external influence on the behaviour of individuals in particular ways. This is not to deny that the actions of individuals are also influenced by their mental state and psychology. But Durkheim claimed that collective action or thought have a reality outside of individuals (1895).

Clearly, in this positivist approach, the internal meanings given by actors themselves of human and social behaviours were of less concern. The areas of sociological study on motivations, feelings, and emotions of individuals were largely ignored, since those mental states cannot be observed and measured by scientific methods in any objective way. In their methodology, positivists were much more concerned with the so-called "quantitative methods" that are closely associated with statistical data. The use of quantitative methods and classifications made it possible to count sets of observable social facts, to classify the social world in an objective way, and so to produce statistics. Since there are several "social facts" observable in the social world, this methodology needs to describe the ways in which the correlations between them can be determined.

In his study of suicide, Durkheim (1897) showed that it was possible to observe a particular type of correlation that exists between several social facts within the social world. In this case he argued that the correlation existed between a particular religion, Protestantism, and a high suicide rate. In other words, quantitative functionalist analysis requires a search for causal connections that may exist between two or more types of social phenomena. One phenomenon is seen as causing the other to happen. A causal relationship could exist between two social facts. Or, a third factor could have a causal relationship to two other social facts.

EPISTEMOLOGICAL QUESTIONS AT ISSUE

Another important methodological issue in the sociology of religions is that all scholars who contributed to the formation of the discipline were from a particular historical and cultural context dominated by a form of Christianity. In other words, the concepts and theories developed within this subdiscipline to explain religion are not only limited culturally, but also historically. In the study of "primitive" religion and other historical religions such as Judaism, or Islam, the historical limitation of sociology of religions is particularly important to note. And, in the study of modern religious phenomenon, we remain captive to both the cultural and historical limitations when we refer to the theoretical definitions of religion—or of modernity. From this, we can see that theory remains central to an understanding of methodology. Despite the cultural bias and historical limitations in the development of the sociological study of religion, religion has remained at the heart of classical sociological theory and study to the present day.

Considering this historical development of sociology of religions, epistemological questions have been a central issue in the debates about the science of the discipline. This is even more true of the positivistic approach to the empirical study of religion.

But the centrality of religion in many societies and in human experience implies that to study religion from an approach that emphasises function or organisation is very limited. Rather, the social significance of religion has to do with its capacity of representation in categories and symbols. On the other hand, religion's social significance is encapsulated in a language that not only seeks to evoke and denote descriptions and evaluations, but, above all, to sustain particular types of emotional responses. Religious language is not only a repertoire of objective cultural and symbolic categories, but also a storehouse of subjective categories, values, and manipulative symbols that are used to fulfil its own needs.

SUBJECTIVE MOTIVATION AS STARTING POINT OF RESEARCH

In September 1993, when I was invited to join the Ecumenical Monitoring Program in South Africa (EMPSA) as an international volunteer who monitored the prevailing political violence during the preelection period, I did not know how sociologically important religious phenomena were in that country. My experience of EMPSA provided me with extensive field observation in KwaZulu-Natal Province, from Pietermaritzburg, the capital of the province, to the rural areas within the region. The EMPSA program was a very valuable opportunity to observe the ongoing transformation of South African society among grassroot black people in the period of transition leading to the first multiracial elections in April 1994. For three months, I worked as a monitor from early morning till late evening every day in various black townships and villages under traditional chiefs. During that period, I spent time in discussions and meetings with various actors involved in the process of transformation, such as the police, army representatives, political party leaders, church leaders, ecumenical organisations, and various local nongovernmental organizations (NGOs). I became motivated to learn more about events in contemporary South African society.

I became interested in understanding the meanings given by religious actors in South African society to their sociopolitical actions, and, above all, to their religious actions in the rapidly changing South African society. In this I followed Max Weber, who had defined sociology as the study of social action that takes account of other members of society. This chance to discover the very meanings given by the actors themselves to their actions would be difficult with quantitative research methods such as a survey questionnaire. Weber believed that an explanation of social action requires an understanding of the meanings and motives which underlie individual and collective behaviours.

Unlike Durkheim, I did not regard as social "things" the meanings and motives supplied by actors for their actions. Meanings do not exist independently, but as part of a social world that is constantly constructed and reconstructed by agents who take into account social interactions among different actors. This was my sociological conclusion after three months of daily field observations of various actors engaged in sociopolitical actions in the townships of KwaZulu-Natal.

I was later called back to South Africa again as an international monitor and election observer for the first multiracial and democratic elections, held in April 1994. This time I was sent to Pretoria, the capital of the country and arguably a highly symbolic city for the Afrikaner community of South Africa. The month that I spent in the greater Pretoria area (including the diamond-rich areas of Cullinan) provided me with very useful and complimentary insights into a region that is not massively affected by the type of political violence that prevailed in KwaZulu-Natal Province. Nevertheless, I found people there to be very fearful about the uncertainties of imminent change in the country—particularly some of the white Afrikaner population.

As my colleagues and I worked in the International Election Observer Teams, I was surprised to see that religion was fully present in all areas of the unfolding transformation of South African society. Apart from providing a platform for change, religion seemed at the same time to offer continuity—and so to assure the collective identity of the group. My observation as an outsider was that religion fulfilled this dual role everywhere, including in the State Joint Security Operation Unit meetings, Independent Electoral Commission, various peace structures, debates, and discussion meetings relating to the April elections. For example, at an election meeting that I observed of the right-of-center Freedom Front Party in the Cullinan area, political leaders and the minister of the local Dutch Reformed Church shared the platform as panelists, and the debate included religious references.[1] Activities such as

Voter Education and Mediation for Peace were conducted by church-related organisations and churches to ensure the peaceful transition to democracy. In addition, churches hosted meetings of civic and political organisations, as well as trade unions in their buildings. Many South Africans that I spoke to commented that they were quite used to this, and would say, "Of course . . . what is so surprising?" But for many non–South Africans like myself, the extent of religious involvement in the transition was quite remarkable.

During my period as an international monitor in the EMPSA program, I tried my best to listen attentively to all actors involved in the transformation so that I could understand the process of sociopolitical change in order to better monitor it. The political power struggle of various actors who tried to manipulate political violence as a possible means of negotiation was particularly noticeable. But the more I spent my time and energies in those townships and rural areas affected by political violence, and in the various related institutions—such as the police, army, and even the churches—the more I was impressed by the omnipresence of religion. And here I am thinking particularly of the various types of Christian beliefs that regulate, in various ways, the lives of actors in all sectors of South African society.

PARTICIPANT OBSERVATION AND SELECTING A RESEARCH OBJECT

My observations of the omnipresence of religious phenomena within South African society, as well as the very complicated relationship between religious and the other sociopolitical phenomena, led me to opt for a study utilising sociological and socioanthropological perspectives.

But I also noticed during my stay that religion, obviously, also manifests itself outside the political field. For example, larger African Independent Churches (AICs) such as the Zion Christian Church (ZCC) mobilised thousands of people for meetings during Easter celebrations. The ZCC is probably the only organisation apart from the African National Congress (ANC) capable of assembling so many people, and had emerged as an important variable for the outcome of elections. This factor led to much concern on the part of leaders of major political parties, who went to great lengths to woo the ZCC faithful during their Easter gathering at their holy site, Moria.

The ZCC example is not just an episodic illustration of changes taking place prior to the first democratic elections. Over a period of five years of field research in South Africa I visited the country several times, staying for three to five months at a time. I observed the emerging and continuing debates on abortion and on the movement from a Calvinist state to a secular state enshrined in the new 1996 Constitution. The amount of tension generated by these questions showed clearly that the contemporary debate on the role and place of religion in the new South Africa is not over yet.

But why did religion play such a primordial role in discussions about the nature of the new South African society that occurred *after* the elections of 1994, resulting in multiple debates carried by the mass media and in protest marches by thousands of Christians to Parliament? Simply, because religion continued to be at issue in various policies proposed by state and regional governments. Education provides a good example. Controversy arose in Gauteng concerning that province's new Education Bill, which allowed children the right to refuse religious instruction. The bill came under attack from Jewish, Muslim, and Christian schools that feared it would outlaw their right to provide religious teaching. Under the new dispensation, the teaching of religion in school required a shift from a Christian National Education model to a multireligious, multicultural, and plural-values paradigm.

And so I was further prompted to work on religious phenomena in South Africa by questions concerning the logic that governs religion, and relating to the modalities that regulate diverse values, beliefs, and subjective meanings given to political and religious events by religious actors.

FORMULATING A HYPOTHESIS VIA THE DEDUCTIVE APPROACH

Once I had chosen as object of my research the relationship of religion to modernity, I then surveyed those sociological theories relevant to this question, after which I weighed different research methods to find the most suitable one. I conducted a preliminary bibliographical analysis to decide what church groups, in terms of their relationship to modernity, could be included in my research field. I selected the white Dutch Reformed Church, the Roman Catholic Church, and—my major focus in chapters 6 and 7—the African Independent Churches (AICs).

Initially, I considered combining quantitative methods and statistical analysis as one possible research method, alongside an inductive approach, but eventually decided not to. I rejected an inductive approach because I did not intend to follow the usual approach for this method, namely to develop a sociological theory from the collected information that can be tested against other sets of data to see whether it is confirmed or not.

I decided against using only quantitative methods in the study of religious phenomena. I felt that quantitative methods would provide too simplistic a base from which to generalize a sociological rule for explaining the individual and collective behaviours of given religious groups. A quantitative analysis of collective behaviour would not enable a researcher to consider the complexity and subjectivity of phenomena where humans attach much importance to their emotions, beliefs, values, and practices.

Instead, I decided to use a deductive approach to test a sociological theory that had already been developed by sociologists of religions, namely secularization, as it concerns the relation of modernity to religions in modern society. Secularization theory speaks of an inescapable decline of religion in modern society. By using this theory, I could then formulate a research hypothesis that could be tested in the sociocultural context of South Africa. I also decided to test a particular definition of modernity as developed in the field of sociology of religions as an interpretative framework. According to this understanding, modernity is described by three major traits. The first trait concerns the logic and the process of institutionalization and its bureaucratization. A second characteristic is the logic and the process of the autonomisation of the subject. And the third feature is the process of the plurality of production and the regulation of diverse values and beliefs systems.

Based on the above understandings of modernity and its relationship to religions, I formulated a research hypothesis that runs counter to the classical theory of the decline of religion in modern society. Based on my observations in South Africa, I believed that in this non-Western society, the classical sociological tradition of secularization is countered by evidence of spectacular growth and increasing religious proliferation among AICs.

I intend to use the concept of modernity not as a sociological theory of the evolution of history, but rather as a working definition. I apply modernity as a tool to understand and interpret some aspects of the continuing sociocultural transformation of South African society in relation to AICs. I argue that AICs help their members to face the modernity of their own society, as well as the callback to earlier forms of African identity and tradition. In this way, AIC members are provided with the potential means to overcome the difficulties presented by changes in society that escape their control. South African blacks are not as yet the major agents of modernization at all levels of their society; yet I would suggest that they invoke African identity and tradition as an implicit, creative strategy with which to engage modernity. They construct and reconstruct a constantly changing identity as members of African Independent Churches. Their practice of reinventing oral and healing traditions (both biblical and African) as a means of accepting the ongoing transformation of society represents the most interesting characteristic of AICs. It is precisely this practice that forms a major feature of modernity as defined above: the logic and the process of emerging autonomous subjects who control their own destiny and history.

In brief, my research hypothesis is that instead of being opposed, the concepts of tradition and of modernity exist in a complex relationship of solidarity to one another in the AICs—as they do in other forms of South African Christianity. The impact of modernity on the religious domain in South Africa is to proliferate churches and organisations, as is evident in AICs, estimated at six thousand separate Christian churches. The purpose of my research was to understand this proliferation in terms of my research hypothesis. That this phenomenon constitutes one of the most visible consequences of a major change in South African Christianity can partly be demonstrated by statistical analysis of data from the *South African Christian Handbook* (Froise 1992), from the population census, and from my survey data (1996–97). The obvious question to ask, then, is why this is so—how can we interpret this phenomenon?

I conducted field research in South Africa from 1993 to 1995 in order to elaborate my research hypothesis; to test both its validity as well as the validity of subsequent predictions. Accordingly, from 1995 to 1998, I conducted field research using a combination of quantitative and qualitative research methods, including the more anthropological approach of field observation. I believe that it is almost impossible to predict the outcomes of an elaborated research hypothesis without doing fieldwork. A second requirement is that a sufficiently long time span is needed for such a study. Both this chapter and chapter 6 are based on the results of field observations, among groups belonging to small- to medium-sized AICs in Guateng and KwaZulu-Natal, that were tested against my research hypothesis.

DELIMITING THE SAMPLE AREA FOR FIELD RESEARCH

My decision to include a sample population of AIC churches in my field research led to the question of how to choose and delimit the sample area. Several factors working in on one another decided the outcome. I needed to conduct observations over a sufficiently long time span to identify the relevant sociocultural phenomena. But this ideal was constrained by very limited human and financial means for field research. Another limiting factor was the extremely precarious context of prevailing political violence and my subsequent physical insecurity. Yet it was exactly the relationship between politics and religion in a context of political violence that seemed of particular importance for the choice of geographical sample area. A final limiting feature of the research context was the degree of multilingual and multicultural diversity. As an outcome of all these factors, I decided to work in the greater Pietermaritzburg area (GPA) in KwaZulu-Natal Province, after previously spending a month doing field observation in Soweto, Gauteng

Province in 1995. I then had to consider the demographic and historical significance of these churches in KwaZulu-Natal Province, as well as ongoing changes in the sociopolitical dynamics of this province. All of the above factors, including race, influenced the information that I collected.

Although fieldwork and observations open up possibilities to better understand some aspects of the sociocultural signification that individuals and groups ascribe to their behaviour, these methods have their own limits. Time and scope of geographical space are examples, since obviously one researcher cannot do field research in different places at the same time. Sociological field research is also usually confined to small-scale studies over short periods of time. Nationwide fieldwork sufficiently large in sample to achieve some degree of representativeness of a society as a whole, covering several geographical regions, is only possible when large amounts of funds and human resources are available.

Given my limited resources, I decided that participant observation conducted during short periods of full immersion (living among the population being studied in the sample area) would be my method of choice.

In the end, my own survey of AICs was conducted from 1995 to 1997 with seventy-eight members, including archbishops, bishops, ministers, and their active adherents in twenty-one AICs present in the GPA, part of the midland region of KwaZulu-Natal. Certain socioeconomic and cultural characteristics were gathered and analysed against larger-scale surveys which had already been conducted. The data confirm the extremely precarious socioeconomic situation of AIC affiliates, who tend to exhibit very low educational level. These factors supported my research hypothesis that the majority of AIC members belong to the lowest social class, and are entirely marginalized in the historical process of modernization as manifested in political, economic, and sociocultural domains in South African society.

THE IMPORTANCE OF INFORMANTS FOR FIELD RESEARCH

One way to overcome the limits posed by smaller-scale field observation over shorter periods is to use informants to collect data, test certain research hypotheses, and interpret the sociocultural significance of gathered information. In my field research, this question of "reliable" informants was extremely important not only in terms of collecting data, but above all in terms of the viability of field observation. This was particularly true when I intended to live with the family of an informant among a selected population group in its cultural and religious contexts.

As mentioned earlier in this chapter, my provenance as a foreign woman who intended to live in a black township posed a number of questions. The most important of these related to security, mobility, and access to people within the area. The viability of my research became more of an issue because political violence intensified in those townships and their geographical regions that I had chosen for my study.

In order to guarantee my own physical security, I had no choice but to make arrangements for my field research with families who enjoyed relatively high respect and esteem within the community. They were often religious or community leaders who therefore had some authority over the local population. Such individuals also enjoyed better socioeconomic and cultural conditions compared to the rest of the population, as evidenced by the very simple fact that they had enough means and space within their houses to accommodate a foreign observer of daily activities in their families and in their religious communities.

In other words, where ethnographic researchers would normally attempt to obtain the maximum acceptance possible within a sample population by living with as representative a family as possible, this option was excluded by the need for personal security as a primary condition. In this way, the external conditions working in on a researcher's choices directly shape research procedures and affect the behaviour of those who are being studied. Moral and subjective value problems then also come into play.

THE LIMITS OF QUANTITATIVE METHOD

The demographic weight and spectacular growth of AICs can be estimated through the analysis of existing statistics such as the population censuses and my own survey conducted in KwaZulu-Natal. The data confirmed that AICs are presently the largest group of Christian churches that are also mostly black: 92% of members are black (1991 census), as are 98% of all Zionists (2001 census). AICs can be considered one of the most significant and important group of churches in South African society today. They are an important religious phenomenon to study if one wishes to understand the religious phenomena as social phenomena in South Africa.

But quantitative methods had relatively limited value as a way of understanding the meaning of collected data—particularly as a system of values and worldviews that govern individual and collective behaviour within a given sociocultural context. This renders a study of religious phenomena with only quantitative methods unsatisfactory, as religion deals with human consciousness, emotions, and cognitive meanings that are constructed by the relevant actors and groups themselves. Researchers also have to consider the important fact that religion does not only perform a social function in society. For example, there has been a phenomenal growth of "coping-healing" practices in the AICs. Stuart Bate (1995, 15) defines "coping-healing" as "all that is involved in healing through prayer, faith and other 'spiritual' means."

SEMISTRUCTURED INTERVIEWS AS A COMPLEMENTARY METHOD

Contrary to the numerical form that quantitative data usually takes, qualitative data is generally presented in words. Descriptions can be drawn from notes of field observations, from a transcript of a semistructured interview, or from a full and in-depth account of how people describe and explain their religious experiences. Compared to quantitative data, the resulting information is generally considered to be richer, more vivid, and more emotionally revealing. Critics maintain that qualitative data is more subjective and possibly less scientific. Yet, when such data reflect the words of actors themselves, a truer picture of a way of life, religious experiences, attitudes, and belief systems can emerge.

Despite my use of semistructured interviews, I still had to face several foreseen but unavoidable difficulties. One difficulty was the cultural gap between my first language (Korean) and that of informants or respondents (Zulu). Other problems included how appropriate the questions were that I asked, and what their implications could be for those not acquainted with sociological research. I conducted most of my interviews through an interpreter, who was embedded in his/her cultural and religious context, but who was not living in the same area as my respondents. I chose to use such interpreters in order to heighten the objectivity of interviews. The content of the interview was not the only thing that mattered. Some skills in interpersonal relationships and intercultural dialogue techniques were needed, since for the majority of AIC members, the interview was often not as important a question as the visit of a foreigner.

Apart from cultural factors related to language and interpersonal skills, time proved to be a very important factor during my research. The majority of AIC members are from the most impoverished population of South African society, who usually possess neither telephones at home nor postal addresses to which I could send a survey questionnaire. Consequently, the time needed for each interview—considered alongside all hazardous events that could be encountered before, during, and after the interview—required a far longer time than I had originally planned.

Spending more time meant having to spend more money. Ultimately, only five interviews could be concluded with AIC members that were manageable in terms of time, financial implications, translation, and mobility in the region. The contents of each interview also proved extremely time-consuming to transcribe. Sociological study is in general an exercise of distilling gathered information into more general observations or theoretical propositions. Thus a large amount of transcribed interview data, representing a heavy time investment, may produce only a very short sentence. This, in my experience, makes the analytical process very frustrating.

THE COMPARATIVE METHOD

The "comparative method" involves comparing collected data and observations with other sets of data. For example, different religious groups that coexist within the same society at the same time—or, at different points in time—can be compared to one another. Unlike fieldwork and observations, the comparative method analyses what is happening, or what has already happened, in the society in question. The data yielded by the comparative method may come from any of the primary or secondary sources used in research.

The comparative method may be used to overcome some of the problems mentioned above in relation to fieldwork, observations, or method of analysis. This method renders the problem of the moral and value involvement of a researcher in the collection of data less problematic, since the data is based upon an analysis of what has already happened and come from existing sources. A comparative method has often been used in sociological study by those who advocate a scientific attitude and approach to a subject, including Marx, Durkheim, and Weber. Durkheim's study of suicide presents a classic example of how detailed statistical analysis involving the comparison of different societies, different groups within society, and in different time periods, can be used to determine the variables that cause a social phenomenon. Max Weber also systematically used this method in his study of *The Protestant Ethic and the Spirit of Capitalism.* He compared early capitalist countries in Western Europe and North America with countries such as China and India to try to show a correlation between early capitalism and a Protestant ethic—in particular, Calvinism.

The other advantage is that the comparative method allows a sociologist to study the results of large-scale social change over long periods of time. The historical development of particular religious groups that can be studied in this way is absolutely not possible with a more limited scope of observation.

ELABORATION OF ANALYTICAL CONCEPTS AS AN INTERPRETATIVE FRAMEWORK

I have argued so far that some sociological approaches are too limited and some methods too inadequate to really understand the process of sociopolitical transformation that makes up the milieu of AICs. Statistical analysis—collecting, analysing, and explaining data through methods such as nationwide surveys or semistructured interviews—prove, at least partly, inappropriate for researching AICs in relation to modernity.

To examine my research hypothesis, and to resolve theoretical as well as practical questions regarding research procedure, I had to elaborate the relevant analytical concepts into an interpretative framework. This meant translating individual phenomena as reported by respondents into a more general, abstract conceptual language. Concepts are themselves formulations that can help researchers to express hypothetical propositions. The analytical concepts that I had to elaborate included working definitions of modernity, religion, and tradition. As an interpretative framework, these concepts would help me to explain the data, which were also tested by my qualitative approach, supplemented by quantitative methodology and a comparative perspective.

I used literature study and the comparative method to trace the consequences of the historical development of modernity for religious phenomena in South Africa. I accepted that the sociocultural transformation of society formed an important part of this historical path. I then tried to discern what the meaning was of the major cultural transformation of South African Christianity as manifested in the AICs, using theoretical tools and notions developed by sociology of religions.

The evolution and transformation of the interior Christian world and of churches in South Africa have profoundly altered the image of Christianity as a *singular* religion, which leads us to the need to define religion. For many South Africans, religion functioned as a framework and realm of significance, as a mechanism of meaning that helped them to overcome the disappointments, uncertainties, and frustrations of daily life. But religion also, without doubt, realised constructions of meaning that were very different to one another. Although in general based on references to a supreme textual authority (the Bible), religion provided differentiated and sometimes contradictory visions of the world for various communities. The realm of religious significance became differentiated within the extremely segregated South African society. While several realms of significance are available for the subjective satisfaction of each community, the question is how to analyse these religious expressions—particularly in the AICs—in relation to the whole of social life.

When no religious institution provides any framework of unity, how do we judge their evolution and their transformation by which religious beliefs are reconstituted, displaced, and innovated? I hoped to do so by adopting a sociological working definition, in which religion refers to "a particular mode of belief which implies, in a specific way, a reference to the authority of a tradition" (Hervieu-Léger 1993, 10, 110). In this way, I thought to avoid the difficulties of being trapped in the endless development of a definition. I also wanted to avoid the difficult debates between substantialists and functionalists, on which the scientific community of the sociology of religion has not reached a consensus. My definition helped me to organize and update the social, political, cultural, and symbolic functions and meanings of religious belief in the era of modernity.

PHENOMENOLOGY AS METHOD OF ANALYSIS

To answer these and other questions, I used a phenomenological method to interpret the political and sociocultural historical process that South African Christianity is undergoing in terms of modernity. This method is particularly useful in allowing the practices through which the religious and political meaning system are organised, produced, and regulated in AICs to be analysed as a manifestation of modernity. Similarly, a phenomenological method was utilised by Johann Kinghorn (1997) in a very brief analysis of the question of "Modernisation and Apartheid" with reference to Afrikaner churches—in particular the Dutch Reformed Church (DRC). His analysis shows how important the debate on modernity in South African society is, and how one particular trait of modernity was developed within the Afrikaner churches.

Phenomenology rejects the possibility of producing causal explanations for human behaviour, thus representing the most radical departure from the so-called "scientific" and quantitative methodologies that can be used to study religious phenomena. Phenomenologists do not believe that it is possible to objectively measure and classify the social world—more particularly, the religious world. For them, human beings make sense by imposing meanings and classifications upon the world. These meanings and classifications make up the social reality that we observe. There is no objective reality beyond these subjective meanings of the social world.

From a phenomenological perspective, the job of a sociologist is simply to understand these meanings with which social reality is constructed. With their exclusive emphasis upon meanings and the social construction of reality, phenomenologists concentrate almost entirely on the subjective aspects of social life that are internal to the individual's consciousness. They tend to use more anthropological or socioanthropological research methods than so-called "scientific" methods.

Using this method, I examined some of characteristics of religious practices of the AICs, concentrating especially on the coping-healing practices that so dominated the religious experiences of many AIC members. Some of the scholars whose work I had used analysed these practices with reference to the political process of transformation. These authors regard AICs to be part of a major manifestation of the acculturation process that is occurring now in South Africa. The results of my own fieldwork show that some aspects of the religious practices of AICs form part of the transformation of religious tradition, and of the transmission of memory, within the Christian churches. So I would agree that coping-healing practices form part of a political process of transformation, characterised by a tradition of independence and rupture from institutionalised structures. This is evidenced by the breakaway of AICs from the denominations and doctrines of missionary and white-dominated, Western-originated Christian churches. According to AIC actors such as Archbishop Nduruso H. Ngada, historically the institutional rapture was due to the desire of AIC members to return to the roots of Christianity, since missionary-controlled Christian churches emphasised Western civilization more than Christianity. The physical aspects of Western civilization were stressed to the extend that the spiritual understanding of Christianity was suppressed a great deal, Ngada argued.

Sociologically speaking, the religious logic of the AICs provides an ideological, practical, and symbolic device through which the individual and collective consciousness of belonging to a particular belief system could be constituted, maintained, developed, and controlled. AICs draw on the immense knowledge and symbolic resources of both Christian and African traditions. One of the most spectacular results is the healing phenomenon, which emerged as a space where AIC members actively reinvent and rearticulate their distinctive religious traditions in the logic of oral transmission of memory. In this particular mode, AIC members self-legitimise the act of believing through reference to the authority of a tradition constructed from both biblical and African traditions. This modality generates the voluntary adhesion of believers to a heritage of belief that in some cases had been newly created—even less than a month ago.

Similar observations are reaffirmed by those who studied the phenomenon of healing within the AICs. Some identify a process of articulation of symbols, while others perceive a black response to an alien world of urban values. Other scholars again point to the creation of a psychologically supportive space within which people feel comfortable and cared for, alongside an emphasis on reintegration. Such analyses underline the importance of the cultural dimension in AICs, for example, by emphasising the symbolic (in a broader sense: words, actions, objects, and intellectual constructs) as "articulated carriers of meaning." Much of what I had observed during my field research in AIC services confirmed such phenomenological analyses. I often observed the use of symbols—

such as prayer, laying on of hands, stepping into a healing circle, and confessing sins—as principal components of religious practices.

Some scholars choose to analyse the significance of AICs as social phenomena, perhaps with an emphasis on communities or subcultures within society as a whole. They regard the cultural factors that comprise beliefs and values, which determine right and wrong behaviour, as based on tradition. In this sense, some suggest that the AICs construct rituals to reform the world in their image (see Comaroff 1985). Many argue that often the religious space of AICs directly fulfils the needs of its members by being a supportive, caring, and giving group. Certain authors place great stress on the importance of a shared worldview in the religious practices of the AICs. Others suggest that the African Independent Churches have grown partly because they are prepared to take African cosmology and worldview seriously.

From the phenomenological perspective, I find it interesting that such issues revolve around the significance of a plurality of worldviews and the epistemological keys that ground them, as well as attempts to construct a metaphysics that can accommodate such a plural vision. Thus, some authors argued that AICs as "indigenous churches enhance the process of modernization in changing attitudes advantageous to progress" (Oosthuizen 1986, vi). Clearly, worldviews and epistemology form the principal source of resources, legitimacy, and strength in the traditions that are so clearly manifested in the AICs. For this reason, some suggest that AICs represent a return to a nonliteracy form of Christianity in reaction to the literary form of the mainline traditional churches.

CONCLUSION

The central topic of this chapter is the suitability of a variety of research methods and theories to a national study of AICs. I situated my discussion within a dialectic relationship that I detected between modernity and tradition, which contributed to a particular proliferation of religious phenomena within South African society. This dialectic makes a sociological analysis of the transformations of religion in the modern era not as simple a matter as it could be—particularly not in the study of AICs in South Africa.

After reviewing the values and limits of different possible research methodologies for my research project, I concluded that any one would be too limited for the analysis of religious phenomena in non-Western or Western societies. Thus, I advocated a methodological pluralism, in which a mixture of quantitative and qualitative methods is used.

This chapter represents a very modest attempt to outline some of the crucial questions concerning the choice and use of methodology for the study of religious phenomena. The appropriateness of the various methods has to be weighed against their utility for interpreting the significance of certain sociocultural transformations within South African society. The discussion was situated within broader, ongoing debates about epistemological and theoretical questions within the discipline of the sociology of religions.

Any study of the complex and transforming religious phenomena that make up AICs in South Africa, consisting of the majority of a poor black population, needs to take account of, but also to proceed beyond, all of these difficulties. This is particularly true when the study is of the relationship between AICs and modernity—a perspective heretofore relatively ignored in the literature.

NOTE

1. During the heated debate about whether or not it was right to take part in the upcoming elections, an elderly woman asked: "How do you dare to ask us to change our opinion and to accept the upcoming elections as the only and right way to secure the existence of Afrikaner community in these time of tumultuous changes? How should I accept this when you all told us for decades that apartheid was the will and mission of God? You told us that this was the plan of God and the only right way to follow. How is it possible that you tell us now, all of the sudden this truth has been changed and God has changed his plan? How is possible that the only way to ensure the existence of Afrikaner community is to take part in these upcoming elections and accept the rule of black people?"

REFERENCES

Bate, Stuart C. 1995. *Inculturation and healing: Coping-healing in South African Christianity*. Pietermaritzburg: Cluster Publications.

Comaroff, Jean. 1985. *Body of power, spirit of resistance: The culture and history of a South African people*. Chicago and London: The University of Chicago Press.

Durkheim, Emile. 1951 [1897]. *Suicide*. Translated by J. Spaulding and G. Simpson. New York: The Free Press.

———. 1947 [1912]. *The elementary forms of the religious life*. Translated by Joseph Swain. Glencoe, IL: The Free Press.

———. 1964 [1895]. *The Rules of Sociological Method.* Translated by Sarah A. Solovay & John H. Mueller. New York: The Free Press of Glencoe.

Froise, Marjorie, ed. 1992. *South African Christian handbook 1993/94*. Johannesburg: Christian Info.

Hervieu-Léger, Danièle. 1993. *La religion pour la mémoire*. Paris: Cerf.

Kinghorn, Johann. 1997. Modernisation and apartheid, the Afrikaner churches. In

South Africa, A political, social and cultural history, ed. Richard Elphick and Rodney Davenport, 135–54. David Philip: Cape Town.

Oosthuizen, G. C., ed. 1986. *Religion alive: Studies in the new movements and Indigenous Churches in South Africa.* Johannesburg: Hodder and Stoughton.

StatsSA. 2004. *Census 2001 by province, gender, religion recode (derived) and population group.* Statistics South Africa. (URL: http://www.statssa.gov.za/SpecialProjects/Census2001/Census/Dialog/varval.asp?ma=Religionbyprovince&ti=Table%3A+Census+2001+by+province%2C+gender%2C+religion+recode+%28derived%29+and++population+group%2E+&path=../Database/Census%202001/Provincial%20Level/Persons/&lang=).

Weber, Max. 1976 [1905]. *The Protestant ethic and the spirit of capitalism.* Translated by Talcott Parsons, introduction by Anthony Giddens. New York: Scribner.

6

The Reinvention of Tradition in African Independent Churches as a Means to Engage Modernity

Lawrencia Kwark

INTRODUCTION

"Tradition" in a commonsense understanding is something to be opposed to innovation, or to modernity. From this perspective, "Africanness" is opposed to transformation of culture,[1] to modernization, and to the Westernization of "African culture." For many of the same persuasion, Africanness—a slogan characteristic of certain movements in contemporary Africa—goes back to African roots, and represents the exact opposite to modernity. In the minds of such people, Africanness and modernization are as opposed to one another as the two end rungs of a ladder. This commonsense notion is not helpful in trying to understand the most spectacular religious phenomenon in South African society today, namely the development of the so-called African Independent Churches (AICs). Certainly, a sociologist of religions would see tradition in a different way.

By contrast to the above commonsensical notion, I argue that far from being opposed, Africanness and modernity relate to one another in a complex solidarity. Members of AICs call for people to return to an older African identity, and to their African roots, in my opinion, as a means to face modernity and the Westernization of their own society. To elaborate this hypothesis, I conducted field research during several visits to South Africa between 1993 and 1998. This chapter presents some of the results of my fieldwork among groups that can be classified as AICs. AICs represent an important locus for researchers who try to understand the religious experience and identity of black South Africans, who make up 79% of the total Christian population. Almost 38% of black South Africans are members of an AIC (2001 census figures).

The object of my research was to investigate the relationship of Christianity—in the form of AICs—to modernity. In this chapter, I refer to a few smaller AICs to investigate how modernity is manifested. The results analysed in this chapter come mainly from a sample population of AIC churches drawn from Soweto in Gauteng Province, and from the greater Pietermaritzburg area (GPA) in KwaZulu-Natal Province.

THEORETICAL PERSPECTIVES AND ANALYTICAL CONCEPTS AS AN INTERPRETATIVE FRAMEWORK

The growth of AICs run counter to a classical sociological tradition that speaks of an inescapable decline of religion in modern society, often called "secularization." Secularization is a systematic concept for the differentiation and institutional specialisation of social domains. In mainstream sociology, this decline of religion forms the pivot of analysis of modernity. But in South Africa, the secularization paradigm is strongly challenged by AICs at the same time that the historical development of the religious and political domains are intersecting with that of modernity itself.

An investigation of religious modernity in the AICs requires an elaboration of the notions of modernity and of religion. Both notions entail very broad fields in which debates are clearly linked to the society that hosts them. An added difficulty, then, is how to define modernity in the South African context rather than a Western one, which does not seem to follow the "paradigm of secularization." But such definitions are necessary if we are to interpret and conceptualise the social significance of the historical process that South Africa is undergoing.

To address these issues—which are theoretical as well as fundamental to my research hypothesis—I revisit the debate on the definition of modernity. To understand the significance of this debate in South Africa, I examined the ongoing transformation of society within a sample of African Independent Churches in the post-apartheid context.

Ambiguity of the Term *Modernity*: An Example

I attempt to interpret the significance of the sociocultural transformations in South African society through the concept of modernity. As the concept is heavily dependent on the Western cultural contexts in which it originated and was debated, *modernity* remains a limited and overburdened term. I therefore do not use modernity as a theory of the evolution of history, but rather as a working definition and as a tool of analysis.

I define the term *modernity* by its three major traits:

- the logic and the process of institutionalization and its bureaucratization;

- the logic and the process of the autonomization of the subject;
- the process of plurality of production and the regulation of diverse values and belief systems.

As an example of how to understand the political and sociocultural significance of the historical process of modernity in South Africa, I find Kinghorn's analysis of Afrikaner churches particularly interesting (Kinghorn 1997). He shows what the practices of organisation, production, and regulation of religious and political meaning systems imply for understanding the term *modernity* in South Africa. Kinghorn's text also indicates how important the debate on modernity in South African society is:

> Predictably the Afrikaner churches initially reacted against modernisation. Not so predictable, however, was the strength of that resistance or the length to which Afrikanerdom would eventually go in an attempt to ward off modernity. The role of Afrikaner churches went deeper than political activism. They nurtured the underlying values, the very soul of Afrikaner mobilisation. Two core values were stressed: the family and hierarchical authority. In the case of the Afrikaners, however, these values were undergirded by religious tradition enshrined as doctrine. Any situation or context, therefore, in which they were perceived to be under threat was to be interpreted as a threat to religion as well. This connection between religion and social values later made it possible to elevate secular apartheid policies to the status of faith and to turn a modern-day inquisition loose on anyone of alternative mind. (Kinghorn 1997, 141–42)

Kinghorn acknowledged that the keystone of the Afrikaner value system was the religious presupposition of a cosmological hierarchy headed by God, the ultimate source of all being, and an all-encompassing descending structure of authorities over all of human existence. As Kinghorn pointed out, "Of course, modernity in general, and natural science, in particular, fundamentally challenged this presupposition." Human rights and democracy became the twentieth-century benchmark for the social manifestation of this challenge. Consequently, threats to this Afrikaner value system were not merely considered to be sociopolitical in nature, but as a challenge to religion. According to Kinghorn:

> until the late 1980s, the Afrikaner churches carried forward the ideal of separate development, which to them was the embodiment of true biblical justice under South African conditions . . . At the next synod in 1986 a new policy document was accepted, and refined in 1990. The discourse was no longer doctrinaire on socio-political issues. Concepts such as "modernism," "godless humanism," etc., disappeared altogether. Peace with modernity had been made. Human rights were now accepted as in accord with biblical justice. This could only happen because the mainstream of Afrikaners was no longer resisting modernity. (Kinghorn 1997, 149–51) .

Defining Modernity

How terms such as *modern, modernism,* and *modernity* should be defined has long been debated. For example, the terms *modern* and *modernity* have been defined as follows: "'modern' refers principally to modern ideas, patterns of thought, philosophies, and their expression in art and literature. Modernity is the intellectual and cultural heritage of the Enlightenment project—namely, the rejection of traditional and religious sources of authority in favour of reason and knowledge as the road to human emancipation" (Sampson, Vinay, and Sugden 1994, 7).

The modern is often defined as opposition to what is past, so that modernity is seen as a rupture with tradition. Here, we mean tradition as a way of seeing things in historical continuity, as a kind of fidelity, as a mode of belief that implies a reference to the values and models of heritage. In the terminology of Georges Balandier, it functions as a "generator of continuity":

> Tradition expresses the relationship to the past and to its limitations; it imposes a conformity resulting in the codification of meanings, and thus in the values that govern individual and collective conduct, transmitted from generation to generation. It is a heritage that defines and maintains an order, while suppressing the transformational action of time, retaining only the key moments from which it draws its legitimacy and strength. It orders, in all senses of the word. (Balandier, quoted by Danièle Hervieu-Léger 1993, 122–23, my translation)

Despite its variety of senses, modernity itself became a kind of tradition—the tradition of newness. Modernity became an ideology of change, of ruptures that push forward constantly. But to what ruptures does modernity refer? How did these ruptures become a reality? What are their sources? Those who defined modernity describe the major changes and ruptures that occurred in diverse fields of human activities in different ways. For example, in the field of knowledge, the fundamental rupture is identified as the emergence of the modern science of nature, which led to the differentiation of knowledge and the separation of different domains of science. In economic terms, the major rupture is often described as the process of development of capitalism, industrialisation, and the ethical code of work. In the political area, the major change is the process of political emancipation, which became synonymous with the emergence of democracy and human rights. In the field of cultural transformations, it is the ever-increasing affirmation of the individual and the autonomy of his/her conscience; a process that contributed to consumerism in modern society. In the religious domain, the major rupture is seen as a protest against the authority of ecclesiastical institutions, which is often described as rejection of God. One result was to create the widely accepted modern belief in an inescapable decline of religion in modern society.

The Signs of Modernity in South African Society

A central question in this chapter is: What are the major characteristics of the sociopolitical, cultural, and economic transformations in South Africa that express some traits of modernity? Due to the limited scope of this chapter, I am unable to include as detailed an analysis of the formation and evolution of South African society as such a question demands. Instead, I will extract certain characteristics of the particular local manifestation of modernity from the works of different commentators.

The era prior to the 1990s was a period of resistance, described by Tom Lodge as "a fundamental crisis in South African society. . . . The resistance of the 1970's provides a startling contrast in terms of scale and duration to the movements of the 1950's and early 1960's. This has reflected a fundamental crisis in South African society, in its origins both economic and political, a crisis which the authorities are apparently incapable of resolving through reform" (Lodge 1983, 321).

The era was characterised by repressed political emancipation, during which resistance to the established apartheid political system was increasing and intensifying. Another characteristic was a crisis of authority of institutions such as state, police, army, judiciary system, schools, media, and municipal councils. Such a fundamental crisis of the authorities reflects a major trait of modernity, as described by most of authors who define the term. Moreover, this total crisis continued for some decades—a duration which reveals the incurable structural contradiction of the apartheid political system.

These characteristics can be related to modernity in as far as they contributed to an emerging movement towards autonomous subjects and towards a proliferation of the religious dimension. Each is addressed in more detail below.

Emerging Autonomous Subjects

During the struggle for political emancipation, a conflictive relationship emerged between the logic of institutionalization and rationalisation of the apartheid state, and the logic of the autonomization of the subject. These logics constitute two dialectic dimensions of modernity, manifested at the political level in South African society. The conflict between them was expressed in the emerging new "value-charged" political culture—expressed as a growing aspiration for equality—that emerged within the resistance movement, alongside a heightening awareness of the social and economic distress caused by apartheid.

But similar characteristics of modernity were present in the historical origin of AICs in the nineteenth century that emerged in the political context of the 1980s and 1990s. The principal motivation for a rupture from the missionary Western churches for AIC founders was their growing aspiration for equality with white missionaries. A desire for political and human emancipation in social and cultural domains was also present, reflecting the relationship between the religious and political domains that seems to form a pivot of "tradition" within the AICs. Such logical patterns and historical consistencies today still govern the reality of the AICs.

Let us briefly analyse how the dialectic relationship between these two different logics of modernity is also manifested at the economic level in South Africa. The historical path of capitalism here shows a rationalisation of the economy that constitutes a major trait of modernity. The development of what is often called "racial capitalism" produced consequences such as the structurally sustained poverty of most black people who form more than 79% of the total population (2001 census).

The combination of political and economic logics in the rationalisation of apartheid produced a deep sociocultural transformation, of which one consequence was a particular architecture of urbanisation. The base for this architecture was the separation of spaces designed by the apartheid regime, and by the economical imperative of capitalism. Urbanisation was rationally organised, controlled, and instrumentalized by the political structure of apartheid to develop "racial capitalism." In Harold Wolpe's analysis, the "urban living conditions deteriorated rapidly and this was a crucial factor leading to the organised mass actions in the townships" (Wolpe 1988, 65). In this context, "mass organisations such as the ANC (African National Congress) were radicalised and extended" (Lodge 1983, 38–39). This led to the "growing African worker consciousness," which would shake South Africa's rulers to the core (Saul and Gelb 1988, 68).

The inexorable process of racialized urbanisation, combined with growing demographic pressures in the 1980s, had calamitous results. Factors that included a housing crisis and the catastrophic conditions of family life generated an even more volatile situation within the black community—particularly in the townships. Such deep socioeconomic and political frustrations and anger proved fertile ground for the growing politicisation of youth, black trade unions, women's and community organisations. The ferment fed into a more organised resistant movement. These factors combined generated a strong sense of the illegitimacy of the regime among large sectors of the black population and fuelled their aspirations for fundamental change. The long continuous crisis of the 1980s was characterized by an "ungovernable" situation and a total crisis of legitimacy for the apartheid regime.

The effects of urbanisation—as Georg Simmel (1903) depicted so well in his analysis—are among the factors that contribute to the emergence of the modern individual. As a newly emerging figure of modernity, the modern individual will, as a "historic subject" of modern consciousness, claim autonomy. In South Africa, urbanisation provided the privileged space from which the modern and autonomous consciousness of subjects grew, whether as a growing "African worker consciousness," a "black Consciousness," or of the self as a "youth activist."[2] Many would also begin to claim to be subjects of history, through references to what became widely known as a "liberation struggle."

But it is in the religious domain where the majority of black people, as emerging subjects of their autonomous consciousness, would experience the most dramatic transformation of modernity, in the development of African Independent Churches. And it is important to bear in mind that the spectacular growth of the AICs from the 1970s to 1990s took place precisely in the residential spaces of the poverty-stricken townships.

Proliferation of the Religious Dimension

The proliferation of Christian churches is a very visible consequence of the paradigm shift towards resistance among black people in South Africa. This phenomenon certainly helps us to understand a major change in South African Christianity: "Between 1980 and 1990 in South Africa, the number of Christians belonging to Mainline churches such as Anglican, Methodist, Catholic and Dutch Reformed Church declined by 25 percent from 12.1 million to 9.1 million" (Froise 1992). During the same period, the number of Christians belonging to AIC churches, offering religious and faith healing, increased from 5.6 million to 9.2 million—a figure that embraced at least 47% of all black Christians (1991 census).

The religious proliferation shows how black people tried to make sense of their lived experiences within the oppressive structures of apartheid society. According to the survey that I conducted from 1996 to 1997 among AICs in Gauteng Province and KwaZulu-Natal, less than 5% of respondents belonged to the AICs because their parents were members. The absolute majority said that they themselves chose to belong to AICs, having been invited by either friends (19% of all respondents) or pastors (38.1%). A further 9.5% of members joined because of faith healing. Of all respondents, the parents of 19.05% belonged to the Roman Catholic Church, and 19.05% in all to Lutheran, Anglican, or Methodist churches.

The various denominations of churches and ecumenical organisations responded in different and even conflictive ways to the repressive circumstances of apartheid. As a result, Christians were more or less overtly divided among themselves. Within particular denominations, certain groups supported the state and rallied to the resolute defence of white power; others sought compromise and reconciliation with the government. Simultaneously, prophetic Christians gathered strength and defied the state; while hesitant at first, they eventually made a spirited and even crucial contribution to the liberation movement.

Given these circumstances, we can understand the ever-growing phenomenon of African Independent Churches as an example of how black South Africans engaged modernity through religious activities. Within this broad religious grouping, I want to briefly attend to the phenomenal growth of "coping-healing" practices in the AICs (see Bate 1995).

Even though specialists in the field often consider Christianity in South Africa to be a divided and fragmented reality as a result of apartheid, I think a Christian "religiosity" or culture does provide a unifying tradition for the majority of the population. South Africans do not share a common culture in the sense of "historically transmitted shared patterns of understanding, that provides a means whereby South Africans can be united through culture rather than being divided by it" (Bate 1995, 17). Yet, as Stuart Bate correctly observed:

> The great Protestant missionary endeavour in South Africa with its emphasis on faith, the Scripture and the personal experience of God's presence, as well as the prophetic witness of faith has showed a depth of faith in the country which has resulted in many people, both Black and White, being practising Christians and the influence of the Church in the society being relatively high. This religiosity actually forms part of the common culture which exists or which is emerging within the country. (Bate 1995, 17)

That is why the religious domain forms an important part of sociocultural transformation of the country.

The Meaning of the Major Transformation of South African Christianity

I now examine the question concerning the meaning of the cultural transformation of South African Christianity, as manifested in the AICs with the help of theoretical tools and notions developed by sociology of religions.

A New Working Definition of Religion

I have adopted a working definition of religion from the sociological point of view, without trying to establish a "definitive" definition. I want to avoid being trapped in the endless development of a definition, or in the ongoing difficult debates between substantialism and functionalism.

I borrow my working definition of religion from Danièle Hervieu-Léger, who refers to "a particular mode of the organisation and functioning of belief. There is no religion without the authority of a tradition being invoked in support of the act of belief." In other words, religion is "a particular mode of belief which implies, in a specific way, a reference to the authority of a tradition" (Hervieu-Léger 1993, 31–34, my translation).

Hervieu-Léger's definition will help us to deal with the phenomena of reconstitution, displacement, and innovation of religious beliefs, which are so spectacular within the AICs and which also characterise religious phenomena in the era of modernity.

A Renewed Approach to Tradition

To better understand the reality of fast-growing AICs, we need to elaborate a renewed approach to tradition. South African society, particularly its cultural and religious phenomena, cannot be understood by means of simple concepts such as tradition/modernity, if these concepts are regarded as similar to past/future.

Belief in witches illustrates this point. A majority of AIC members do not exclude witches from their set of beliefs. My own survey conducted in the townships around the greater Pietermaritzburg area in KwaZulu-Natal showed that more than 76.2% of respondents clearly stated that they believe witches exist. Only 9.5% said that they do not believe, while 14.3% refused to give a response.

A recent opinion survey about culture, ethnicity, and religion, produced similar results on this topic. The majority of respondents, regardless of denominational affiliation, agreed with the sentence: "Although evil is everywhere, it can take possession of some people, and the community must get rid of such people, even if it means that they have to be killed" (Kotze 1997, 14–15). So it seems that there is an important element of religious belief that brings people, a majority of people, to share a punitive conception of evil in South Africa.

I noticed during my fieldwork that the phenomenon of witches, or the new interpretation of this phenomenon, explains for many people why group conflicts occur in South Africa. The political fight against the "people's enemies" is understood as a fight against witches. Subsequently, many people transposed political concerns to everyday life issues (witches); political life is not located outside the everyday struggle for personal and family integrity. Many people experienced the end of apartheid in South Africa as a time of chaos, of rapid changes, and of the reign of a spirit of evil over the country.

In this context, the political vocabulary often lent support to the religious vocabulary. Contrary to the commonly accepted image of the AICs as being apolitical, nearly 24% of AIC churchgoers in my 1996–1997 survey said that they had participated in the struggle by praying for liberation and peace in the country. But 62% said that their AICs did not have any particular position on apartheid. More than 38% said that they continue to support the transition to democracy by praying for peace. This is not surprising to me. I witnessed many times how the AICs had been actively involved in caring for communities and in conducting funerals for victims of political violence in the volatile townships of KwaZulu-Natal. This happened prior to the 1994 national elections and the regional elections in 1996. Sometimes these victims belonged to other church denominations. Some were not churchgoers at all, but their parents had belonged to the AICs. In some instances, AICs simply took charge because the mainline church pastors were viewed as "partisans" who could therefore not fulfil their duties. The AICs emerged as the only "viable and neutral" churches able to look after the families of victims in the townships. The most telling example was provided by a massacre that happened on September 1992 at Bisho, in the Ciskei. Numerous members of AICs were victims. On this occasion, the leaders of the AICs—particularly the African Spiritual Churches Association—wrote a protest letter and sent a delegation of nine persons to the Ciskei's military leader, Brigadier Oupa Gqozo. Their delegation stopped along the way at the place of the massacre, to pray for those who had been killed and injured.

In South Africa, political fights were often understood as religious fights. ANC leaders identified the white leaders of the apartheid regime and the Afrikaner organisations as sorcerers. They revived the famous call of Zulu king Dingane when he had the Voortrekker leader Piet Retief and his followers killed: *"Bulalani abathakathi!"* (Kill the sorcerers!) The death squads of the Inkatha Freedom Party ravaged the trains to the townships, killing ANC affiliates with the same call: Kill the sorcerers! In this way, political leaders were identified as witches and sorcerers, as evil persons manipulating supernatural instruments of power to perform violent harm. From this perspective, the only legitimate response to such persons and to "political" rites was forceful resistance.

The presence in South Africa of the invisible world in the form of witches and sorcerers is not a legacy of the preindustrial and premodern world, which economical development will soon eradicate. To the contrary, the invisible world seems to offer a means of interpreting the transformations of the contemporary world. Even someone who does not believe in witches and sorcerers will have to take into account the beliefs of people—especially if they are voters! The belief in witches and sorcerers is a reserve of legitimate memory that, particularly for black South Africans, constitutes an authorised tradition—a religious tradition. People whom I interviewed did not understand belief in sorcerers as being anti-Christian (as it would be in modernised and Western-rationalised Christian belief) but as part of a game of power between the spirit of evil and the spirit of good.

Dealing with this kind of religious belief, as a renewed tradition dealing with contemporary "political" issues, generates many reflections about the meaning and definition of tradition and "religion." The working definition of religion that I adopted (a particular mode of belief that implies a reference to the authority of a tradition) focuses particular attention on the question of tradition in my research. This is because two opposed dynamics of modernity have been manifested in South Africa during the historical development of apartheid and—in particular—of Christianity. On the one hand, missionaries originated mainline churches, and on the other, indigenous peoples developed and evolved AICs. AICs thus form an interesting example of the successful and spectacular revolt of conscience and of the autonomization of the subject as these processes unfolded in the religious domain.

How do AICs then refer to the authority of a tradition as a particular mode of belief within their churches? To clarify the question, quoted below is part of my interview with Archbishop Nduruso H. Ngada, president of the African Spiritual Churches Association (founded in 1969):

> Africans have always been a religious people. They worshipped God with all they had. God provided them with all what was necessary for their lives. He was worshipped by young and old, male and female, alike. They observed their culture, customs and traditions. There was no Bible during that period. Their Bible was their hearts, as King Moshoeshoe I once told the missionaries that, "Your laws are exactly like ours except that while yours are written on paper, ours are written in our hearts." People believed that God was with them. When there was drought, people would speak to God through their traditional ways of worship and God would answer them. Things changed after the missionaries came. The missionaries introduced a new way of worship and a new kind of people who came to be known as believers. Almost everything that Africans believed in was also termed as heathenism. Even God was called a heathen God. And the African ancestors were called demons. According to the missionaries, to be a Christian, you had to deny your natural and traditional way of life, and adopt the Western way of life. That's why our ancestors wanted to create our spiritual churches for the African people. (Ngada 1998)

Obviously, tradition has become a major force for mobilising power, and for contributing to conflicts in society. There is no unique tradition in South Africa that provides an authoritative reference to the past and is valid for all. Tradition is at the heart of all these problems because it is rooted in all actions and produces a particular mode of belief for each group with which it is associated: an imaginary projection of the present into the future. This is regardless of the fact that the Christian tradition in its evangelical form appears to provide the one unifying tradition in South African society.

What is essentially at stake here is not so much the content of belief produced by the act of believing, but rather the mode of production of a particular belief. The mode mobilises people to imagine a link across time and space, and so forms the basis of political and religious adhesion for members of different communities. This modality generates "the self-legitimacy of the act of believing by reference to the authority of a tradition," while aligning itself to a heritage of belief. It thus constitutes the principle source of conflict, since belief is a matter of interpretation, of selection, of sorting through traditions that institute the self-legitimacy of the content of beliefs (Hervieu-Léger 1993, 117–20).

The self-legitimisation of belief, and the validation of this act of believing by others, raises the question whether a consensus society is possible. This matter is a source of vigorous debate in South Africa—particularly among those actors in the political and religious fields who have contributed to theological-ethical disputes on the interpretation of Christian tradition, gospel, and Bible.

Archbishop Nduruso H. Ngada (1998) provided an example of how white Christians self-legitimise their act of belief, while condemning the act of traditional belief by Africans:

> Now since White Christians took it that they knew everything, the differences between White Christians and Black converted went further and further. A Black Christian would be suspended for brewing African sorghum beer [used in ancestral rites], while in church he is allowed to drink wine as Holy Communion. This wine he drinks at church is brewed by him at work, as he is taught by his White master. In all the church activities the White man was the leader and the Black man a follower with no objections. Even when Black Christians could read the Bible themselves, the White Christians enjoyed dominating them in the church until the Black Christians could no longer agree to be dominated by the White Christians in the church.

The discussion shows that tradition in South African society is not doomed inevitably to lose influence. On the contrary, tradition is becoming a force for mobilisation in the political domain as in the religious domain. Disputes about interpretation create differences between actors in the political, social, and religious arenas, especially among the leadership classes in all sectors of society. As for AIC believers, they have tried to delegitimise this "modernity" that was invented, in their view, by white Christians to claim the legitimacy of their traditions over those of others. In this way, AIC members exhibit a trait of modernity: the autonomy of modern consciousness in the act of believing.

According to Hervieu-Léger (1993, 119), "a religion is an ideological, practical and symbolic device through which the individual and collective consciousness of belonging to a particular belief system is constituted, maintained, developed, and controlled" (my translation). Thus, the question is: How can the respective estimated six thousand AICs claim to belong to the same tradition of Christianity as a "religion"? What is the role of that Christian tradition? Does it work as a "generator of continuity," or as part of the "imperative of change"?

REINVENTION OF TRADITION IN THE AIC AS MEANS OF ENGAGING MODERNITY

The reinvention of tradition is manifested in the day-to-day life of black South Africans in the religious context.

In South African society, a renewal of the cult of ancestors is under way, not only in rural areas but even more so in townships, as can be seen from certain rites. For example, consider the inauguration of a tombstone. In this rite, all the members of an extended family have to return to their village. Together they go to the cemetery to assist in the laying down of the tombstone of an ancestor. In most cases, such ancestors passed away a long time ago. Why then do they organise this ceremony only now? To buy a tombstone and to organise a big ceremony where a large family will be present requires money. Sometimes a family needs several years to save the necessary amounts of money for this purpose.

This practice can be viewed under the rubric of a new rite, as many informants with whom I had worked in townships told me that the rite does not originate in African "tradition." Nevertheless, this tradition is becoming increasingly important for black people who want to show that they honour their ancestors. The rite is certainly an innovation; a mixture of traditional African ancestral veneration and certain habits adopted from whites. Even poor people engage in such renovated rites—spending a lot of money on tombstones (sometimes made from marble) and on the travel costs and alimentation of the whole family who participates in the ceremony.

This cult has emerged as an obligation for all black people, regardless of whether they belong to traditional African religion, AICs, or historically established mainline churches. Due to the belief that ancestors comprise a force that is able to modify the present situation of the living—in death and life, health, and professional achievement—this ancestral rite survives as a renewed tradition in modern South Africa. In my survey of the greater Pietermaritzburg area, 90.5% of AIC respondents said that they practice ancestral veneration. The impact of this new tradition can be easily measured in the growing boom of funeral businesses.

How does one describe such a practice—as tradition, modernity, or the innovation of old habits? The rite probably embodies everything at the same time: an old tradition in new clothes—a way for tradition to survive in the modern world through renewed forms.

Examined below are some of these questions regarding the religious practices of the AICs, in particular the coping-healing practices present within the AICs—which have also been called spiritual churches, or coping-healing churches. Here, we use the work of Bate (1995, 67–176) as a main resource of this analysis.

Bate analyses the coping-healing phenomenon in the AICs as "part of the political process of transformation to which the country is being called," and as a major manifestation of the acculturation process that is occurring in South Africa now. Archbishop Nduruso H. Ngada explained that there was too much emphasis on Western civilization in Christianity in the white missionary controlled Christian churches:

> As missionaries continued to work among Africans, they also continued to change our way of living. They would not allow our people to attend the "church" services in African traditional clothes. To be a Christian, you were expected to forsake your people, your culture, customs, your traditions even your traditional dress and your name. You were expected to wear Western clothes, speak a foreign language and to accept a foreign name because you would not be a Christian using your African name which was termed heathen name. Thus the Western civilization was taken as Christianity by the African. (Ngada 1998)

In coping-healing AICs, members draw on symbolic resources both from the Christian healing tradition of the Bible and from the African tradition of traditional healers as they actively reinvent and articulate recently developed religious traditions in the logic of transformation of memory. This is not so surprising if we consider the socioeducational background of the majority members of the AICs. The most striking characteristic that AICs have in common is that their members come from the poorest and most excluded black population of South Africa, and usually have very low education and socioeconomic levels. The size of AICs might vary from a few dozen members to the enormous network of Zion Christian Churches (ZCC) with a possible two to three million adherents who go to Moria near Pietersburg during the Easter week. AICs usually do not have their own church buildings. They typically meet on street corners, near a river, in a bishop's house, or in an empty classroom. My 1996–97 survey confirmed that more than 50% belonged to the lowest social class, and were typically employed as manual or domestic workers. More than 29% were unemployed, including housewives. In terms of education, more than 56% had not completed Standard 10 (Grade 12)—a figure that could have been even higher, given that 24% of respondents refused to answer this question. The majority of the pastors, bishops, and archbishops of the AICs either belong to the lower working class or are pensioners who did not receive a salary from their churches.

Because many AIC members and officials are illiterate and do not have conventional theological training (apart from a few who completed courses in Bible schools), the majority have developed a very significant Christian tradition—an oral form of transmission of their faith. This oral tradition forms a principal part of their rituals, which are often combined with singing, music, and dances when they are moved—as they would say—by the "Holy Spirit" during their church services. So AIC services comprise religious experiences based on an oral tradition of Bible stories, which are reinterpreted during services with the assistance of pastors, bishops, and prophetesses. The oral tradition is expressed in terms of their own religious experiences of daily life, and includes dreams, visions, sickness, and various problems of the community. Archbishop Ngada (1998) says, "When Black man could read the Bible himself, he came to understand that the White man in the church was not teaching him the Bible only but his culture also. This situation changed even further when the Bible was translated into most of the African languages."

Since AICs provide members with the faith that functions as possibly the only available means with which to interpret their life experience, it is little wonder that this faith is formulated, lived, and experienced in terms of African culture. The legitimacy of the origin of AICs comes historically from the rejection of the control of Western culture over Christianity. For this reason, AIC members are free to affirm an African sense of community, family ties, respect for elders and ancestors, belief in spirits, customs of initiation, and the African way of worshipping by singing and dancing.

Many scholars have underlined the importance of the cultural dimension in the functioning of AICs, particularly where they interpret healing as a process of the articulation of symbols. I observed during my fieldwork that symbols such as prayer, laying on of hands, stepping into a healing circle, and confessing sins constitute the principal part of an AIC's religious services. The coping-healing phenomenon also fulfils other important functions in AICs, as a ministry that meets the needs of people on a very basic and accessible level. The services of AICs can also be seen as adaptive structures, which provide a "coping" social environment that operates within an easily understandable and simplistic cultural framework. This provides a refugee for those unable to cope with the complexity of modern life. The time spent within the subculture is therefore a time of reconstruction of humanity.

Certain scholars suggest that some AICs identify the source of a person's illness as a kind of "social deviance," which can be understood as "social deprivation." "Deviance" here refers to the person's situation as someone who does not receive the normal benefits of society. This implies also a wider understanding of "social disorganisation," where society as a whole is seen to "deviate" from what a normal society is, and so finds itself in crisis. For such scholars, this social deprivation and alienation occurs as people feel powerless and alienated from the societies they belong to and the values they profess. The cultural factors comprising the beliefs and values that determine right and wrong behaviour are based on tradition.[3] So to heal people means also to respond to the deviance. In this sense, Comaroff (1985, 197) suggests that, "the Zionists construct rituals so as to reform the world in the image they have created, to establish a dynamic correspondence between the self and the structures that contain it."[4] Many other authors also highlighted this question of status and respect denied by the society and affirmed within the AICs. The religious space of AICs directly fulfils these needs by being a supportive, caring, and giving group.

Others emphasise the importance of a shared worldview in the healing practices of the AICs. David Chidester (1989) suggests that the term *worldview* be broadened to include "a multidimensional network of strategies for negotiating person and place in a world of discourse, practice and associations." He suggests that AICs are concerned with the process of reestablishing human identity for people whose daily experience is one of dehumanisation. Sundkler (1961) points out that the religious worldview that Zionism employs manifests both similarities to and changes from the traditional African worldview. Bate (1995) observed that a centre of theological and missiological debate today concerns a paradigm shift. Chidester (1989) argues that the study of religion is a discipline of worldview analysis. He suggests that the African Indigenous Churches are clearly involved in the process of negotiating "a human identity through contact with superhuman powers in a dehumanising environment." Similarly, for Oosthuizen (1986, vi), AICs enhance modernization and attitudes that favour progress.

According to Dorothy Farrand (quoted in Bate 1995, 142–43), "the infiltration of Western attitudes and thought patterns has led to the emergence of a two stage process, 'in which the sick person first goes to a Western doctor to get the illness cured and then goes to an indigenous healer to determine and alleviate the cause of the illness.'" She also showed that people move towards faith healers and away from traditional healers because they consider the former more "oriented to an industrial and urban environment." Consequently, they view faith healers as more effective at amalgamating "the traditional black worldview and belief system with a Western religious approach." This is an interesting observation, which my own fieldwork during 1995–97 confirmed. When they are sick, 57% of AIC respondents consult an indigenous healer, while 14.3% go to a Western doctor. A further 14.3% of respondents consult faith healers and use the blessed water and prayers of their AICs, while 9.5% use all these approaches.

CONCLUSION

The concern in this chapter has been to ask whether the logic and dynamics that govern AICs in South Africa are the same as those operating at political and socioeconomical levels. I attempted to clarify the significance of certain sociocultural transformations in the South African society through attention to the development and life of AICs, using modernity as a working definition. In my analysis, I referred to different studies of the growth of AICs and their healing practices.

I concluded that certain major traits and two logical processes of modernity can be observed in the political, economical, and sociocultural domains of South African society that also generate a profound transformation of the religious domain. Similar transformations of religion form part of a globalized phenomenon that is evolving in non-Western society. The logic and the dynamics of modernity manifest in the constant and conflictive tension of a dialectic relationship between its major characteristics. At the religious level, the consequence of the dialectic produced a particular form of proliferation of religious phenomena in South Africa—a characteristic of the transformation of religion in the modern era. This transformation revises "religious content from within, without emptying them of their religious authenticity, since it is in fact the means by which they are able to conserve a cultural relevance and thus survive modernity, in a renewed manner" (Hervieu-Léger 1993, 103, my translation). The development of AICs manifests, in a particularly creative and visible way, the active revision of religious content, based on the concrete experiences of life under the repressive apartheid system and in the dehumanising context of modernization in South Africa.

The particular historical path followed by South African society generated a plurality of values and a proliferation of religious phenomena instead of secularization. AIC members—as autonomous subjects—participated very actively in the production and the regulation of their worldviews. They constructed a new meaning of life through a complex and creative process of rearticulation. AICs played a major role for many black people in South Africa as a framework of symbols and significance with which to overcome the disappointments of daily life. The religious domain became one of the most privileged and visible fields in which the subjective dynamics of reconstruction, displacement, and innovation occurred in the era of modernity in South Africa. The subject of this dynamic needs a particular mode of the organisation and functioning of beliefs. The religious domain became a major force for mobilisation and a reference to an accessible tradition in the context of a total crisis of legitimacy of the authorities in apartheid institutions.

NOTES

1. Readers should be aware that the complex definitions and theoretical debates about the meaning of *culture* acquired an added segregationist dimension in apartheid-era South Africa. "The term 'culture' was abused by

the apartheid ideologues who constructed the myth of separate nations with separate cultures in separate areas who nevertheless had to participate in a single socio-economic and socio-political entity as though culture was somehow divorced from these latter two fundamental realities" (Mary De Haas 1989, quoted by Bate 1995, 16).

2. According to Lodge (1983, 323), "In July 1969, the South African Students' Organisation (SASO) was launched at Turfloop and an important vehicle for the spread of the Black Consciousness movement was born. The main goal of SASO was to restore Black pride, dignity and confidence in Black students' ability to lead and direct the struggle for emancipation . . . The analysis of SASO differed from the analysis of the Africanists of the late 1950s, . . . Blacks were not defined as such ethnically: from the start the Black Consciousness movement involved Indians and Coloureds as well as Africans." Langefeld (1993, 46) states, "The influence of Black Consciousness spread beyond the campuses and resonated with the broader community of Blacks especially in the townships. Although the organisational aspects of this new movement were restricted to literacy campaigns, health projects, cultural activity, community projects and a general workers' union, the influence of the movement was extensive. Steve Biko became its central figure and symbol."

3. Authors such as Sundkler and Itumaleng Mosala suggest that many Western approaches lacked an adequate social and cultural analysis of this phenomenon. Sundkler (1961) notes that the emergence of these churches from 1913 to 1945 related to the Land Act, while also involving a reaction to the mission churches. Mosala (1989) argues that the concepts "working class" and "blackness" are key to the investigation of African Independent Churches.

4. Comaroff (1985, 228) affirms that "both ritual and healing provide two responses to the society within which people live: an experience of resistance to the society on the one hand and an experience, on the other hand, of reconstruction of the human person. This reconstruction, both of dignity and of humanness occurs in the counter society, the church, within which such human dignity is both affirmed and enhanced."

REFERENCES

Bate, Stuart C. 1995. *Inculturation and Healing: Coping-healing in South African Christianity*. Pietermaritzburg: Cluster Publications.

Chidester, David. 1989. Worldview analysis of African Indigenous Churches. *Journal for the Study of Religion* 2: 15–29.

Comaroff, Jean. 1985. *Body of power, spirit of resistance: The culture and history of a South African people*. Chicago and London: The University of Chicago Press.

Froise, Marjorie, ed. 1992. *South African Christian handbook 1993/94*. Johannesburg: Christian Info.

Hendriks, Jurgens. 1995. Facing the facts. In *Meeting the future: Christian leadership in South Africa,* ed. Duncan Buchanan and Jurgens Hendriks, 25ff. Randburg (South Africa): Knowledge Resources.

Hervieu-Léger, Danièle. 1993. *La religion pour la mémoire.* Paris: Cerf.

Kinghorn, Johann. 1997. Modernisation and apartheid, the Afrikaner churches. In *Christianity in South Africa: A political, social and cultural history,* ed. Richard Elphick and Rodney Davenport, 135–54. David Philip: Cape Town.

Kotze, Hennie. 1997. Culture, ethnicity and religion: South African perceptions of social identity. Occasional Papers, April. Department of Political Science, University of Stellenbosch.

Langefeld, Christiaan. 1993. *An emerging ecclesial practice: A socio-theological study of the theory and practice of a church youth group in the period 1980–1988.* MA dissertation, University of Natal, Pietermaritzburg.

Lodge, Tom. 1983. *Black politics since 1945.* Johannesburg: Ravan Press.

Mosala, Itumaleng. 1989. *Race, class and gender as hermeneutical factors in the African Independent Churches' appropriation of the Bible: A final report to the Human Sciences Research Council.* Research Report. Pretoria: Human Sciences Research Council.

Ngada, Nduruso H., Archbishop. 1998. Personal interview with the president of the African Spiritual Churches Association at their Research and Theological Training Institute, Braamfontein, Johannesburg.

Oosthuizen, G. C. (ed.) 1986. *Religion Alive: Studies in the New Movements and Indigenous Churches in South Africa.* Johannesburg: Hodder and Stoughton.

Pretorius, Hennie, and Lizo Jafta. 1997. 'A branch springs out'—African Initiated Churches. In *Christianity in South Africa: A political, social and cultural history,* ed. Richard Elphick and Rodney Davenport, 211–26. Cape Town: David Philip.

Sampson, Philip, Samuel Vinay, and Chris Sugden, eds. 1994. *Faith and modernity.* Oxford: Regnum Books.

Saul, J. S., and S. Gelb. 1988. *The crisis in South Africa.* Rev. ed. London: ZED.

Simmel, Georg. 1903 (1989). *Philosophie de la modernité.* Paris: Payot.

StatsSA. 2004. *Census 2001 by province, gender, religion recode (derived) and population group.* Statistics South Africa. (URL: http://www.statssa.gov.za/SpecialProjects/Census2001/Census/Dialog/varval.asp?ma=Religion by province&ti=Table%3A+Census+2001+by+province%2C+gender%2C+religion+recode+%28derived%29+and++population+group%2E+&path=../Database/Census%202001/Provincial%20Level/Persons/&lang=).

Sundkler, Bengt G. M. 1961. *Bantu prophets in South Africa.* 2d ed. London: Oxford University Press.

Wolpe, H. 1988. *Race, class and the apartheid state.* London: Unesco.

PART IV

A GLOBAL PERSPECTIVE

Applying a World System Perspective to a Literature Study of African Independent Churches

Dawid Venter

INTRODUCTION

This chapter outlines the implicit methodology that underpins my case study of the emergence of Apostolic-Zionist churches in chapter 8. Discussions of methodology in a narrower sense usually deal with how a researcher collects data. But chapter 8 represents tertiary analysis that seeks to reinterpret or extend data that previous researchers had already collected and interpreted. Therefore, I instead concentrate on a broader understanding of methodology, which includes both the steps that I took during analysis to meet my research objective, as well as the set of assumptions that led me to take *these*—rather than other—analytical steps. Accordingly, I also reflect on the rationale for selecting various presuppositions and preexisting theoretical concepts, which I blended into a perspective that guided my interpretation. In common with many researchers, then, I neither invented new methods, nor used all possible existing ones.

I refer to an "implicit" methodology, as my analysis proceeded in a relatively intuitive way. To recover my methodology, I had to consciously retrace the sequence by which the research unfolded, with special emphasis on analysis. The first step, theoretical interest, followed a chance remark about the world system made by a fellow academic. His comments led me, secondly, to theoretical engagement, in which I read a number of theories about the world system, including globalization theories. These theories provided certain presuppositions about the nature of social reality, which prompted me to phrase the research objective in a particular way. In turn, the objective became the lens for rereading J. De Wet's (1994) presentation of data on Zionist churches. In other words, my methodology comprised a dialectical process between the objective, with its attendant subquestions, and the steps that I took to answer them.

Yet there are also more explicit aspects of my methodology, as I had set out with a consciously formulated objective rather than a research question. In general terms, I wanted to know how a global perspective could help to explain why Zionist churches emerged in a southeastern region of South Africa, the Transkei, that had proven particularly resistant to Western and Christian influences. More specifically, I wanted to demonstrate theoretically how globalization trends—and the resulting global formation—articulated with national socioeconomic developments in South Africa to contribute to the rise of African Independent Churches (AICs).

A critical question is whether my presuppositions, procedures, and results are valid, which requires some attention to the unit of analysis, levels of analyses, and type of research. Although none of these are explicitly indicated in chapter 8, they were not too difficult to bring to the surface.

The *unit of analysis* is the belief system of a particular sociopolitical and linguistic group within a particular geographic area: Xhosa-speakers in the southeastern subregion of the Transkei. I reinterpreted changes within this local unit of analysis as the consequence of interactions between dominant and subordinate groups. One group comprised colonial and postcolonial political authorities, and the other, Xhosa-speakers. I perceived the interactions between these two groups as having occurred within three interlinking *levels of analysis*. The first level of analysis is local, with a focus on society-wide change in the southeastern Transkei subregion. At the second, national level, I viewed developments in South Africa as a whole as affecting local socioeconomic and political changes in the subregion. A third level of analysis is global, in which I regard world systemic structures and dynamics as linked to the national and subregional geographic areas (South Africa, the southeastern Transkei).

As a *type of analysis*, chapter 8 represents a diachronic investigation that covered a specific but long historical period, spanning both the colonial and the subsequent apartheid regimes. My use of "case study" to refer to the contents of chapter 8 suggests that I am biased towards an idiographic—rather than a nomothetic—interpretation. My study of the emergence of Zionist churches in the Transkei remains an examination of a *single* case, which I interpreted by reference to the world system. This does not mean that I was completely uninterested in nomothetic explanations, as my desire to explain the case by reference to a global structure shows. But a nomothetic approach would require that I gear my research to analyze the world-economy (Wallerstein's term) itself, rather than the other way around. My study seeks rather to demonstrate the *intra*national effects of the global system on a particular phenomenon.

Note that I use the phrase *world system* without a hyphen, as my approach differs to some extent from *world-system* analysis, though not in a particularly radical manner. The major elements of this perspective remain those outlined by Immanuel Wallerstein in relation to his seminal discussions of the world system. Like world-system analysts, I accept that economic linkages (e.g., trade agreements) make up the foundation of the world system. But, in addition to incorporating insights from this preeminent world-system theorist, the writings of others who reflect on the different dimensions of the global system strongly informed my methodology. These scholars include Peter Beyer (1994), Roland Robertson (1992), John Meyer et al. (1997), and—to a lesser extent—Niklas Luhmann. The major difference between my work and world-system theorists is that I assume the global system comprises more than economic dimensions. As a result, I try to give equal attention to cultural, political, and social linkages when I tackle the question of how the global system affected the African Independent Churches.

I now turn to a fuller discussion of methodology in which I raise specific issues, each forming a section of the chapter:

- First, I concentrate on the elements that I selected from various theories about the global system to build my own variation of a *world system perspective*. I attempt to make explicit that which is implicit in this concept, namely a set of *presuppositions* that guided my analysis;

- Second, I describe how I analysed the preexisting data. This defines my work on Zionist churches of the Transkei as tertiary literature analysis. Such a reworking of secondary data has certain consequences when it comes to debating whether the analysis has any validity—as the third section of this chapter shows. (Further discussion of "tertiary data"—information based on already-processed data—can be found in the glossary and in research methodology books); and

- Third, I address the issue of how to assess the validity of my work. To what degree does the evidence support my reinterpretation of the emergence of Zionist churches in terms of the effects of the world system?

ELEMENTS IN THE CONSTRUCTION OF A WORLD SYSTEM PERSPECTIVE

Even Immanuel Wallerstein, the scholar most responsible for reinforcing the idea that the modern world comprises a single economic system, does not make his methodology explicit. At closer range, Wallerstein's work suggests that his findings are based on a dialectic movement between a number of concepts about the world-economy (with a hyphen) and economic historical evidence itself. Walter Goldfrank (2000, 166) agrees that for Wallerstein "reconceptualization in tandem with reinterpretation *is* his method" (emphasis in the original). Goldfrank points out that Wallerstein's theory comprises *structural elements*, such as the notions of a single division of labor between the core on the one hand, and the periphery and semiperiphery on the other. The *dynamics* of the system include long-term cycles of expansion and contraction, as well as the unequal exchange through which the core extracts resources from the periphery. Wallerstein's interpretation proceeds from viewing the world-economy as the ultimate unit of analysis for analyzing social change (150). With reference to our overall theme, a world-system perspective denies that states "develop" from tradition to modernity in the manner of athletes competing in separate, staggered lanes. Instead, the system depends on maintaining the differences between the core and the periphery (170).

While theorists on the global system tend to mirror Wallerstein's inattention to explicit methodology, there are a few exceptions. Within the world-system field, Christopher Chase-Dunn and colleague Tom Hall (1997) have offered extensive discussion of methods. Similarly, John Boli and his coworkers represent exceptions in world-polity theory (Boli and Thomas 1999). Undoubtedly, this tendency not to outline methodology also unconsciously influenced me to adopt a similar implicit approach in chapter 8.

The world system comprises—at least—the outcomes of the globalization of capitalism on the one hand, and on the other, the globalization of institutions that regulate the interstate system. But religious institutions, which clearly influenced interstate relations up to the colonial period, by themselves constitute some of the earliest globalized forms of social organization. Consequently, alongside colonial administrative structures, religious proselytization formed a major transnational linkage between South Africans and others elsewhere across the world. The strong European and missionary presence in South Africa led to the establishment of education institutions that promoted "civilized" Western notions and economic practices. Indigenous appropriations of Christianity in the form of African Zionist churches were exported to other southern African states. Clearly, the world-economy is dialectically linked to cultural change, with cultural hegemony accompanying the expansion of the world capitalist system. For example, a global language system that favours English has emerged as part of the cultural structure of the world system.

My repeated use of the term *system* so far should alert readers that I assume the global structure consists of components that interact with one another. With systems theory analysts, I do not take this to mean that all components of the system are equally powerful. Instead, the system comprises interacting elements that have differing degrees of significance. Because systemic elements are independent and interconnected, what happens in one part of the system affects other parts of the system to varying degrees. Local phenomena may affect the global system; while certain local effects may be *systemic*—that is, can be said to derive from the dynamics or structure of the global system.

It should be noted that *world-economy* and *world system* are not used as synonyms. I take the world-economy to refer to the economic dimension of the world system. I accept with world-system theorists the importance of structure in the global formation, and of the significance of the world-economy in producing that structure through increasingly dense financial and trade networks. I also recognize that to a large extent the world-economy, as a totality, encompasses most systemwide dynamics (Boswell and Bergesen 1987, 4). I also accept that a global division of labor exists between periphery, semiperiphery, and core zones. At the same time, I find the arguments that cultural and political logics can function systemically and independently of the world-economy equally compelling. For this reason, I reject the notion that the world system is structured only by a single economic logic.

The methods used in the case study, then, are based on my implicit assumption that the concept of a world system should be linked to the processes that comprise globalization. I regard globalization as a process that establishes a global structure (the world-economy) and worldwide institutions (the world-polity). Both formations in turn affect political, economic, and cultural structures. I deem the spatial and structural stratification of the global system by the operation of the world-economy into the core, semiperiphery, and periphery analytically relevant.

ANALYTICAL STRATEGY FOR REREADING PREEXISTING DATA

My analysis centres on cultural change as a particular social phenomenon occurring among people that comprise, in sociological terms, a single unit of analysis. Yet the analysis itself moves between three different levels (a subregion of South Africa, South Africa as a whole, and the global system), each of which is regarded as necessary for a more complete perception of the processes at work. Obviously, the methods used to analyse the three levels differ from those used to understand the unit of analysis.

While I wanted to explore the interaction between the global and the local, my study focuses on a particular local phenomenon, which I relate to the global. In other words, the case study is *not* a study of the world system as such, but of the possible ways in which the world system could have affected the local. I use empirical data to describe change within the local unit of analysis, but at the global level, my interpretation is based on theories about the world system.

I embarked on the case study as a result of an initial desire to understand what African Independent Churches are. As I came to know more about them, I also wanted to know how such churches emerged. Both these steps led me to review the literature on AICs in southern Africa, as well as elsewhere in Africa. I compiled lists of books and articles on AICs from electronic databases (such as that offered by the American Theological Library Association, ATLA) and read those that seemed relevant and available. During my preliminary review of literature on the AICs, I noticed that no author had so far offered an analysis of their emergence using a world system approach. I became particularly interested in what insights a world-economy perspective could bring. In other words, I had unconsciously and arbitrarily selected a particular perspective in which economic analysis featured prominently.

I was stimulated to think about economic analysis by J. De Wet's 1994 study, which explained the emergence of Zionist-Apostolics in the Transkei in terms that recalled for me the global political economy. In particular, De Wet's discussion, although not posed in such terms, mirrored the way in which the global has a dialectical effect on the worldview of some Xhosa. To me, this suggested that there was an affinity between *world-economy* theory and explanations for the emergence of the AICs.

But De Wet's insistence on the changes in worldview among Transkei Xhosa that accompanied changes from a preindustrial to an industrial mode of production also seemed to have an affinity with globalization theories. While the prominence that De Wet lends to economic systems aligns him with world-economy theorists, his reference to cultural ideologies allows me to bring in globalization theories. I regard globalization as the process through which a world system emerges, linked primarily but not exclusively through the world-economy. De Wet's economic interpretations allow me to ask how changes in local modes of production are prompted by an emerging global economy. The prominence that De Wet places on economic analysis emerges most clearly in his discussion of the association between the rate at which Xhosa-speakers in the Transkei were incorporated into migrant labor and the rate of their affiliation to Apostolic-Zionism. His cultural references permit me to ask how changes in localized cultures are affected by globalizing identities—not only by economic changes. So, Zionism can also be described as a globalized form of American Pentecostalism, which in time became an indigenized form of Christianity.

The discussion so far suggests that in order to reinterpret data in world system terms, an appropriate text—which demonstrates some affinity to the theories that an analyst wishes to employ—has to be selected. The bibliographical work of Hennie Pretorius (1995) and David Chidester (1997) represents other obvious places to find references to texts on AICs.

Not all cases appear equally appropriate to an investigation using a world-economy approach. In a recent attempt to explain contemporary cultural change in language statuses by reference to the world system (Venter 2000), I found world-economy theories only partly successful. Perhaps this has to do with my own proximity in time to the unit of analysis: the effects of the world-system may become more obvious the further away the analyst stands from the period being studied. The fact that in chapter 8 I used a diachronic strategy of analysis for the AICs and a synchronic strategy for the language study (2000) suggests that perhaps diachronic strategies lend themselves more to world-economy explanations than synchronic ones. The opposite may be true: that synchronic research strategies have a greater elective affinity to globalization theories.

To review briefly, in order to achieve my central objective, I had to apply world-economy theories to an existing interpretation and to its supporting data so that I could extend that explanation beyond the national to the global level of analysis. This was the covert purpose, and in effect formed a secondary research question. In this way, the data could be understood in a new light, which in turn would extend theories about the world system. My implicit interest was to provide a theoretical contribution to the study of AICs as much as to the study of the world system. For this reason, my discussion here is not limited to purely methodological explanations, but also explores associated theoretical dimensions. I regard theory and methodology as closely intertwined.

Having elected to reanalyse De Wet's work in terms of a world system perspective, I needed to understand what the world system is, and how its structures and dynamics are thought to affect national development. Another review of literature ensued, this time on world system theories, through which I became acquainted with world-economy and globalization concepts, associated primarily with the work of Immanuel Wallerstein and Roland Robertson, respectively. Essential elements from such theorists were then applied to De Wet's analysis.

I reinterpreted De Wet's data in terms of the relationships between the dynamics of cultural change among the Transkei Xhosa and the dynamics of the world system. The economic cycles that play a central part in world-economy theory seemed relevant here. This, in turn, prompted me to recall the notion of hegemonic succession, particularly as explained by Peter Smith (1986). Smith argued that hegemonic succession could be used to explain cultural hegemony in the world system, as I explain in more detail in chapter 8. The extent to which homogeny or heterogeny features in the world system is debated, of course. The suggestion in globalization theories that both occur seems accurate to me. A movement towards homogeneity alongside a retention of heterogeneity appeared as a likely explanation in the case study. I concluded that Xhosa-speakers retained within their newly adopted Apostolic-Zionist identities some aspects of localized traditional culture alongside the incorporation of globalized identities.

At this point, the purpose of the chapter 8 case study can be restated as concerning the analysis of a sociocultural phenomenon in terms of world system theory. This focus requires some detailed discussion, as the analysis of culture—like the analysis of religion—poses particular difficulties for world-economy analysts. For globalization theorists, the debate about culture is rather about the relation of the local to the global, and of homogeneity to heterogeneity.

METHODOLOGICAL QUESTIONS RELATING TO GLOBALIZATION

Roland Robertson and William Garrett (1991, xiv) maintain that theories of globalization "must define the role of cultural factors in establishing the parameters of that order by which the world is apprehended as 'one place.'" For Robertson, globalization concerns the construction of global meanings, and so implies a world culture upon which the respective units are compelled to draw. This does not lead to a hegemonic perspective of what constitutes the system, but to competing views. Despite such elaborations, Robin Holton claims that globalization theories still offer unsatisfactory explanations of cultural dynamics, due to their underdeveloped nature. Consequently, the analytical usefulness of globalization theories is curtailed, as they comprise "general programmatic statements . . . little more than broad orientations to analysis" (Holton 1998, 196).

Robertson and Garrett's challenge regarding cultural factors implies that the role of religious elements must be explained, a task that again provides a variety of responses, of which Robertson and Garrett note four. First, theorists who argue that cultural factors have a limited role in globalization tend to side with radical secularists, while those who acknowledge the function of culture tend—at the least—to be more ambivalent (Robertson and Garrett 1991, xiv). Second, theorists who accept that globality comprises norms, but not those directly linked to religious sources. Norms governing international law and global treaties could serve as examples here. Third, theorists who accept the basic secularity of globalization, but admit that religions can occupy certain niches in the world order. Fourth, those who believe that religions contribute "significantly to the development of patterns of universal order," though in forms not directly associated with denominational organizations (xv). The latter position coincides most clearly with that of Robertson. My own approach combines aspects of the second and fourth explanations for the role of religion in the world system.

The question of how religion interacts with the world system is relevant, as chapter 8 concerns the intersection of global and local institutions in a subunit of a *religious* institution. The nature of the interaction can, firstly, be viewed in terms of the possible contribution that religious institutions make to globalization processes. A second approach would concern the reverse, the effects of the global system on religious institutions. A third way would be to discern the dialectic dynamics of these two processes.

For Robertson and Garrett (1991, xii–xiii) any attempt to understand the role of culture has to outline how religion interrelates with the social order; economic, cultural identity; and socialising agents of the global system. They consider the global social order to be constituted by states, political parties, ideologies, cultural symbols, society, and "patterns of political legitimation." Economic institutions are formed by businesses, unions, organizations, welfare systems, and "attitudes to work." Cultural identity includes national bodies, ethnicities, classes, associations, interest groups, and the media; while socialising agents comprise "the family, neighborhood, reference groups, peer groups."

While the articulation of religious elements with these components is historically demonstrable, in an increasingly differentiated and pluralizing postmodern world, the relationships are admittedly complex (Robertson and Garrett 1991, xiii). For example, secularization can be viewed as related to global processes in different ways (xii–xiv). Some would argue that globalization results in "deep structural secularisation," which will mean the "inevitable eclipse of religious hegemony." Others view religion as having been exorcised from the macrostructural to the microstructural realm, where it provides symbolic sustenance to individuals. Or, secularization can be seen as a special European case, premised on a particular alliance of religious and class elites in a specific political context. Then it follows that outside of Northern Europe "modernity and religious decline have not been coterminous" (xiv). This sentiment is echoed in Jules-Rosette's (1989, 156–57) evaluation of new African religious movements as cultural responses to modernizing and secularising influences; and by Lawrencia Kwark in chapters 5 and 6 of this book.

Frank Lechner (1991) points out that in the past, certain religions not only functioned "as global institutions," nor merely existed as limited world systems (e.g., the Holy Roman Empire), but also played causal roles in establishing the world system. In short, Lechner (1991, 272) argues that religion plays an important role in processes of institutionalization as "an obvious source of values." His argument prompts the question what the role of religion is in the institutionalization of global values. Where differences of values occur, this may hinder such institutionalization.[1]. Lechner warns that when religion is considered in global terms, idealist perceptions of the world system may emerge that would highlight values to the exclusion of other categories (265). Surprisingly, Lechner concludes that the current world system is essentially secular, despite counterevidence in the form of religious revivals, high levels of belief, or continued salience of religious institutions. He does not provide support for his argument in any way.

J. H. Simpson (1991) believes that Robertson's perspective on the role of religion in the world system contains great flexibility and has the advantage of explicitly thematizing religion. For example, Robertson departs from the received notion of modernization as he proposes the possibility of a "new typological social complex," which combines "symbols, structures, and cultural elements of *Gemeinschaft* and *Gesellschaft*." This allows Robertson not only to include institutional differentiation, but also to imagine "the 'recombination' of autonomous institutions," so that in globalization processes religion can be viewed as "seeking institutional 'partnerships'" (Simpson 1991, 13).

Like Robertson, Simpson argues that no single thematization of the role of religion is adequate. All the major theories are defensible, including those that emphasise "exchange processes" (Wallerstein), "myths of progress" (Meyer), "logic of interaction and perception operating within an admixture of traditional and modern institutions that perforce lead to the direction of co-operative systems or systems governed by the tempered conflict of pluralism" (Robertson) (Simpson 1991, 14; compare Beyer 1994, 28).

For Simpson (1991, 15), Wallerstein's theory "raises the question of the structure of the relationship" between religion and other institutions at the global level. Wallerstein seems to regard religion, like culture, as "structurally dependent on processes of exchange." His position raises unanswered questions about whether the envisaged relationship between economic and religious institutions is necessary, and the extent to which that relationship varies across time and space.

John Meyer's contribution to the debate, according to Simpson, is to outline the conditions under which certain ideas (Simpson's "myths") come to "organize a context of action." This follows from Meyer's conclusion that in the contemporary world system "the myths of progress and science" possess "the greatest organizing capacity". Simpson maintains that Robertson's perspective does not exclusively concern the role of religion in globalization, but the construction and perception of identities at different levels "in the field of global interaction." Religion is important because of its function as one of the major generators of frames of reference in identity formation (Simpson 1991, 15).

Simpson concludes that a theory combining aspects of Wallerstein, Meyer, and Robertson's analyses is needed. Such a theory would outline "the structure of institutions and their relationship to exchange processes, the varying capacities of different types of myth to organize action, and the dynamics of symbolic interaction between selves, societies, and the system of nation-states at the global level" (Simpson 1991, 16).

What would such a combined examination of global processes involve from a methodological perspective?

For Lechner (1991, 264), "the problem of institutionalization of global forms of thought and action needs to be at the heart of world system analysis. Two other issues to address are (a) the historical process which produced (b) this particular world system." Research requires a focus on how the cultural construct (globality) achieves social form (263). That is, a study of "globally institutionalized modes of communication and association . . . which involve interaction on an unprecedented scale . . . guided by normative principles of unprecedented scope." Lechner argues that to explain global order as "natural" in either utilitarian notions (i.e., as the outcome of interactions) or idealist notions (i.e., as the outcome of sacred principles) is unacceptable. "Global forms of thought" that have been generated include specific notions of "nation-states, ethnic groups, language communities, religious enclaves," which serve to preserve identities. From this viewpoint, even insistence on national sovereignty can be read as a manifestation of global involvement (Robertson and Garrett 1991, xix), as it involves globally understood concepts.

Apart from John Meyer (1980, 1983), Meyer et al. (1997), and Boli and Thomas (1999), scholars seldom apply theories about culture in the world system. Even where they do, the level of theoretization remains highly abstract. Consequently, I fuse the concepts and theories of world-economy and world-polity in the backbone of my arguments, supplemented by insights from other scholars when necessary.

VALIDITY IN NONQUANTITATIVE WORLD SYSTEM ANALYSIS

My intention to analyze local events by means of processes that integrate the globe into a single system—and so, against the widest possible scope—raises questions regarding the validity of my interpretations. The discussion on validity and related issues in the following sections draws partly on the work of Lawrence Neumann (1994) and Johann Mouton and H. C. Marais (1990).

A discussion of the validity of research findings can be framed in terms of external validity, internal validity, and falsifiability.

External validity has to do with generalizability, with the capability to show that the findings of a particular study can be applied to all other similar instances. In discussions about generalizability, questions regarding the size and representivity of samples tend to receive more attention than other issues. I would add that the appropriateness of the methods used for data collection (and analysis) to the subject matter is just as significant. Data collection methods must stand a good chance of yielding an answer to a research question or to fulfil the research purpose. Selecting appropriate methods for data collection increases the degree to which conclusions become generalizable. The same applies to choosing relevant methods for analyzing data. Inappropriate methods, like inconsistent analysis, yield distorted results. In this regard, methodologists tend to speak of the reliability of data collection methods; of whether retracing the same steps would ultimately yield the same conclusions. Obviously, appropriate data collection methods do not necessarily guarantee adequate analysis. This is why attaining internal validity is necessary, which requires researchers to show that their analysis of information proceeded in a logically consistent manner.

Internal validity refers to the ability to demonstrate that the findings represent the best possible explanation, taking into consideration the evidence and supporting arguments presented. Mouton and Marais (1990) suggest that internal validity can encompass various subelements, such as the validity of the concepts used (theoretical validity), of the way in which measurements are defined during operationalization (measurement validity), of the steps taken to collect information, and of the inferences drawn during analysis (inferential validity).

Falsifiability has to do with the ability to specify what would render the findings false. From the discussion so far, we can see that validity is related to falsifiability, and that external and internal validity are also related.

As will become clear, my conclusions at the end of chapter 8 depend more on internal consistency than on external validity, and so inferential validity is most relevant here. For purposes of discussion, then, I will use internal and inferential validity interchangeably.

I will now argue more extensively why external validity and falsifiability, while not irrelevant, are less important to chapter 8 than internal validity.

External Validity

External validity is generally associated with quantitative research based on a statistically random sampling strategy, known as a probability sample.

By contrast, chapter 8 represents a qualitative study of a single phenomenon, selected as a nonrandom, purposive sample, and so the findings are neither quantitatively nor universally valid.

Yet qualitative studies—like that in chapter 8—can lay claim to a greater degree of external validity by including samples that are more representative. For example, I could achieve greater external validity by investigating a representative sample of South African AICs; then, of southern African AICs; and, finally, of AICs in the rest of Africa. Ultimately, I would have to study a representative sample of indigenous forms of Christianity under comparable historical and material conditions across the world to see whether similar explanations could apply.

As indicated earlier, validity does imply the question whether the world system paradigm represents an appropriate methodological tool with which to analyze the AICs. Such measurement issues constitute face validity, the requirement that a method (or measurement) must be a suitable source of data for the topic under investigation. I argue that world system paradigm is suitable for an analysis of AICs, as this approach allows additional insights that would not have emerged otherwise. After all, De Wet's secondary analysis provided conclusions without recourse to the idea of a world system. And my findings do not contradict or invalidate those of De Wet. My approach allows the sociopolitical and economic forces that De Wet identifies to be tied to a wider theory, which helps us better understand their origin and consequences. For instance, we can interpret labor migrancy in the Transkei in terms of the early expansion of global industrial capitalism, and in terms of the globalization of alternative global cultural identities. These two processes are interrelated, with economic globalization undermining identity representation in terms of local ideas and practices, and cultural globalization offering alternative representations. In the final analysis, though, I would agree with the idea that local agencies, while severely curtailed, are not completely obliterated.

Can a single case provide additional insight into the world system paradigm? In other words, does an analysis of AICs represent an appropriate means with which to study the world system? As this was not my primary motivation, the question is, again, not directly relevant to my study. But I believe that the findings could add to our understanding of the effects of globalization and of the world system. Christopher Chase-Dunn (1989, 310) maintains that studies of other units of analysis such as individuals, organizations, classes, states, and zones are not "irrelevant for our understanding of the world-system. Indeed, our conception of the world-system as a holistic structure includes these levels." He continues that "some world-system processes must be studied by examining smaller units of analysis." The case study in chapter 8 falls into the latter category.

Internal Validity

In chapter 8, inferential validity relates to my description of the local factors that played a role in the emergence of AICs, my outline of the global dynamics that contributed to the presence of these factors, and my interpretation that local change is linked to global processes.

The pertinent questions relating to internal validity—in the sense of inferential validity—in chapter 8 are (a) whether the logical jump between local and global processes is legitimate; and (b) whether the extent to which microagency is neglected in such a macrosociological approach does not imperil my conclusions. These questions are not unrelated, as critics of my preference for explaining mesolevel phenomena (AICs) in terms of a macrological structure (a world system) could argue that I neglect the individual agency of Xhosa-speakers. But for clarity's sake, I will deal with each issue separately.

Validity of the Local-Global Assumption

Concerning the logical jump in the case study, the question is how I can be certain that cultural production in a particular locale is affected by global structures, agencies, and norms. Could cultural shift among Transkei Xhosa not equally well have been explained by other means, especially those that pay more attention to individual decision making?

The question of how the local and global relate to one another raises the issue of how those factors that may be attributable to globalization can be distinguished from those that cannot.

Ethnographic work in South Africa demonstrates that some distinction is possible with relation to earlier (traditional) and more recent (modern) modes of production and of consumption, kinship structures, residential patterns, and political and belief systems. The industrial mode of production, for example, indicates the local presence of global forces in the form of the establishment of mines, European-based schools, Western-derived residential patterns, migrant labor, colonial administrative systems, and capitalist modes of production. The industrial mode has long been regarded as one of the keystones of modernity.

The emergence of indigenous churches in the late colonial period (1880–1925) followed on the European globalization of capitalism. This process converged with the simultaneous globalization of U.S. Pentecostal and European forms of Christianity, which ultimately led to migrant laborers becoming the carriers of new cultural identities.

In short, factors that indicate globalization become evident when and where::

- people refer to, use, or become part of global phenomena (transnational processes, identities, events, organizations);

- the phenomenon under discussion can logically be linked through other intervening phenomena to a global process (this presupposes that global processes should first be identified);

- institutions exist through which global cultural and ideological artefacts are transmitted (globalized education systems of the core);

- individual agency is influenced by norms operating at the national level, which in turn articulate with global structures and global norms; and

- structures can be identified through which globalization occurs, and which emerge as the result of globalization (nation-states, education systems).

In other words, it is possible to draw distinctions between global and local factors; but the undertaking is not without difficulties.

Global factors that affect a local phenomenon probably would not remain constant over time, which requires that researchers pay careful attention to similarities and differences between historical periods. At various periods of history, different globalized aspects of the world system will affect specific countries more than at other times, when other features come into play. For example, in chapter 8, the consequences of South Africa's *economic* incorporation into the world system during the colonial period were easier to trace. By contrast, my study of language in multiracial churches found the role of the state in mediating global norms to be more obvious (Venter 2000).

My point is that different features of the global system become prominent at various times. While global economic, political, and cultural processes all function simultaneously and dialectically, like strands in a rope, the effect of the one strand on the others varies from time to time. Any attempt to construct a theory about their origin and development should account for the variation among AICs at different points in time and in various locations. Additionally, the continued relevance of factors that led to the emergence of AICs in the past should be weighed against those that characterised later stages of its history, or that sustain it in the present (Daneel 1987, 68). For instance, Ethiopian churches emerged as a response of protest against white domination, and initially expressed a pan-Africanist desire for liberation. Such seminal factors slowly dissipated, and obviously no longer motivate current Ethiopian churches (38, 51). By contrast to the earlier Ethiopians, protest did not play a significant causal role among the Shona AICs of Zimbabwe. And, unlike their southern African counterparts, AICs in West Africa did not arise primarily because of sociopolitical, economic, or ethnic factors (compare 71, 100).

Validity of Emphasizing Macrostructures over Microagencies

Critics may argue that my study lacks attention to individual Zionists and to their attitudes towards Zionist-Apostolicism, and so neglects microlevel individual agency—the outcome of cumulative choices. Clearly, individual motivations behind affiliation to AICs remain empirically unsubstantiated in De Wet's work, as they do in my own, and so were not methodologically catered for in my research design.

Instead, my analysis assumed an interaction between a macrosociological structure (a world system) and a mesolevel entity (AICs in the Transkei). Neil Smelser (1997) maintains that macrolevel analysis examines the state and society as a whole, while microlevel studies emphasise the individual in relation to the social. The term *mesolevel* is best understood in comparison to these two terms. Mesolevel studies focus on communities, voluntary associations, political parties, and trade unions. Smelser actually recognizes four levels of sociological analyses, as he adds the global level, by which he refers to suprastate aspects of the social system. Myra Ferree and E. J. Hall (1994) discuss the three levels as part of stratification theory, in which they argue that gender is a microphenomenon that results from socialization, race a mesofactor that involves group interaction, and class a macrophenomenon that can be used for cross-national comparisons. Ferree and Hall propose that feminist theory incorporates an alternative model that analyzes these phenomena at all three levels as interactive processes.

I will briefly review and critique both macro- and micrological analytical approaches in order to motivate my argument that my option for the former does not imperil the conclusions reached in chapter 8.

A microanalysis assumes "that the key to understanding social systems is the individual . . . that individual decisions are predictable but free; and that the proper focus of social research is the analysis of individual decisions" (Tollefson 1991, 28). Analysis that favors microvariables, located within the individual, as analytic tools to explain behaviour has been characterised as "neoclassic" (26). A microstudy attends to the "shifts in personal and group values and goals" in a community setting (Kulick 1992, 19).

Applied to my study, the question at the microlevel is why Xhosa-speakers came to interpret their lives in such a way as to abandon or modify their beliefs. De Wet (1994) answered this by pointing to changes in the worldview of the Babomvu, brought about by their enforced participation in migrant labor and later urbanization, as well as the consequences of drought. Such experiences made them more receptive to Zionism, which they no doubt encountered during their sojourn as migrant laborers. Comparable evidence is supplied by the emergence of

AICs in Zimbabwe and Swaziland after encounters with Zionism on the gold reef near present-day Johannesburg.

De Wet's argument is supported by Don Kulick's ethnographic study in Papua New Guinea, which demonstrated that villagers were motivated to modify cultural practices because of changes in their perceptions of themselves and their world. Kulick studied Gapun, a village of ninety-eight, whose inhabitants came to associate their vernacular (Taiap) with "badness," backwardness, and "paganness." On the other hand, they came to view a pidgin lingua franca (Tok Pisin) with goodness, modernity, and Christianity (Kulick 1992, 20–21). In Kulick's analysis, cultural practices and beliefs occur within a dynamic cultural framework. Traditional cultural categories can be used to interpret and act upon new situations in such a way that the categories themselves become altered (17, 19).

But Tollefson has critiqued the neoclassic microvariable approach for inadequacies such as a tendency to neglect factors external to the individual, and to disregard questions of equity. Historical and structural factors tend to be underestimated, and the contributing roles of political and economic interests may not be accounted for (Tollefson 1991, 28). In other words, the neoclassical model cannot explain variations in a group's ability to retain a particular cultural trait or not, nor the conditions under which policy decisions bring about cultural change. From within the neoclassic microvariable paradigm, sociocultural change tends to be perceived as "natural" (29).

The pertinent question is whether I manage to avoid the micrological charge that theories that highlight macrosociological causative factors are mechanical," while possessing limited explanatory and predictive abilities (Kulick 1992, 8).

The opposition between micro- and macrological interpretative strategies can be overstated, as studies are possible that combine functionalist structural analysis with attention to the roles of individuals. Such a synthesis traces how microprocesses intervene between macrosociological factors, and so affect choices regarding options between traditional belief systems and ritual practices (compare Kulick 1992, 8). From this perspective, what is crucial is how macrosociological change comes to be interpreted by individuals so that social practices in their community are altered (compare 9, 12). But such ethnographic attention to individual motivation, due to my choice of unit of analysis (belief systems in a specific region during a particular historical period), was ultimately beyond the scope of my study. Any comments I make that may infer individuals' decisions about the relevance of their religious practice must remain theoretical speculation. Yet, because my inferences are based on other existing studies, my arguments remain empirically informed—even if secondhand.

Ultimately, I preferred a macroperspective precisely because world-polity theory allows for attention to mesolevel phenomena, just as a world system approach can incorporate micro-macro-interactions. A world system perspective offers a helpful synthesis of individual, national, and global levels of analyses that can be applied to AICs. Theorists like Peter Beyer have posited a global culture, global polity, and a global economy that combine to form a single global society. Spybey has also used both individual and global levels of analysis to argue that individuals feature strongly as agents within the global economy, the nation-state, in communications, and in world order structures—all which, in turn, affect them. Holton (1998) argues that Robertson's model of the interactions between individual selves, nation-states, the world system of societies, and humankind in the global field offers the most fruitful analytical avenue.

So a world system approach allows me to argue that global economic and political norms promote the relative efficacy of Western over non-Western belief systems. The global can be presented as affecting the local indirectly, as global institutions are mediated by the state—itself legitimated by the world interstate system and bestowed the authority to act on behalf of societies.

Falsifiability

The question of falsifiability has to do with whether conditions can be specified under which a particular set of conclusions can be shown to be false. While validity requires me to demonstrate that my conclusions are legitimate reflections of what transpired, falsifiability requires me to show that alternative explanations are invalid.

There are two arguments in particular that could be used against my conclusions that the emergence of AICs in the eastern Transkei is linked to economic, political, and cultural features of the world system. One possible line of argument could be that local economic change in the southeastern Transkei was not influenced externally. Along similar lines, someone could propose that the changes that occurred in the belief system of Xhosa-speakers could have occurred without global influences, as far-reaching changes in the linguistic and religious systems of what later became Xhosa-speakers resulted from historical interactions between Zulu-speakers (Nguni) and the San (Bushman) nomads that they subjugated.

As falsifiability asks whether the emergence of Zionist-Apostolic churches can be adequately explained without reference to features of the world system, the key phrase is "adequate". Obviously other explanations are possible, and numerous ones have already been advanced. But the central assumption of a world system perspective is that the world comprises a single system. World system analysis for this reason allows a researcher to proceed from the base assumption that a global entity exists. Analysis shifts between this whole and its constitutive parts. To explain a phenomenon by reference to the local only, or even to the relation between the units, yields partial results - at best. Per definition, a world system paradigm must attempt to describe the linkages between the global and the local.

CONCLUSION

In conclusion, the world system serves as a macroenvironment that constrains levels of diversity and homogeneity in state as in civil society organizations. The diffusion of core cultures, which accompanied the expansion of the world-economy, continues to occur today through the adoption of global mass education and religious institutions outside of core states. Along with the dispersion of the Western model of the nation-state came the increasing importance of having a constitution as foundation stone. Compared to the previous constitution, the latter reflects the increasing integration of South Africa into the world-polity and its global norms of equality. For example, language rights were instituted in constitutions as part of the globalization of human rights, as happened in South Africa.

All that remains is to ask how effective a world system approach, comprising world-economy and world-polity perspectives, is as theoretical tool for cultural analysis. World-system theory seemed more easily applicable to analysis of turn-of-the-19th-century developments than to contemporary phenomena. Despite the reticence of many world-system theorists about culture, I think that theory's inherent historical materialism is very helpful in indicating how earlier phases of systemic integration affect cultural practices. Yet my attempt to yoke world-system theories to world-polity theory also suggests my misgivings about the ongoing usefulness of the former as heuristic device in the present context. World-polity theory seems to me to offer a clearer understanding of the organizations (states, international nongovernmental organizations, education systems) as mechanisms, operating at different levels, through which global norms are institutionalized in local state and nonstate sectors. These macrolevel and intervening mesomechanisms help explain how isomorphism, and so homogeneity-heterogeneity, is diffused within the world system.

NOTE

1. Lechner (1991, 273–76) summarizes competing arguments in this regard, and provides counterexamples. Some theorists claim that diverse cultural

value systems exist that hinder universal understanding. Moreover, these differences support a range of political structures that "prevent the institutionalization of a legally grounded global order" (274).

REFERENCES

Beyer, Peter. 1994. *Religion and globalization.* London: Sage.

Boli, John, and George M. Thomas. 1999. *Constructing world culture: International nongovernmental organizations since 1875.* Stanford: Stanford University Press.

Boswell, Terry, and Albert Bergesen, eds. 1987. *America's changing role in the world-system.* Westport, CT: Praeger.

Chase-Dunn, Christo pher. 1989. *Global formation: Structures of the world-economy.* Cambridge, MA: Blackwell.

Chase-Dunn, Christopher, and Tom Hall. 1997. *Rise and demise: Comparing world-systems.* Boulder, CO: Westview.

Chidester, David, ed. 1997. *African traditional religion in South Africa: An annotated bibliography.* Bibliographies and indexes in religious studies, No. 42. Westport, CT: Greenwood.

Daneel, Marthinus L. 1987. *Quest for belonging: Introduction to a study of African Independent Churches.* Mambo Occasional Papers—Missio-Pastoral series No. 17. Gweru: Mambo Press.

De Wet, J. 1994. Social change, resistance and worldview of a community in the Transkei. In *Afro-Christianity at the grassroots,* ed. G. C. Oosthuizen, M. C. Kitshoff, and S. W. D. Dube, 137–64. Leiden: E. J. Brill.

Ferree, Myra M., and Elaine J. Hall. 1994. *Bringing the feminist revolution to sociology: Transforming stratification paradigms.* University of Connecticut, Storrs: Unpublished paper. (Source: Sociofile).

Goldfrank, Walter L. 2000. Paradigm regained? The rules of Wallerstein's world-system method. *Journal of World-Systems Research* VI (2): 150–95. (URL: http://www.csf.colorado.edu/jwsr/archive/vol6/number2/pdf/jwsr-v6n2-goldfrank.pdf).

Holton, Robin J. 1998. *Globalization and the nation-state.* Basingstoke: MacMillan.

Jules-Rosette, Benetta. 1989. The sacred in African new religions. In *The changing face of religion,* ed. James A. Beckford and Thomas Luckmann, 147–62. London: Sage.

Kulick, Don. 1992. *Language shift and cultural reproduction—Socialization, self, and syncretism in a Papua Nieu Guinean village.* Cambridge: Cambridge University Press.

Lechner, Frank J. 1991. Religion, law, and the global order. In *Religion and global order,* ed. Roland Robertson and William R. Garrett, 263–80. New York: Paragon House.

Meyer, John W. 1983. Institutionalization and the rationality of formal organizational structure. In *Organizational environments: Ritual and rationality,* ed. John W. Meyer and W. R. Scott, 261–82. Beverly Hills: Sage.

———. 1980. The world polity and the authority of the nation-state. In *Studies of the modern world system,* ed. Albert Bergesen, 109–38. New York: Academic Press.

Meyer, John W., John Boli, George M. Thomas, and F. O. Ramirez. 1997. World society and the nation-state. *American Journal of Sociology* 103 (1): 144–81.

Mouton, Johann, and H. C. Marais. 1990. *Basic concepts in the methodology of the social sciences*. Pretoria: Human Sciences Research Council.

Neumann, W. Lawrence. 1994. *Social research methods—Qualitative and quantitative approaches*. 2d ed. Boston: Allyn and Bacon.

Pretorius, Hennie L. 1995. *Historiography and historical sources regarding African Indigenous Churches in South Africa.* Lewiston, NY: Edwin Mellen.

Robertson, Roland. 1992. *Globalization: Social theory and global culture.* London: Sage.

Robertson, Roland, and William R. Garrett. 1991. Religion and globalization: An introduction. In *Religion and global order,* ed. R. Robertson and W. R. Garrett, ix–xxiii. New York: Paragon House.

Robertson, Roland, and William R. Garrett, eds. 1991. *Religion and global order.* New York: Paragon House.

Simpson, J. H. 1991. Globalization and religion: Themes and prospects. In *Religion and global order,* ed. R. Robertson and W. R. Garrett, 1–18. New York: Paragon House.

Smelser, Neil J. 1997. *Problematics of sociology: The Georg Simmel lectures, 1995.* Berkeley, CA: University of California Press.

Smith, Peter. 1986. Anglo-American religion and hegemonic change in the world system, c. 1780–1980. *British Journal of Sociology* 37 (1): 88–105.

Tollefson, J. W. 1991. *Planning language, planning inequality.* New York: Longman.

Trochim, William M. 2000. *The research methods knowledge base.* 2d ed. (URL: http://www.trochim.human.cornell.edu/kb/index.htm (accessed August 20, 2000).

Venter, Dawid. 2000. Cultural reproduction in the world system: Case studies from a semiperiphery, 1872–1997. *Society in Transition* 31 (2): 184–95.

8

Globalization, World System, and African Independent Churches in the Transkei

Dawid Venter

INTRODUCTION

Macrostructural explanations are usually neglected in accounts of the rise of African Independent Churches (AICs), due to an affinity among AIC specialists for a focus on microvariables. Where analyses incorporate macrovariables (e.g., Barrett 1968, Daneel 1987), they tend to focus on the effects of colonialism within the national sphere. Both individual decisions and national forces are important and legitimate concerns. Consideration of how they relate to globalization presents an important additional analytical level, which researchers should not ignore. Applied to religious phenomena, globalization theories—which explain the emergence of an interdependent world system (compare Chase-Dunn and Hall 1994; Chase-Dunn and Grimes 1996)—provide the largest possible macroframework against which to view both societal and individual interactions.

The application of globalization theories to religious movements is relatively undeveloped, and so what follows is by necessity exploratory. Roland Robertson, the pioneer in this field, has analysed how state-religion tensions across the globe arise from the politicization of religion, and the religionization of politics—the result of globalization (Robertson 1985, 1987a, 1989, 1992). Other attempts at harnessing globalization theory to religious phenomena include an analysis of Anglo-American religion (Peter Smith 1986), Catholicity (Robertson 1987a), Japanese religion (Robertson 1987b), and Islam (Akbar and Donnan 1994). Several anthologies have examined the relationship of religion to globality, particularly in relation to the political order (e.g., Swatos 1989; Robertson and Garrett 1991; compare McNeill 1994). More recently, Peter Beyer (1994) offered a theoretical and applied examination of the topic, while Raymond Bulman (1996) examined the implications of theology for world-system analysis.

My overall purpose in this chapter is to demonstrate theoretically how globalization trends articulated with national socioeconomic developments in South Africa to contribute to the rise of AICs, by using J. De Wet's (1994) description of the emergence of Zionist-Apostolic churches in the former homeland of Transkei. My modest intention is not to construct a new theory about the emergence of the AICs, but rather to converge two existing discourses in the social sciences and missiology, namely globalization theories with discussions on the emergence of the AICs. My general argument is that globalization contributed to the emergence of AICs by affecting African religious identities through radically altering economic and cultural systems.

In the rest of this chapter, I first summarize J. De Wet's theory about Transkei Zionism before moving on to a brief presentation of Peter Beyer's sketch of four major globalization theories. In a third section, I apply elements from the theories to the emergence of AICs. I first link changes in African cultural and religious identities to the initial expansion of the world economy and its need for cheap migratory labor, sustained by the engine of "development" and its drive towards modernization. Then, I bring global cultural hegemony into focus. The emergence of the AICs as new forms of African cultural and religious identities is connected to the cycles of core state hegemony within the world polity, accompanied by a global extension of cultural products (e.g., language) and institutions (e.g., education, religion).

The separation of economy from culture implied in this discussion is theoretically possible, but analytically difficult to sustain, as both articulate with one another. Strictly defined, economy has to do with the production, distribution, and consumption of commodities. Culture has to do with the communal production and transmission of patterns of thinking and acting. The distinction between religion and culture faces similar difficulties. Religion can be defined as the cultural interpretation of the supernatural, and so distinct from belief systems (acceptance of suprahuman—but not superhuman—entities). Logically, not all cultural practices are religious in nature.

Despite these conceptual problems, my position remains that the globalization of Western systems of education, language, economy, and religion clearly effected not only the division of labor between core and periphery (and within the periphery itself), but also radically altered social structures and belief systems.

My theoretical point of departure is that of a world system approach, which is an eclectic blend of world economy, world polity, and globalization theories. Consequently, I synthesise elements from the materialist and functionalist points of view that underpin these theories.

A materialist perspective—such as Kruss (1985) provides—is able to link directly with Wallerstein's world economy. Below I explore more fully just how helpful it is to link the emergence of AICs to global economic trends.

To better illustrate the articulation of global economic dynamics with cultural change, I now turn to J. De Wet's extended case study of Zionist-Apostolics in the Transkei.

EMERGENCE OF ZIONIST CHURCHES IN THE TRANSKEI

De Wet (1994) focuses on social, political, and economic reasons for the emergence of Zionism among Transkei Xhosa. He traces the historical roots of this development to the two cultural responses that emerged among the Xhosa in reaction to colonialism during the nineteenth century: the formations of a traditionally oriented Babomvu (or "Red") worldview in contrast to a Christian-oriented (or "School") worldview (De Wet 1994, 139; see Pato 1990 for a similar treatment).

De Wet (1994, 137, 161) argues that the low numbers of people in this area who claimed affiliation to Christianity up to 1980 demonstrate that most people in the Transkei were Babomvu. As recent as the 1960s, 77% of the indigenous people living in the eastern Transkei claimed no church affiliation, while the overall figure for rural Transkei areas was between 41.8% and 48% (145, 149).

At first, those who espoused Babomvuism were in the majority, managing to maintain traditional cultural practices by shunning all things Western, including Christianity and Western education. Babomvu would not allow their children to mix with School children, for fear of cultural contamination. They also resisted being drawn into the emerging migrant labor system. Most Babomvu could practice a subsistence living on ancestral lands, exercising their traditional beliefs and cult, for which purposes (among others) cattle were kept. In this way, their economic, religious, kinship, and political system intertwined and remained intact, additionally insulated by the remoteness of their rural homesteads.

Towards the end of the nineteenth century, social change in the Transkei happened because of the cumulative effect of a number of events. A severe drought, crop failure, and cattle disease destroyed the economic base of the Babomvu culture. Slowly, the Babomvu were drawn into migrant labor and a monetary economy for short periods, so that they could build up their homestead. When they lived in towns as migrants, they continued to practice a cultural separatism and consumer asceticism towards all things Western, so that the essential features of the Babomvu ideology remained intact (De Wet 1994, 137, 146). The *Abantu baBomvu* ("Red People") dressed differently, "kept apart from school and town people," and only bought Western goods as was necessary (148). The Babomvu ideology was retained through the development of rites of passage, departure, and purification—which cast the new migratory experience in a traditional light, as McAllister (1980) has described (De Wet 1994, 147).

Under a government-enforced development programme known as the Betterment Schemes, proclaimed in the 1930s and implemented in the 1950s and 1960s, Xhosa-speakers in the Transkei were moved from their traditional homesteads into towns, were they had to live next to strangers instead of kin. This severely disrupted their land-based ancestral cult. Under the scheme, people received limited grazing land for cattle, so that many were forced to reduce their herds. The provision displayed gross ignorance of the role of cattle in maintaining ritual and political structures through the kinship system (De Wet 1994, 151).

Subsequently, the material and relational base underpinning the Babomvu worldview was substantially weakened. Their geographical insulation was broken with the extension of roads, telephones, radio services, and education systems throughout the Transkei (De Wet 1994, 150). No longer able to survive through subsistence farming, they became increasingly drawn into migrant labor. The longer absences of males from home due to migrant labor made maintaining the ancestral cult even more difficult.

According to De Wet's interpretation, in this situation of extreme social change, the worldview of the *Abantu baBomvu* could no longer adequately service their altered needs and they were forced to adopt another. They were unwilling to assimilate to Western culture, or to choose between the mission Christianity of the School people and the Ethiopian alternative. As all three options contained an unpalatably radical rejection of ancestral beliefs, they increasingly found a home in Zionism (De Wet 1994, 152). Zionism offered a midway route between preserving selected traditional practices and Africanized Christianity as vehicle for adjusting to a modernizing environment.

De Wet's arguments can be summarised as follows:

- Initially, the Babomvu were able to resist alteration to their traditional structures and belief systems by sustaining their material conditions and cultural isolation, supported by the construction of a vigorous worldview;

- during a second period, the material and political base of the Babomvu were undermined, causing alterations in ritual and social patterns; and

- finally, due to increasing participation in migrant labor and cultural pressure, the Babomvu had to abandon most of the old worldview for a Zionist-Apostolic ideology, yet managed to retain some older ritual aspects. (De Wet 1994, 154).

Consequently, Zionist churches emerged in the Transkei of the early 1930s, but became visible only in the 1950s, and grew significantly between 1960 and 1980. Dependency on wage labor increased between 1910 and 1930, so that by the late 1930s, about a quarter of all economically active males were involved. This period saw the emergence of a small number of Zionist churches in the Transkei. Labor migrancy was spurred on by the implementation of Betterment Schemes between the 1950s and 1960s, coinciding with an increase in Zionist affiliation. By the 1980s, some 80% of all males over the age of sixteen were engaged in migrant labor, by which time 10–15% of the population of the Transkei had affiliated to AICs—of which 71% were Zionist-Apostolic.

GLOBALIZATION AND WORLD SYSTEM THEORIES

The primary feature of globalization theory is that its unit of analysis is the entire globe, perceived as a single social system with distinct properties, which constrains and enables all other social forms such as polities and cultures (Beyer 1994, 14, 16). Robertson argues that there are four possible ways for "conceiving global order" based on Toennies' classic *Gemeinschaft/Gesellschaft* distinction. These account for how societies perceive both of their own ideal order and of how the global system should look (Beyer 1994, 28):

- one Gemeinschaft (communitarian) image is of a system of "closed societal communities" and "more or less incommunicable identities";
- a second Gemeinschaft image desires "a single global community";
- one Gesellschaft image views the global system as "an association of open societies";
- a second Gesellschaft image is of a global order deliberately organised as a system, e.g., under a world government. (Beyer 1994, 29)

For Niklas Luhmann, there are three ways in which the global society can be perceived (Beyer 1994, 40), namely in terms of:

- "what it is not" (e.g., Wallerstein's socialist future);
- premodern categories (e.g., Robertson's communitarian orientation);
- substituting a part for the whole (e.g., Meyer's world polity).

Some globalization theories can loosely be grouped into those that focus on centripetal processes that draw the world into a single place, resulting in the concentration of power and capital in certain states. Other theories tend to focus on centrifugal processes that decentralize power and capital

Globalization as Centripetal Processes that Lead to the Continuous Expansion of the Global Economic System

Globalization theories that emphasize centripetal processes describe the continuous expansion of the global economic system (Wallerstein 1984), accompanied by the consequent globalization of cultural structures (Robertson 1992), organizational structures (Meyer 1983), and religious structures (Beyer 1994). As a consequence, the core is strengthened while the relative weaknesses of the peripheries are reproduced. As a result, Western cultural forms dominate local material and nonmaterial cultural forms.In the following, I depend heavily on Beyer's succinct summaries of the contributions of four proponents of globalization theory: Immanuel Wallerstein, Roland Robertson, John Meyer, and Niklas Luhmann. Readers should note that Beyer's summary, although generally accurate, is his interpretation of the theorists, and so ideally should be supplemented by reading their work. I follow his argument here to the extent that it furthers my own discussion later on.

The Global System as a World Economy—Immanuel Wallerstein

For Wallerstein, the global system is a *world economy* with a single division of labor, which emerged in Western Europe in the fifteenth century.[1] In his view, nation-states are a "dependent function" of "a single logic of the world-economy" (Beyer 1994, 18). The world economy led to the rise of the modern nation-state, and created three geographical divisions: the periphery, the semiperiphery, and the core. States do not control the world economy, but are themselves controlled by it (17). The position of nation-states in the global division of labor determines its place (in the core, periphery, semiperiphery), strength, and its position in the class structure of the world economy. So, for example, semiperipheral areas function as a middle class. The world economy is driven by class conflict, disguised as racial or ethnic conflict by a global "ideas-system." Globalization has been described as a historical-political project driven by the state managers of the core in conjunction with their counterparts in the periphery (McMichael 1996).

Core states are complex, exhibiting mixed economies and combining high technologies with high wages. Periphery nation-states supply the core with staples and raw materials, and are characterised by low-wage labor and low technology. Semiperiphery states (e.g., Brazil) form a permeable barrier between the core and periphery, exploiting the periphery and being exploited by the core. The semiperiphery prevents wholesale revolt thus stabilising the system, demonstrating that in essence Wallerstein conceives of the nation-states within the world system as classes (Beyer 1994, 17). Core states redistribute wealth internally in order to protect the vested interests of the ruling class. Periphery states are generally speaking weak, as their ruling classes are often complicitous with the ruling class of core states, who also subvert the peripheries through various measures (18).

Another dependent function is the emergence of an idea system to overcome contradictions in the world economy. The world economy requires both the removal of all social barriers that hinder the operation of the market, and the unequal distribution of wealth necessary for the accumulation of capital. The universalistic-egalitarian ideas promoted by the first requirement are countered by particularistic-inegalitarian notions generated by the idea system, such as race, ethnicity, and nationalism. These cultural notions are so pervasive that antisystemic movements that oppose the world economy cannot but take them into account (Beyer 1994, 18).

The world economy is characterised by cyclical trends, through class conflict between those who benefit from it, and those who do not (Beyer 1994, 18). But cycles also result from the contradictions within the capitalist mode of production. Capitalism needs "constant expansion to maintain profit margins," and new economic opportunities have to be found continually—"often in different areas" (19). This process causes economic upturns and downswings (19). Linear trends also occur from one type of social system to another, which in the future will lead to a new type of system, mediated by antisystemic agents (e.g., socialist movements) (20).

The World System as a System of Nation-States—John Meyer

For John Meyer, the globe is conceived of as *a system of nation-states*—what Robertson calls a world-political culture (Robertson 1992, 105). Here, a nation-state's internal strength is not determined by its position in the division of labor of the world economy. Instead, the degree to which it conforms to world norms determines whether its legitimacy is accepted by other states (Beyer 1994, 23). Legitimacy is a reward for conforming to two particular world cultural norms: equality and progress. States that profess conformity to these norms are allowed internal monopolies of power. So for Meyer, it is possible that strong, centralized states can develop in the periphery—not only at the core (23).

In other words, the world-polity system functions independently of the world-economic system, as illustrated by the internal dynamics of states. That is, it contains two logics: polity and economics. Further, Meyer believes that the world polity is decentralised, and is held together by a world culture (Beyer 1994, 25). Meyer's arguments are made possible by his theoretical distinction between polity and economy, based on different systems of value creation (22). The economy creates value through commodification, while polity creates value through collective authority, by constructing and bestowing value on selected activities. These values are not determined by market forces, but by the authority of the polity. For example, the state as a dominant agent of collective authority can place a high value on social services. Polities include religious and cultural organisations (22).

The World System as a Global Culture—Roland Robertson

For Roland Robertson, globalization is a process that results in a *global culture*. He defines globalization as "'the overall process by which the entire world becomes increasingly interdependent, so as to yield a 'single place' . . . a world society.'" So, "subunits of the global system can constitute themselves only with reference to this encompassing whole. This is what Robertson means by relativization." Globalization relativizes identities: national identities can now be constructed only by reference to "the global system of societies," while individual identities have to refer to "humankind." In other words, globalization universalizes the particular (distinct national/individual identities) and particularises the universal (global order/humankind) (Beyer 1994, 27, 28).

The globalization process involves a paradox: (a) the world becomes a single place, in which (b) the expectation exists that societies "'should have distinct identities'" (Beyer 1994, 28). The process is not supported by a single dominant image of global order, supplied by a world culture. Instead, societies construct their own images (national identities), which not only reflect what the world should be like, but conflict with those of others (27). In their attempts to deal with these conflicting images, a global culture is produced around the idea that the world is a global whole (27).

According to Robertson, five phases can be distinguished in the development of globalization:

- a germinal phase (fifteenth to eighteenth century) through
- an incipient phase (mid-eighteenth century to 1870s),
- a take-off phase (1870s to mid-1920s),
- a struggle for hegemony phase (mid-1920s to late 1960s), to
- an uncertainty phase (late 1960s to early 1990s) (Robertson 1992, 58–59; 1990, 19, 27).

Robertson believes that religion can encourage the formation of particular national-individual identities, or provide world theologies that promote an inclusive view of humankind (Beyer 1994, 29, 30).

Globalization causes church-state tensions, as religion is becoming increasingly politicised, while politics are becoming increasingly theologised (30). Jules-Rosette (1989) raises a similar point when she talks about a resacralizing that includes political goals.

The world system as a global society—Niklas Luhmann

Niklas Luhmann argues that a *global society* exists because communication "extends continuously around the globe" (Beyer 1994, 31). In other words, Luhmann provides insight into the structure of global society (33). He argues that society is a social system in which actions occur based on meaningful communication (30). And so, "increasingly, meaningful communication can and often does take place between any two points" (30). Communication, in turn, depends on relatively stable social structures, based on expectations (36). The kind of communication that has become globalized is cognitive or adaptive; for example, scientific, technical, news, travel (36). Modernization leads to globalization, and so to a world society (38).

One of the most important shifts between premodern and modern societies is from a normative to a cognitive (learning) way of responding to disappointed expectations (Beyer 1994, 37). Learning is increasingly important in modern social structures (36).

Another shift is from the dominance of stratified differentiation to that of functional differentiation (34):

- in *stratified* differentiation, people are ranked on the basis of status, so that their actions are interpreted according to strata membership. Stratified societies are characterised by the dominance of a ruling strata, which control most of the power. The boundaries of society are determined by "the reach of their communication" (Beyer 1994, 35);

- in *functional* differentiation, people and their actions are categorized on the basis of the function that they fulfil in specific (political, economic, educational, religious) systems (Beyer 1994, 35). Such systems "specialise in specific modes of communication" (37). By implication, this sets boundaries that are relatively independent from one another, so that one system cannot control others. The "only boundary that remains possible for the encompassing societal system is then the globe itself" (38). World society is characterised by "the dominance of functionally differentiated subsystems" (40).

Globalization as Centrifugal Processes that Lead to Radical Fragmentation

In contrast to the above, alternate globalization theories exist, which focus on centrifugal processes that are seen to radically realign the world system: globalization-as-fragmentation at the political and economic levels. One version is present in Samir Amin's notions of multipolarity within the world system (e.g., Amin 2000), or in the arguments by Jonathan Friedman (1994) for a decentralisation of capital. Whether viewed in terms of centrifugal or centripetal conceptualizations of the world system, the notion that the change began in 1970 seems widely supported (compare Featherstone 1990).

In Friedman's (1994) opinion, globalization can act as centrifugal process that decentralizes power and capital, resulting not in the disintegration of the world system, but in its radical realignment. Fundamental changes are brought about by a decentralisation of capital, which weakens the centre while strengthening the periphery. The decline of hegemony leads to the fragmentation of homogeny, and so to an increase in expressions of different cultural and social identities.

GLOBALIZATION AND THE EMERGENCE OF AICs IN THE TRANSKEI

My modest intention is to show that globalization contributed to the emergence of AICs by altering African economic and cultural systems, and so, ultimately, religious identities. In the first subsection below, I argue that the initial expansion of the world economy and its need for cheap migratory labor—sustained by "development" and its drive towards modernization—altered preindustrial modes of production and therefore the cultural systems supported by them. In this way, an earlier period of economic globalization can be linked to changes in African cultural and religious identities. In the second subsection, the consequences of global cultural hegemony are the primary focus.

AICs and the Expansion of the World-Economy

To describe the effect of globalization on African religious and cultural identities, I use Africa's incorporation into the world economy as point of departure. The descriptions are pen sketches and largely confined to South Africa, but my analysis proceeds from a global perspective. Events unfolding in South Africa are viewed against the global system as primary constraint. By implication, the global system created similar effects elsewhere—such as new religious movements across Africa, Asia, and Latin America—but these would take different forms depending on the local configurations of, for example, the political economy.

Colonialism was part of the early expansion of the capitalist world system, which led to the formation of nation-states in Europe and in the colonies. Pre- and postcolonial sub-Saharan African societies were peripherally integrated into the world economy. This dependency was mirrored internally with the emergence of urban centers and rural peripheries. "Globalization is not simply a matter of societies, regions and civilizations being squeezed together in various problematic ways but also of this occurring with increasing intensity inside nationally constituted societies" (Robertson 1992, 104).

By the end of the colonial period, the global "hegemony of the Western free-market economy" had been well established in South Africa as elsewhere (Heugh 1995, 330). South Africa was incorporated into the world-economic system as part of the periphery, and exploited by the colonial core for mineral and other commodities. By the end of the nineteenth century, South Africa was the largest producer of gold in the world. Gold exports formed 60% of exports between 1909 and 1937 (Milkman 1979, 269). African economic and political systems were radically altered, particularly as the need for cheap labor resulted in the absence of males for extended periods from the homestead due to migrant labor. Ritual systems that required their presence disintegrated, or acquired new forms to match the new form of labor. For example, rites of passage emerged around migrant laborers' leaving home for urban areas (McAllister 1980). On a larger scale, the effects on African belief systems included (a) the desacralization of African belief systems; (b) structural differentiation; and (c) the transfer of religious meanings to a secular setting (Jules-Rosette 1989, 153). In such a context, the development of indigenous churches, prompted by the experience of migrant laborers at their places of work, "inevitably acquired overtones of ethnic and tribal defiance" (Van Binsbergen 1994, 154).

During the period following World War II, South Africa became a semiperiphery[2] (compare Martin 1990, 219; Wallerstein and Vieira 1992, 5; Milkman 1979, 262). After 1948, a manufacturing industry developed, supported by direct foreign investment. Restrictions were imposed on consumer imports, parallel to the development of an import-substitution industry, and importation of capital goods (Milkman 1979, 261, 266–67). Yet, by 1972, 60% of all exports continued to be of raw materials, of which 37% was gold (272). South Africa's potential to be eventually incorporated into the core was constrained by the policies of the apartheid regime and its failure to take advantage of changes in the world system—most notably, the movement of manufacturing to the periphery. Stagnation occurred; South Africa not only remained in the semiperiphery, but also at present appears to be spiralling downward, due largely to forces beyond its control.

During the apartheid period, an internal form of colonialism racialized class divisions. Mamdani (1996) proposes that the apartheid state continued the quintessential form of state established in the late colonial period. Just like indirect rule, apartheid created racialized urban citizens, with tribalized rural subjects under a native authority "supervised by White officials" (Mamdani 1996, 287). "Whites of all political and ideological persuasions" became so "comfortable with the privileges which Apartheid offered them in the form of cheap Black labor that they found no need to learn African languages—they were in a situation which never demanded that they associate with the African working class as equals at any time" (Maake 1994, 117). In the post-apartheid era, the interests of the ruling class are increasingly tied to the economic structure, which means that, state policies to the contrary, a change in the conditions of the working classes is unlikely.

State responses to the AICs mostly took the form of nonrecognition (Claassen 1995), and even occasionally attracted direct state opposition. The case of the Israelite massacre at Bulhoek by state forces demonstrates that AICs were sometimes viewed as potentially disruptive to "civic political commitments by virtue of their ability to mobilize masses of people in activities which are not directly . . . controlled by the state." Such repressive actions mirrored state violence against, for example, the Kimbanguists in the Kongo (Jules-Rosette 1989, 155). The readiness of the white populace to ascribe Ethiopian complicity to the 1906 Bambata rebellion echoed a general mistrust of the political intentions of AICs.

South Africa's status in the world economy is relevant insofar as the movement from periphery to semiperiphery was accompanied by increasing rates of incorporation of the African population into migrant labor. De Wet's work shows that in the Transkei region, an escalation of migrant labor coincides with increasing affiliation to Zionist churches, so that the first factor seems directly related to the second. In both of South Africa's world zone incarnations, a large segment of migrant labor continued to feed into the mines, first along the gold reef and later further afield. South Africa's shift to a semiperiphery through post–World War II industrialisation was accompanied by increasing recruitment of migrant labor. As the major industries were, like the major mines, also initially situated primarily on the reef, or in the nearby Pretoria and Vereeniging urban areas, migrant laborers were drawn to the same region, where they encountered Zionist evangelists. Labor migration is the dependent variable and the presence of Zionist recruiters among labor migrants at the place of work the independent variable. That is, labor migrants encounter Zionism and take it back home through a point-to-point diffusion. This explains the emergence of Zionism among low-paid manual workers.

The close link between the spread of AICs and migratory labor can also easily be demonstrated for the rest of southern Africa, for example, in the founding of AICs in the 1920s among the Kalanga of Botswana (Daneel 1987, 102; Van Binsbergen 1994). The establishment of Shona and Swati AICs happened through the interlinking of southern Africa through this system, due to mining—a function of the core in relation to the periphery in the global economy. The First Ethiopian Church among the southeastern Shona in Zimbabwe was founded by Mupambi Chidembo, who, as a migrant laborer in the Transvaal from 1890 to 1910, encountered Ethiopians. He returned to Zimbabwe in 1910, as an ordained bishop, to establish congregations there (Daneel 1987, 51). Similarly, the founder of the African Congregational Church in the Chipinga District had made contact with the Zulu Congregational Church in the 1930s (52). Likewise, Zionist churches in Zimbabwe were established after the experience that their founders (Makamba, Mtisi, Masuku) had as migrant laborers with the Zion Apostolic Church of South Africa (est. 1917) and with the Zion Apostolic Faith Mission in 1923 (54–55, referring to Samuel Mutendi who cofounded the ZCC).

While membership of AICs affirms local identities, they alter them in significant ways, through rejection of certain traditions and through promoting education and agricultural innovation (Daneel 1987, 56). Conversion to Christianity in the colonial era was linked to the acceptance of certain economic practices, such as commercial agriculture—and arguably, broadly speaking, still favours capitalism. To convert from African Traditional Religions (ATRs) and to reject African practices is to become part of a global project that militates against the expression of local identities, structures, and kinship patterns; that is, modernizing (Kritzinger 1992, 301). In this way, AICs contributed to the more individualistic role required by a globalized capitalist system, which is one step removed from the primary communal emphasis stressed in ATRs. By contrast, ATRs function to support local identities and to maintain the functions of traditional kinship, and economic and political systems. AICs seem to offer continuity with selected aspects of a traditional past, while orienting their members to the realities of the present, as shown by Zionist churches in the Transkei.

AICs and Cultural Hegemonies in the World System

Peter Smith (1986) has theorized that religion is strengthened inside a core state as that state achieves hegemony within the world system. Subsequently, the core state extends its religious system to the periphery. The dominance of a religious system within the world system waxes and wanes with the fortunes of the core state with which it is associated, as it does within that state. The dominance of Christianity in Anglophone sub-Saharan Africa is thus primarily a residue of the successive core states (particularly Britain and the United States) that dominated this region.

During the colonial period, South Africa was incorporated in the world economy as a periphery. An internal replication of the core-periphery dualism followed, with "homelands"—like the Transkei—constituting the periphery. The accompanying European cultural and linguistic hegemony meant that labor migrants who opted to remain outside the education system also became peripherally integrated into the economy. Wim van Binsbergen (1994, 147) demonstrated a similar process for the Nkoya of Zambia.

When British hegemony was declining in the world system, a global conflict ensued to establish a new dominant state in the core. In South Africa, this struggle assumed economic, linguistic, and racial forms, evident in, for example, the elevation of English and Afrikaans to official languages and the devaluation of indigenous cultural forms—including belief systems. During the apartheid era, mother-tongue teaching during the initial years of education in black schools, followed later by the introduction of both official languages (Afrikaans and English), structured the racial division of the labor market, while ensuring the effective functioning of the economic market. A small, educated black elite class was created, capable of cooperating in the divide-and-rule strategies over distant rural areas and of participating in the extension of Western institutions.

AICs emerged during the late colonial period (1880–1925) as an African initiative to span the rural/urban, African/Western, local (African) and global (Western) continuums generated by the process of globalization of capitalism. Shifts from traditional African religious identity to AICs is linked to attempts to overcome the peripheral position assigned to Africans in the world system. Christianity, like Islam, offered Africans entry into a global identity through conversion to a world religion. Like other newer forms of African religion, and unlike mainstream religion at that time, AICs provided possibilities of "inter-ethnic and transcultural associative networks" through "overarching symbols and doctrine" (Jules-Rosette 1989, 157).

In post-apartheid South Africa, the continuing spread of English as the language of choice in state and civil society, despite multilingual official policies (see Venter 1996, 2000) entrenches class divisions of labor, and the core-periphery continuum between metropolitan and rural areas. Similar situations occur elsewhere, as differential access to English, dependent on the level of state funding of education, structures and integrates marginal groups into the peripheral economy (Tollefson 1991, 132–33).

One effect of cultural globalization on African identities was to promote assimilation into the hegemonic culture, seen as inevitable and even desirable. Maria Brandel-Syrier (1978) in her study of the emergence of an African elite in South African townships in the 1960s, outlines the mechanisms of assimilation that accompanied the acceptance of Christianity. These include enrolment in Western education systems, which produces an elite eager to assimilate Western society.

Brandel-Syrier (1978) insists that the effect of modernization on Africans is to cause cultural and social mobility—cultural in that

Africans adopt Western practices and surrender traditional religious beliefs, social in that Africans have difficulty in relating to their kin. Assimilation is also implicit in the lack of attention to cultural diversity in English and Afrikaans-speaking churches. This is partly due to the colonial equation of Westernization with civilization, and the expectation that Africans who converted should reject African traditional religious practices—particularly those associated with ancestor cult. Brandel-Syrier acknowledges (without comment) that assimilation alienated black elites from the political struggles of the 1960s townships, brought about class division within black communities, and caused role confusion in relation to peers.

A second effect of cultural globalization is acculturation, in which some aspects of African identities are retained and others altered. This is the case with Zionists, as shown by Jim Kiernan in chapter 2. Through the experiences of urbanisation and poverty, Africans construct new religious identities that combine aspects of traditional belief systems and rural ethnic identities with Christianity to form an indigenous religion (compare Pato 1990 for similar arguments).

Martin West's (1975) belief-cult distinction is useful to describe the effects that the globalization of Western forms of Christianity had on African belief systems. For West, *cult* refers to practices involving the placation of the ancestors (such as the slaughtering of an animal), while *beliefs* indicate acceptance of the existence of ancestors, shades, or ancestral shades. Seen in this light, a variety of outcomes in African belief systems emerge, which can be summarised as:

- a range of *beliefs*, from (i) weaker forms, in which the ancestors are seen as unimportant or sleeping; to (ii) somewhat stronger forms, in which the ancestors are powerful, but only important in crises; to (iii) forms in which the ancestors are important and powerful, sometimes seen as acting as intermediaries between humans and God (West 1975, 203–204);

- a range of *cultic practices*, in which (i) strong beliefs correspond to strong expression of cult (regular offerings or prayer); and (ii) weak beliefs and weak cult (where offerings disappear, or occur only during crises); or (iii) weak belief or strong belief and weak cult (West 1975, 204–205).

From the perspective provided by West's distinctions, local responses to pressures towards a global identity can take many forms: Africans can be both Western and African, both Christian and traditional. Through contact with Christianity and pluralist township situations, Africans can adjust their cult and beliefs in several ways, ranging from strong beliefs and practice of cult to weak beliefs and little or no cult. Or, altered beliefs emerge as a result of the strong influence of Christian ideas on traditional ones. Religious identity involves both cult and beliefs, and the pluralist urban situation leads to changes in one or the other, or in both.

CONCLUSION

I do not want to provide what Robertson calls a monocausal explanation of AICs. As Robertson has suggested, analysis in terms of the global system should include attention to the voluntaristic nature of change, particularly the involvement of individuals (Robertson 1992, 104). The articulation of the individual—communal, national, and global—has to be accounted for. De Wet's (1994) analysis of the emergence of AICs in the Transkei provides a good example of the articulation of the individual and communal, while providing the basis for an analysis of how these interact with national and the global dynamics.

Robertson's view of globalization as a process that constrains individuals and societies to structure themselves with reference to the idea of global humankind and of the existence of the global is not obviously applicable to AICs. Religious systems with a global orientation fit in better, such as the Unification Church or Catholicity (Robertson 1987a, 42). Yet, as De Wet's (1994) analysis shows, religious change relates to sociopolitical structures, which in turn responds to ideas generated and accepted globally (e.g., "development"). The world-political culture promotes individualism (alongside poly-ethnicity) and encourages its institutionalization through state structures, but also through the activities of nongovernmental organisations—such as development organisations (Robertson 1992, 105, compare Boli and Thomas 1999).

The emergence of new African religious movements—such as AICs—have to be linked in particular to two connected global phenomena: (a) the spread of the nation-state, which became the primary unit in the world division of labor between the core and the periphery; and (b) colonialism, which brought about Westernization and the decline of traditional authority (Jules-Rosette 1989, 153). The development of the nation-state is aided by the globalization of education as a system of social control, by which cultural hegemony is established by the state over its subjects. In a context of linguistic and cultural pluralism, education (particularly in a nonindigenous language such as English) serves to structure the division of labor between bureaucrats and technocrats who are essential for the functioning of the state within the world system, and the rest, who are marginalized (compare Tollefson 1991).

The globalization of the world-economy promotes change to traditional religious beliefs and authority systems in non-Western societies (Jules-Rosette 1989, 153). Yet, Jules-Rosette argues, these changes are double-edged, entailing the return to traditional religious concepts that are redefined in a context of "changing political and social demands." Industrialisation is often accompanied by the formation of a substitute preindustrial kinship group, as certain AICs tend to provide, a reestablishment of mechanical solidarity (compare Kiernan 1990a, Jules-Rosette 1989, 154). Obviously, in some cases the kinship group remains the base for rural AICs—although it is unusual for the whole village to belong to the same congregation.

In other words, historical and global processes tend to transform local contexts in several ways. Alternative cultural identities are imported into local contexts for indigenous peoples to assume in order to obtain legitimacy. Assimilation and resistance are two possible responses to this situation, but over time tend to move towards one another so that a synthesis occurs. The forced choice between older and recent, alternative identities are also associated with acceptance of alternative economic, political, and social processes. Local political and social processes of state and ethnic formation are disrupted, along with the preindustrial mode of production. The supporting material and cultural (including religious) base of local identity is inhibited, and class differentiation promoted. Economic and cultural resistance occurs, cast in more traditional patterns, with adjustments to incorporate unavoidable newer social relations. Class differentiation occurs.

The extremely strong link that exists between participation in the AICs and the economic position of their members seems to indicate that membership involves a somewhat transitional structure. Membership is transitional in two senses: increased individual economic welfare militates against continued membership in AICS (Kiernan 1990a), just as increased unemployment feeds into the AICs as well, while recruitment of educationally mobile youth intensifies the movement towards modernity. In the first instance, then, membership is transitional in an economic class sense. People who become economically mobile leave the movement; those who lose their jobs or cannot find unemployment (an estimated seven out one hundred school-leavers in South Africa will find formal sector employment in 1998) tend to become affiliated. In the second instance, a shift within the educational standing of members moves the movement as a whole towards a different place, ideologically speaking.

AICs have an antisystemic function to the extent that they attempt to construct alternate economic and social realities, but this project would be radically altered should their members be drawn into the emerging black middle class. Note that AICs are not antisystemic in Wallerstein's sense of representing either a nationalist or a socialist movement that attempts to counter or establish an alternative to the world-system (compare Wallerstein 1984, 22–24). This is partly because they often organize in small groupings that are either not at all or weakly connected to others. But as the case of Transkei Zionists demonstrates, some AICs have roots in resistance movements against colonial domination and in attempts at resisting the dominant economic system.

The antisystemic function of AICs is evident to the extent that they resist, perhaps unintentionally, being drawn into globalized identities, and construct alternative identities to those offered by either the world system or by an idealised traditional past. By extending mutual financial care, AIC members counter the negative local effects of unequal exchange. Where they are large enough, as in the case of the ZCC, they can attempt to set up alternative economic and social systems (compare Onyango 1996). In contrast to mainstream Christianity, which arguably contributed to the establishment of a global European cultural hegemony, the emergence of Zionism can be seen as an attempt to retain some measure of local identity. But because this development was constrained by the global system, even local forms of identity—African Zionism—have to refer to the global—that is, Christianity.

NOTES

1. Jonathan Friedman (1994)—like Andre Gundar Frank—argues that the world became a global system through trade and conquest long before the middle 1500s, which is Wallerstein's point of departure.

2. According to Milkman (1979), South Africa's movement happened during *and* after the Second World War, but Martin comments that South Africa was restructured during the interwar period, with the southern African subregion as a whole restructured after the war.

REFERENCES

Akbar S. A., and H. Donnan, eds. 1994. *Islam, globalization and postmodernity.* London: Routledge.

Amin, Samir. 2000. The political economy of the twentieth century. Translated by Pascale Ghazaleh. *Monthly Review* 52 (2). URL: http://www.monthlyreview.org/600amin.htm.

Barrett, David. 1968. *Schism and renewal in Africa: An analysis of six thousand contemporary religious movements.* Nairobi: Oxford University Press.

Beyer, Peter. 1994. *Religion and globalization.* London: Sage.

Boli, John, and George M. Thomas. 1999. *Constructing world culture: International nongovernmental organizations since 1875.* Stanford: Stanford University Press.

Brandel-Syrier, Maria, M. 1978. *Coming through: The search for a new cultural identity.* Johannesburg: McGraw-Hill.

Bulman, Raymond F. 1996. Discerning major shifts in the world-system—Some help from theology? *Review* 19 (4): 383–400.

Chase-Dunn, Christopher, and P. Grimes 1996. World system analysis. *Annual Review of Sociology* 21: 387–417.

Chase-Dunn, Christopher, and Thomas D. Hall. 1994. The historical evolution of world-systems. *Sociological Inquiry* 64 (3): 257–80.

Claassen, J. W. 1995. Independents made dependents: African Independent Churches and government recognition. *Journal of Theology for Southern Africa* 91: 15–34.

Daneel, Marthinus L. 1987. *Quest for belonging: Introduction to a study of African Independent Churches.* Mambo Occasional Papers—Missio-Pastoral series No. 17. Gweru: Mambo Press.

De Wet, J. 1994. Social change, resistance and worldview of a community in the Transkei. In *Afro-Christianity at the Grassroots,* ed. G. C. Oosthuizen, M. C. Kitshoff, and S. W. D. Dube, 137–64. Leiden: E. J. Brill.

Featherstone, Mike, ed. 1990. *Global culture: Nationalism, globalization and modernity.* A *Theory, culture and society* special issue. London: Sage (1993 printing). Published simultaneously as Vol. 7, issue 2/3 of *Theory, culture and society.*

Friedman, Jonathan. 1994. *Cultural identity and global process.* London: Sage.

Heugh, Kathleen. 1995. Disabling and enabling: Implications of language policy trends in South Africa. In *Language and social history: Studies in South African sociolinguistics,* ed. R. Mesthrie, 329–50. Cape Town: David Philip.

Jules-Rosette, Benetta. 1989. The sacred in African new religions. In *The changing face of religion,* ed. James A. Beckford and Thomas Luckmann, 147–62. London: Sage.

Kiernan, James. 1990a. *The production and management of therapeutic power in Zionist churches within a Zulu city.* Lewiston, NY: Edwin Mellen Press.

Kritzinger, J. J. 1992. The development of African Independent Churches. In *Empirical studies of African Independent/Indigenous Churches,* ed. G. C. Oosthuizen and Irving Hexham, 291–312. Lewiston: Edwin Mellen.

Kruss, Glenda. 1985. *Religion, class and culture: Indigenous churches in South Africa, with special reference to Zionist-Apostolics.* MA thesis, University of Cape Town.

Maake, N. P. 1994. Dismantling the tower of Babel: In search of a new language policy for a post-apartheid South Africa. In *African languages, developments and the state,* ed. R. Fardon and G. Furniss, 111–21. London: Routledge.

Mamdani, Mahmood. 1996. *Citizen and subject—Contemporary Africa and the legacy of late colonialism.* Cape Town: David Philip.

Martin, William G. 1990. From NIC to NUC: South Africa's peripheral regimes. In *Semiperipheral states in the world-economy,* ed. W. G. Martin, 203–24. Westport, CT: Greenwood Press.

McAllister, Patrick A. 1980. Work, homestead, and the shades: The ritual interpretation of labor migration among the Gcaleka. In *Black villagers in an industrial society,* ed. P. Mayer, 205–53. Cape Town: Oxford University Press.

McMichael, Philip. 1996. Globalization: Myths and realities. *Rural sociology* 61 (1): 25–55.

McNeill, W. H. 1994. The fall of great powers: An historical commentary. *Review* 17 (2): 123–43.

Meyer, John W. 1983. Institutionalization and the rationality of formal organizational structure. In *Organizational environments: Ritual and rationality,* ed. John W. Meyer and W. R. Scott, 261–82. Beverly Hills: Sage.

Milkman, Ruth 1979. Contradictions of semi-peripheral development: The South African case. In *The world-system of capitalism: Past and present,* ed. Walter L. Goldfrank, 261–84. Beverly Hills: Sage.

Onyango, Maurice. 1996. Independent churches and development. *Africa News,* December. (URL: http://www.peacelink.it/afrinews/9_issue/p5.html).

Pato, Luke 1990. The African Independent Churches: A socio-cultural approach. *Journal of Theology for Southern Africa* 72: 24–35.

Robertson, Roland. 1992. *Globalization: Social theory and global culture.* London: Sage.

———. 1990. Mapping the global condition: Globalization as the central concept. *Theory, Culture and Society* 7 (2–3): (June), 15–30.

———. 1989. Globalization, politics, and religion. In *The changing face of religion,* ed. James A. Beckford and Thomas Luckmann, 10–23, 162. London: Sage.

———. 1987a. Church-state relations and the world-system. In *Church-state relations: Tensions and transitions,* ed. Roland Robertson and Thomas Robbins, 39–52. New Brunswick: Transaction Books.

———. 1987b. Globalization and societal modernization: A note on Japan and Japanese religion. *Sociological Analysis* 47: 35–42.

———. 1985. The sacred and the world system. 1985. In *The sacred in a secular age: Towards the revision in the scientific study of religion,* ed. P. E. Hammond, 347–58. Berkeley: UCLA Press.

Robertson, Roland, and W. R. Garrett, eds. 1991. *Religion and global order.* New York: Paragon House.

Siqwana-Ndulo, N. 1997. *The aftermath of Betterment Schemes: Land struggles in three districts of Transkei.* Paper presented to the annual conference of the South African Sociological Association, Umtata, July 6–10.

Smith, Peter. 1986. Anglo-American religion and hegemonic change in the world system, c. 1780–1980. *British Journal of Sociology* 37 (1): 88–105.

Swatos, William H., Jr., ed. 1989. *Religious politics in global and comparative perspective.* Westport, CT: Greenwood Press.

Taylor, P. J. 1997. Modernities and movements: Antisystemic relations to world hegemony. *Review* 20 (1): 1–17.

Tollefson, J. W. 1991. *Planning language, planning inequality.* New York: Longman.

Van Binsbergen, Wim. 1994. Minority language, ethnicity and the state in two African situations: The Nkoya of Zambia and the Kalanga of Botswana. In *African languages, developments and the state,* ed. R. Fradon and G. Furniss, 142–90. London: Routledge.

Venter, Dawid 2000. Cultural reproduction in the world system: Case studies from a semiperiphery, 1872–1997. *Society in Transition* 31 (2): 184–

195.

———. 1996. It may be art, but is it culture? The ANC's conceptions of culture and orientation towards ethnicity in the 1994 RDP booklet. *Politikon* 23 (2): 4–21.

Wallerstein, Immanuel. 1984. *The politics of the world-economy: The states, the movements and the civilizations*. Cambridge: Cambridge University Press.

Wallerstein, Immanuel, and S. Vieira. 1992. Historical development of the region in the context of the evolving world-system. In *How fast the wind? Southern Africa, 1975–2000,* ed. S. Vieira, W. G. Martin, and Immanuel Wallerstein, 3–15. Trenton, NJ: African World Press.

West, Martin. 1975. The shades come to town: Ancestors and urban independent churches. In *Religion and social change in southern Africa,* ed. M. G. Whisson and Martin West, 185–206. Cape Town: David Philip.

PART V

EPILOGUE

9

The Future of African Independent Churches in South Africa

Robert Garner

INTRODUCTION

What does the future hold for the African Independent Churches (AICs)? The spectacular growth of the movement—from a handful of churches at the turn of the century to more than eight thousand denominations by 1990[1]—has generated persistent interest from social scientists, and much speculation on the causes of its success. While the prospects for the numerical increase of the movement were generally held to be limited in the 1960s and 1970s, much scholarship of the last two decades has anticipated further growth.

This chapter centres on two propositions. First, that AIC membership in South Africa has probably peaked: the forces that produced the growth of the movement through the twentieth century are no longer key, and the newly pertinent influences are likely to be evenly balanced. Second, that the distribution of AIC membership is set to change, with a shift away from Zionist towards Apostolic affiliation. Given the problems of differentiating between these two related types from survey responses alone, as indicated in chapter 3, this shift may be hard to discern at that level. This shift will further muddy the already complex relationship between the "charismatic" AICs and Pentecostalism, as I discuss below.

These propositions will be interwoven into a discussion of three important influences: development—embodying rising levels of education and income—and the trend towards urbanisation; the persistence of the rhetoric of Africanism; and the effects of the AIDS epidemic.

But first, let us examine the evidence for the propositions advanced. Table 9.1 shows data collected on religious affiliation among South

Table 9.1:
Recent Data on Affiliation of Black South Africans[a]

Dataset	*1991 Census (Blacks only)*	*1990–91 Soshanguve*	*1996 Census (Blacks only)*	*1997 Edendale*
Sources	*Central Statistical Service 1994*	*Anderson 1992*	*StatsSA 1999*	*Garner 1998*
Mainline	27.6	37.5	32.1	46.6
Pentecostal	0.6	8.9	8.0	4.3
Other Christian[b]	6.5	n/a	2.9	2.5
AIC Non-Zionist	n/a	10.4	4.5	7.4
AIC Zionist-Apostolic	n/a	32.4	28.5	24.9
AIC Total	31.4	42.8	33	32.3

Notes:

a. Although these data sets are comparable in theory, they differ in terms of method, bias, and scope.

b. It is likely that many of these churches, especially in the census data, are Pentecostal, but it is not possible to verify this.

Africa's black population during the 1990s: the census data of 1991 and 1996, and that of two small-scale township studies—Anderson's of Soshanguve outside Pretoria, and my own of Edendale near Pietermaritzburg.

Some predictions in the late 1980s were for the AICs to attain 40% or more of the black population. Such an expectation has been confirmed only in Anderson's (1992) research—and this was conducted in a northern area of South Africa, where membership of the Zion Christian Church (ZCC) is particularly high. The other surveys suggest that, after several decades of growth, AIC affiliation has stabilised at around one-third of black South Africans.

The second proposition—that of a shifting distribution within the AIC category—is harder to establish from the surveys cited above. The later discussion will examine the undercurrents, especially in relation to Pentecostalism. However, tables 9.2 and 9.3 present data from the latest national survey, the 1996 census (StatsSA 1999), on differences between

Table 9.2:

Church Types in the Urban/Rural Black Population of South Africa, 1996

Mission Churches	*Urban %*	*Rural %*	*African Independent Churches*	*Urban %*	*Rural %*
Mainline	36.2	29.2			
			Non-Zionist AIC	5.0	4.3
			Zionist-Apostolic AIC	26.2	30.6
Pentecostal	8.1	7.9			
All Mission Churches	47.7	39.6	All AICs	31.2	34.9
Other Churches	3.4	2.5	No Religion	10.8	16.4
			Refused to Answer	9.4	8.8

Source: StatsSA 1999.

the urban and rural populations, currently of roughly equal size at 21.2 million and 18.6 million people respectively.

Given that the black population is almost certain to continue its relocation towards the urban, the current picture of affiliation in that category may well represent the future. And it suggests a slight diminution of AIC support, falling from 34.9% rural to 31.2% urban, with the mainline churches apparently benefiting (29.2% rural rises to 36.2% urban). The implication—a migration from AICs to mainline churches in the urban context—goes against the trend noted by several researchers, that AIC growth was fuelled by the disenchantment of mainline members who left for independent churches. It may be that this historic trend has now run its course, and is even beginning to reverse. There is also a rather counterintuitive fall in the number declaring "no religion" in urban areas. Among black South Africans, apparently, the city need not be "secular." A parallel finding emerges from the Edendale data: the "No Church" category is strongest among the poor, and falls as income, education, and occupational status rise.

Table 9.3 clarifies the nature of the shift within the AIC ranks. In urban areas, the ZCC-related and Shembe churches suffer decline, the Apostolic and Ethiopian churches gain. These shifts are not coincidental. They reflect the higher levels of income and education in the urban population, and the preference for a "rational," literate (and perhaps more

Table 9.3:
Urban/Rural Differences within AIC Membership, 1996

	Urban	*Rural*
ZCC and related	8.8	15.3
Other Zionist	6.9	6.9
Apostolic	10.5	8.4
Shembe	1.2	1.7
Ethiopian	3.1	1.8
Other AIC	0.7	0.7
Total AIC	31.2	34.9

Source: StatsSA 1999.

orderly), religious discourse.

PAST EXPLANATIONS FOR THE RISE OF THE AICs

Although I contend that the factors responsible for the historical growth of the AICs will no longer be primary, they form an essential backdrop to our discussion. This section hence considers, very briefly, some of the contributions to this debate.

The movement's growth, alluded to at the outset of this chapter, has led to a great deal of research. Much of this has concentrated on the Zionist-Apostolic category, which is the largest subdivision of the AICs and also the most colourful. The first table in chapter 4 has outlined some of these contributions, situating them within an interpretive taxonomy.

The majority of these accounts take economic circumstances and forces as the key explanatory variable for increasing growth. Scholars in the materialist tradition have drawn attention to the strong connection between affiliation and location in the mode of production, and have explained the geographical and numerical expansion of the movement in terms of the phases of capitalist development in South Africa. Other commentators, combining materialist and functionalist perspectives, have portrayed the movement as a more or less conscious form of resistance to capitalism. "Purer" functionalists have seen the growth of AICs as an attempt to create an alternative community of hope and meaning in the context of severe poverty, especially in urban areas, with the object of adapting to capitalism. Other accounts, which give greater weight to noneconomic variables such as health, culture, religious trends, and globalisation, have also produced valuable insights, and I refer to them occasionally.

Kruss (1985) provides an excellent example of a comprehensively *materialist treatment*, interpreting the growth of the AICs in a sociological-historical framework that discerns three phases of growth:

- The first phase is Ethiopianism, which flourished under the slogan "Equality for Africans" during the last two decades of the nineteenth century—especially in the Eastern Cape and on the Witwatersrand. This corresponds to the early incursions of capitalism into black culture, and the anger of successful peasant farmers at their exclusion from full participation in the structures of democracy, capitalism, and Christianity. Kruss (1985) characterizes this movement as the expression of the black petty bourgeoisie, and notes that it shared the perspective, and often membership, of the South African Native National Congress, founded in 1912, the forerunner of the African National Congress (ANC). The ANC's anthem, *Nkosi Sikelele iAfrica* (God Save Africa—now the national anthem), was an Ethiopian hymn.

- A second phase of AIC growth occurred between the two world wars and centered on the theme of "Zion City and the Land." "Messianic" churches grew under the leadership of charismatic men like Isaiah Shembe and Engenas Lekganyane of the ZCC. Theologically connected to the Zion Pentecostalism of Zion City, Illinois, and the ministry of John Alexander Dowie, these churches are interpreted as protests against the progressive theft of land from rural Africans through the passing of the Land Acts of 1913 and 1926. In the Transkei, where access to land was even more restricted, these churches abandoned the legislative quest for their own property and adopted a more militant millenarianism. The most tangible example is represented in the Bulhoek Massacre of 1921, which occurred when Enoch Mgijima's (1858–1929) Israelites refused to move from land they had repossessed.

- A third wave of AIC growth, Zionist-Apostolic churches emerged after the Second World War as an expression of cultural-ideological protest by the thoroughly proletarianised African population. Kruss shows how these churches flourished where this process was furthest advanced. That is, where the African working class, either employed or unemployed, experienced the harsh realities of capitalism "from below." Using a Marxist framework in which material conditions define the range of possible religious expressions, Kruss argues that Zionist-Apostolic healing is a form of ideological protest that fits such limits: their faith is a religious-cultural innovation of the dominated, which succeeds in subverting the hegemony of Western Christianity, in reappropriating the means of salvation, in the form of their healing ministry (Kruss 1985, 265).

Comaroff's (1985) work represents a *materialist-functionalist interpretation*, which explains the historical rise of Zionism among the Tshidi of Mafeking as a symbolic resistance to the encroachments of colonial and neocolonial capitalism. British Methodism had brought in its train a legitimation of capitalism's fundamental requirements—the acceptance of economic inequality and the validity of an industrial working class. But the same faith tradition also carried within it the seeds of protest, in the affirmation of spiritual equality. Methodism became the religion of the petty bourgeoisie among the Tshidi by stressing the first of these themes and downplaying democracy. In other words, equality was confined to the spiritual realm in the dualistic framework of Western Christianity.

Zionism, which arrived from the United States at the turn of the century, provided the poor with an alternative, holistic spirituality. Comaroff (1985) sees its cultural expression as the product of dialectic between the categories of neocolonialism and indigenous culture; a coded resistance of the type that emerges when overt resistance is unfeasible, evidencing a complex relationship between symbol, consciousness, and agency. Rituals embody the quest for control in a hostile and alienating environment. This approach captures the materialist insight that Zionism is a response to circumstances beyond its control, while introducing elements from the functionalist perspective in the form of conscious resistance, agency, and transformation.

Other scholars who work with a functionalist-materialist synthesis include Linda Thomas (1994), Robin Petersen (1996), and Dawid Venter (see chapter 8). Based on fieldwork in a Western Cape township, Thomas (1994) follows Comaroff and Kruss in interpreting healing rituals as a symbolic reappropriation of power, and as a form of sociopolitical resistance. This is in contrast to Schoffeleers (1991), who argues that any healing church will *necessarily* be apolitical. Petersen's (1996) analysis of the AICs also straddles the materialist and functionalist positions. His concern is to create a theological bridge between prophetic (liberation) and popular (Zionist) theologies, but in so doing, he uses a range of anthropological research to assert the validity of the semiconscious, encoded resistance to domination that he discerns in the AICs. Although the thrust of Petersen's work is materialist and economic, his approach relates epistemologically to that of the Comaroffs, adducing theological and anthropological explanations for the growth of the AICs. Venter's account in chapter 8 of AIC growth as an excrescence of globalization is another interpretation that straddles the materialist and functionalist categories.

These sophisticated reinterpretations of the AIC movement are attractive, but by no means uncontentious. Observers less inclined to allow the imagination free rein may find them unnecessarily elaborate. Their value lies in retaining economic reality as the prime cause, while introducing a greater degree of agency and independence into the understanding of AIC growth.

A more prosaic functionalism has shaped most scholarship on AICs. This view explains religious change as a response to changes in social, economic, or physical circumstances.

Pillay (1994) outlines three versions of functionalism in his treatment of Pentecostalism among South African Indians that can be applied to the AIC movement. The first is "Social Disorganization Theory," where social chaos or dislocation provokes a change in religious affiliation. The growth of the AICs has certainly been marked in South Africa's rapidly expanding urban peripheries, such as those around Johannesburg and Durban. The sense of disorganization in these urban and peri-urban settlements is indeed acute. But critics may counter that the AICs have also been strong in the rural areas least affected by such disorganization (see table 9.3).

The second version of functionalism is "Deprivation Theory," which purports that socioeconomic or psychological deprivation prompts a change in religious conviction or affiliation. Sundkler (1948, 1961) saw the rise and growth of AICs as a response to the social reality of deprivation faced by blacks under a system of segregation, and this interpretation has been prominent ever since. For example, Barrett (1968) explains the continent-wide AIC movement as a response to the cultural and racial insensitivity of Mission Christianity. Kiernan (1977, 1990, 1991) has challenged, or at least qualified, this view. Zionism, especially in its urban form, is not so much a response to racial segregation, as Sundkler supposed, as it is a response to poverty. "Zionism supplies the poor with a single organizational means of helping themselves and one another, and of establishing some control over their own circumstances" (Kiernan 1991, 9). Hence, the alternative he suggests—that Zionism is a source of meaning and a mechanism for gaining control over a part of one's life—while distinct from Sundkler's, also falls within the deprivation paradigm. Elsewhere, Kiernan suggests that an economic miracle, however unlikely, that lifted the poor out of such deprivation might diminish the appeal of Zionism; otherwise, it will continue to expand (1995, 127).

Despite a certain amount of sparring for epistemological primacy, there would appear to be little difference between this position and the materialist view. Kruss (1985) sees Zionism as a religious protest against the anomie caused by proletarianization (the sigh of the oppressed). Zionism's stress on healing reflects the actual conditions of malnutrition, wages below subsistence levels, and poor housing and sanitation, for which materialists blame capitalism, but which functionalists take as an ideologically neutral "given."

Pillay's third version of functionalism is "Psychological Deviant

Theory," which portrays conversion as a response to personal dissatisfaction, inadequacy, or cognitive dissonance. While Pillay's labelling of this category may offend, it can be transposed to accommodate what is arguably the most important element of AIC practice—that of healing. Healing in all its forms—physical, emotional, and psychological—is central to the discourse of Zionist churches, a fact so widely observed as to have become a commonplace. In a survey conducted among members of the ZCC, 39% of respondents cited "therapeutic" reasons as the most important reason for joining and staying in the church (compare Naudé 1995, 65). Some 97% of Anderson's Zionist-Apostolic respondents claimed that healing took place in their churches, and although the focus is certainly on physical healing, emotional and psychological healing must be included. So Zionism's appeal to the psychologically vulnerable should not be completely discounted.

A milder variant of this position argues that AICs, and Zionism in particular, appeal primarily to the poorly educated. In an erudite excursion through the cultural discourse informing church affiliation in Langa, a Cape Town township, in the early 1960s, Mafeje (1975) locates Zionism at the bottom of the social and educational hierarchy. The unstated implication of his analysis is that AIC membership should fall, and mainline church membership should grow, as education improves. However, although education levels have steadily risen since Mafeje's fieldwork, the AICs have gained ground, very much to the detriment of the mainline churches.

A smaller number of contributions manifest a theological or idealist perspective. Some of these occupy territory adjacent to, or even overlapping with, that of functionalist interpretations. Archbishop Tutu (in Oosthuizen, Kitshoff, and Dube 1994, vii) positions himself here when he comments on the precipitous growth of the AICs, at the expense of the mainline churches: "Reluctantly . . . we had to admit that it appeared there was a need that these churches were meeting which our own churches with their more cerebral theologies and dignified liturgies were certainly failing to do." Daneel, a prolific commentator on AICs in Zimbabwe, can also be located in this hinterland, seeing Zionism as a *Quest for Belonging* (1987). Cox moves further into idealist ground. He attributes the worldwide growth of Pentecostalism, of which he considers Zionism an African expression, to the rediscovery of "primal" spirituality, the religious impulse usually suppressed in the "spiritual emptiness" of modern, and especially urban, life (1996, 81). Deep in idealist territory (or perhaps in another country altogether), Anderson (himself a Pentecostal pastor) argues that anyone who does not recognise the work of the Holy Spirit in the growth of Pentecostal and Zionist-Apostolic churches has simply missed the point (1992, 116). Such an analysis, however, can hardly inform sociological prediction: the Spirit, by His own admission (John 3:8), is capricious, blowing where He will.

This leads us into the question of the relationship between Pentecostalism and certain AICs. The charismatic religious experience on offer in some of these (Zionist-Apostolic) churches, and the timing of their emergence, has led several observers (compare Cox, Anderson, Daneel, Ranger, Oosthuizen, and Maxwell) to equate them with African Pentecostalism. And there is some plausibility to this identification. Within these AICs, the Holy Spirit (*uMoya oNgcwele*) is frequently invoked in worship. There is an acute awareness of the demonic, and Satan is named in many of the choruses.[2] More Zionists claim to pray in tongues than do Pentecostals; cacophonous prayer is very common. Church members are invited to give testimonies of God's intervention in answered prayer. The noisy and dramatic healing rituals, which involve bodily contact, weeping, and frenzied prayer, have many similarities with the liveliest Pentecostal churches. Defining such AICs as Pentecostal would also provide an explanation for an unresolved enigma: the surprisingly small number of Pentecostals in South Africa, vis à vis the rest of Africa, and other developing regions such as Latin America. Are there, in fact, Pentecostals in South Africa that are being counted as something else?

However, churches at the Zionist end of the continuum embody some practices that are inimical to genuine Pentecostals. Uniforms, elaborate altars decorated with candles, and African drums, while theologically neutral, are seldom or never found in Pentecostalism, of either foreign or indigenous provenance. An example of practices that are viewed by Pentecostals as ignorant at best and demonic at worst include sacrifices of sheep or poultry, introduced with passages from Leviticus, which may result in the congregation being sprinkled with the animal's blood, or at least with the water used to wash the knife. Another example is provided by the persistence of ancestor reverence, accompanied by the burning of special roots (*ukushisa imphepho*), and the drinking of traditional beer *(utshwala)*. Further, the language of exclusion, so crucial to Pentecostal—and, in the Twelve Apostles Church in Christ (TACC), Apostolic—identity, was muted in the Golden Christian Society of Zion (GCSZ). As Kiernan (1974) has argued, Zionists do create barriers between themselves and "the world" in several ways. They use uniforms that can only be worn with the consent of the leadership, a right that may have to be both earned and purchased. Zionism prohibits drinking, smoking, and sex outside of marriage. Affiliates create an alternative subculture that permeates, or rather dominates, work and leisure time as well as church. But, in the GCSZ, these barriers were porous. Breaches were not punished by exclusion or even rebuke. My point is not that Zionism does not manifest exclusion; rather, that the level of exclusion is inconsistent, and that this is significant, representing a point of distinction between that category and Pentecostalism, where such exclusion is more consistent and indeed theologically imperative.

Can these differences be ascribed to contrasting cultural canvases, on which similar religious brush strokes are mounted—a charismatic religious experience articulated through the alternative channels of the West and of Africa? Perhaps: the line is certainly blurred. In the end, where to draw the boundaries of a taxonomy is the subjective call of the researcher. And this fluidity, or opacity, will always complicate prediction and analysis of dynamic religion.

AN UPDATED PERSPECTIVE: THREE INFLUENCES ON FUTURE AIC MEMBERSHIP

As we have seen, most commentators emphasise the overarching importance of economic factors in the history of the AIC movement to date. Although the precise mechanisms at work are disputed, AIC growth is widely acknowledged to have been driven by the alienating experience of the imposition of the capitalist economy onto the South African population.

Table 9.4:

Predictions of the Direction and Effect of the Three Influences

Influence	*Likely Direction*	*Likely Effect on AICs*
Development	Levels of income and education will rise, although endemic unemployment will maintain a large percentage of the population in indigence.	Those who attain higher levels are unlikely to remain in or join Zionist AICs; but the movement itself may evolve towards Ethiopian, Apostolic, or quasi-Pentecostal forms.
Africanism	The popularity of this doctrine may decline, but not immanently.	When it does decline, the shift towards Apostolic and Pentecostal churches will accelerate.
AIDS	Catastrophic effect on poor families, both in terms of income and life indicators. These households will experience extreme anomie as well as deprivation.	Will add to the popularity of Zionist AICs to an unpredictable but considerable degree.

As this process of economic colonisation is now effectively complete, I argue that the future of the movement will be shaped by three new influences: (1) the internalisation of the reality of a market economy and the development paradigms implicit in that reality; (2) the persistence of the ideology of Africanism in the "new" South Africa; (3) and the devastating social impact of AIDS.

Following is a detailed discussion for each of these influences, in terms of their likely direction and effect on AICs, as table 9.4 indicates.

AIC Membership and Development

AIC membership is frequently characterized as the preserve of the poor and the poorly educated, those marginalized in (or, arguably, by) the process of development.[3] This section argues that development in South Africa will gradually erode and shift AIC membership, as a larger section of the population come to embrace and function within the development paradigm, rather than feel crushed by it.

The discussion focuses on education and income. These are not the only facets of development, but are two for which data exist, and whose importance can hardly be doubted. This section will present data from Edendale that confirm the assumed connections, and then probe a little deeper to clarify the relative influence of income and education. The link between education and income is hard to unravel: those with low income also happen to be those with least access to education. While this correlation holds to some extent the world over, it is particularly acute in South Africa. There is no free education in South Africa: even government schools charge a nominal fee, and university fees are several thousand rand per annum.

Oosthuizen has disputed the association between the AICs and low education, yet Anderson's data suggests that the differences are still considerable. Oosthuizen (1986, vi) probably overstates his case when he argues that, "the gap between AIC educational level and that of adherents of the established churches is very small indeed." By contrast, Anderson (1992, appendix B) shows that only 1.7% of Zionist-Apostolic respondents had received any tertiary education, compared to 9.2% in the mainline churches, and a surprisingly high 15.6% in the Pentecostal churches.

The Edendale data (table 9.5) tell a more familiar story: by any measure, the average level of education is highest in the mainline churches, just as it is clearly lowest in the Zionist-Apostolic category. These AICs lose their appeal as education increases, a trend that accelerates at the highest levels. Of the 120 respondents who had completed the last year of high school (grade 12), 17.5% attended Zionist-Apostolic churches; but among the forty-eight who had received

Table 9.5:
Characteristics of Church Types: Education, Income and Occupation

	No Church	*Mainline*	*Pentecostal*	*AIC Zionist-Apostolic*
	%	%	%	%
(n)	(33)	(147)	(21)	(88)
Education				
Average years of schooling	8.2	9.2	7.7	7.3
Primary education or less	30.3	19.2	35.0	41.4
Some tertiary education	6.1	17.1	10.0	2.3
Completed tertiary education	0	2.7	0	0
(n)	(138)	(466)	(43)	(248)
Household Income				
Extreme poverty (below R 570 per month)	33.7	18.1	30.6	34.3
Relative affluence (above R 3 000 per month)	10.1	22.3	4.7	4.8
Occupation				
Unemployed	47.1	32.1	32.6	41.7
Low Skill	15.9	9.2	18.6	17.7
Medium Skill	17.4	17	11.7	10.4
High Skill	2.9	13.4	7.0	2.0
Students	10.9	14.4	18.6	13.3

Source: Garner (1998)

some tertiary education, this had fallen to 8.4%.

Table 9.5 also shows how the predicted pattern emerges in income category and occupational status: as these rise, the probability of Zionist-Apostolic membership falls. But it seems that education (itself the precursor to higher income and status) is the primary determinant. Zionism is indeed a response to poverty, but it is one adopted primarily by those with lower levels of education.

AICs and the Rhetoric of Africanism

Like all ideological concepts, Africanism embraces a potentially disparate set of ideas. For some, it implies simply the need for Pan-African solidarity to assert African *interests* in the wider world. This need not imply any rejection of Western forms of thought or social organisation, only of the domination of Western nations. For others, Africanism embodies an assertion of African *culture*, a celebration of traditional African values. Such an advocacy must entail some measure of conflict with the Western and/or the modern, with their emphasis on individualism, and, in the religious sphere, on either secularism or a Western rendering of Christianity. It is not always clear which of these two senses is in mind when the terms Africanism or African Renaissance are employed. Indeed, there is a great deal of scope for interstitial refinements, and I have discussed the possibility of creative and productive syntheses of African and Western ideas in chapter 4. Nevertheless, for the purposes of this discussion, we assume that Africanism implies the assertion of African culture, in a manner somewhat in conflict with Western ideas. This assumption is certainly open to contestation, but I adopt it nevertheless.

For most of the twentieth century, Africanism received little encouragement from the mainline churches, either in its ritual expression—such as ancestor reverence and sacrifice—or in its implicit rejection of Western cultural superiority. In this respect, the mainline churches were undoubtedly out of step with the majority of black South Africans, a failing that contributed to the numerical decline of those churches. Mainline members flowed into the AICs, where the philosophy and practice of Africanism received overt suport. The AICs of Edendale provide plenty of evidence for the persistence of this support—although the priority of different African values is variable (see Chapter 4).

The recent efflorescence of "respectable" Africanism in intellectual and ecclesiastical circles[4] has reversed this trend, and is probably an important part of the explanation for the stabilisation in membership levels in the mainline and AIC categories. Nowadays, it is the educated middle classes in the mainline churches who are the most ardent advocates of (Zulu) cultural forms, and who reject the cultural hegemony of Western culture and the English language. This rhetorical stance is certainly paradoxical. The increasingly Western lifestyle most of these people have adopted is dependent on their proficiency in English and their adoption of certain Western thought forms and attitudes, as I have argued in chapter 4. Nevertheless, no stigma now attaches to Africanism within mainline Christianity; and, consequently, an affinity for it can no longer be cited as a basis for AIC growth.

Two questions arise. Will the rhetoric of Africanism continue to prosper? And, what will be the effects on AIC membership?

Of pertinence here is South Africa's status as the last country in sub-Saharan Africa to rid itself of "colonial" rule. It may be argued that the current assertion of Africanism here mirrors the articulation of Pan-African consciousness in the earlier liberation struggles of Kwame Nkrumah, Julius Nyerere, and Jomo Kenyatta.

In a recent study of Christianity throughout the African continent, Gifford (1998) argues that the current popularity of Pentecostalism, and the apparent fizzling out of the AIC movement, are directly attributable to popular disillusionment with the Africanism spawned by the anticolonial struggles of the past.

The general feeling that the Nationalist experiment has failed, and the expectation that salvation in material and political terms will come from the neoliberal West, has fed the desire for the religion of that domain, perceived to be Pentecostalism. Might the same happen in South Africa, when enthusiasm for the new political dispensation has faltered, a few years hence?[5]

To predict that the Africanist star of South Africa's new firmament should so soon decline is perhaps a premature conjecture, but it is not an implausible one. It may prove to be significant that fully-fledged cultural Africanism, understood as being in conflict with Western ideas, enjoys less currency among the young. If the philosophy and its articulation recede from prominence, it is very likely that this will feed the religious shift towards the Apostolic and Pentecostal churches—and, potentially, towards the mainline churches, in so far as they de-emphasise their rediscovered cultural indigenousness.

The establishment of the New Partnership for Africa's Development (NEPAD) in 2001—like the ongoing construction of the African Union since 1999—will enable us to trace the trajectories of Africanism and neoliberalism. NEPAD may appear to be a successful renaissance of African cultural values; I would argue, however, that it will be successful nly insofar as it embraces the values of the (Western) international institutions and governments. As a pure reinvention of African culture, its influence will be severely limited.

AICs and the AIDS Epidemic

The previous two sections have outlined forces that are likely to diminish the appeal of the AICs, and especially Zionism, in the coming decades. We must now address one that potentially could totally overwhelm those tendencies and lead to further increases in those churches. Table 9.6 shows some current projections of the extent of HIV infection, and the inevitable consequences of AIDS sickness and death.

The impact of these statistics will be felt at every level of South African society, but, of course, will wreak greatest havoc among the poor.

By 2010, the incidence of adult death (c. one million per annum) will be three times its current level, and life expectancy will have fallen from sixty-five to fifty-five years, or probably even lower.[6] A massive deterioration in the health profile of black South Africans cannot but fuel the indigenous churches, especially those that are Zionist. The healing and social support offered by such churches, always a major reason for membership, will become newly significant. And the epidemic will also maintain in dire poverty a section of the population who could otherwise have edged up the development ladder. The extent of these tendencies, however, is as yet impossible to quantify.

CONCLUSION

The overall prediction for AIC membership is that it will probably hold constant. While development progress and the eventual waning of Africanism will tend to reduce it, the wild card of AIDS is likely to boost it. But while the aggregate standing of the AIC movement may remain steady, the distribution of membership will shift towards more rational and quasi-Pentecostal AICs, and away from traditional Zionism.

Table 9.6:

Projections of the Extent of HIV/AIDS in the South African Population[a]

Year	*% of Adults (15–59) HIV+*	*% of HIV+ Women/Men*	*Number HIV+ (million)*	*Number AIDS Sick (thousand)*
1990	0.2	0.2/0.1	0	0
1995	4	5/3	1.0	20
2000	12	14/9.5	2.9	170
2005	18	22/14	4.9	410
2010	22	27/17	6.5	650

Note:

a. These figures were derived from Metropolitan Life's "Scenario 80" Projections, in early 1997; their more recent estimates do not greatly differ. The generosity of Metropolitan Life's actuarial unit is gratefully acknowledged.

What makes this prediction any more plausible than that advanced by a former generation of soothsayers, that AIC membership would fall as education for blacks improved? To begin with, scholars of two and three decades ago clearly underestimated the extent of alienation experienced by South Africa's poor. The persistence and vehemence of that alienation propelled AIC membership far more powerfully than did the reverse trend of improved education. And it would be rash to rule out the possibility that the ravages of the AIDS epidemic might replicate such anomie in the coming decades. Such an instance would outweigh the aspects of development to which we have drawn attention. Second, Mafeje, whom I have perhaps unfairly singled out in this regard, underestimated the abiding appeal of the supernatural, the numinous. This is revealed by his following, rather disparaging, comment on the AICs: by insisting on antiquarian Christian values such as healing by the Holy Ghost, prophesying, substituting gibberish for real, analytical communication they have not only reduced to a dangerous point their own sense of reality but are also fostering general false consciousness among their followers. (Mafeje 1975, 174)

Today's researchers are much less likely to share these sentiments. The trend towards secularization and a rationalism that would preclude the supernatural no longer appears a one-way bet to social scientists. The marriage of 'rational' and, occasionally, ordered religious discourse to a vigorously transcendent worldview (within Evangelical and Pentecostal Christianity, and mirrored in the Apostolic AICs) has met this persistent human requirement, and thrived globally upon it.

NOTES

1. The literature charts this growth: eight hundred in Sundkler (1948) had risen to 2,200 by the time of the second edition (1961), and three thousand cited by Monica Wilson (in her foreword to West 1975). The figure of eight thousand is supplied by the Durban based NERMIC, run by Professor G. C. Oosthuizen. The numerical expansion of AIC membership is documented by Kruss (1985, 70).

2. One chorus from the Zionist congregation in Edendale translates as follows:

   "There he is, Satan, looking out for Christians; he won't find us, there he is, there he is!

   He arrived, Satan, I lifted up the holy book, he didn't know what to say."

3. Due to limitations of space, these connections—easily established by an analysis of national survey data—cannot be included here. For a fuller discussion, see Garner (1998, chapter 2).

4. As epitomised in President Thabo Mbeki's call for an African Renaissance, but anterior to it.

5. These comments reflect the author's conversations with Gifford, as well as the cited work.

6. For more detail regarding these projections and their relationship to socioeconomic and religious life, see Garner (2000).

REFERENCES

Anderson, Allan H. 1992. *Bazalwane: African Pentecostalism in South Africa.* Pretoria: University of South Africa.

Barrett, David. 1968. *Schism and renewal in Africa.* Nairobi: Oxford University Press.

Central Statistical Service. 1994. *Provincial statistics 1994, part 10, Republic of South Africa 00-90-10.* Pretoria: Central Statistical Service.

Comaroff, Jean. 1985. *Body of power, spirit of resistance.* Chicago: Chicago University Press.

Cox, Harvey. 1996. *Fire from heaven: The rise of Pentecostal spirituality and the reshaping of religion in the twenty first century.* London: Cassell.

Daneel, Marthinus L. 1987. *Quest for belonging: Introduction to a study of African Independent Churches.* Mambo Occasional Papers—Missio-Pastoral series No. 17. Gweru: Mambo Press.

Garner, Robert C. 1998. *Religion and economics in a South African township.* Ph.D. Dissertation, University of Cambridge.

———. 2000. Safe sects? Dynamic religion and AIDS in South Africa. *Journal of Modern African Studies* 38 (1): 41–69.

Gifford, Paul. 1998. *African Christianity: Its public role.* London: Hurst.

Kiernan, James P. 1995. The African Independent Churches. In *Living faiths in South Africa,* ed. Martin Prozesky and John W. DeGruchy, 116–28. Cape Town: David Philip.

———. 1991. The healing community and the future of the urban working class. In *The contribution of South African religions to the coming South Africa.* Conference papers, University of Natal, Pietermaritzburg.

———. 1990. *The production and management of therapeutic power in a Zulu city.* Lampeter: Edwin Mellen Press.

———. 1977. Poor and puritan: An attempt to view Zionism as a collective response to urban poverty. *African Studies* 36 (1): 31–43.

———. 1974. Where Zionists draw the line: A study of religious exclusiveness in an African township. *African Studies* 33 (2): 79–90.

———. Not Dated. Modernity and the African Independent Churches—Adaptations of an indigenous Christianity. Unpublished paper.

Kruss, Glenda. 1985. *Religion, class and culture: Indigenous churches in South Africa, with special reference to Zionist-Apostolics.* MA thesis, University of Cape Town.

Mafeje, Archie. 1975. Religion, class and ideology in South Africa. In *Religion and social change in southern Africa,* ed. M. G. Whisson and Martin

West, 164–84. Cape Town: David Philip.

Maxwell, David. 1999. Historicizing Christian Independency: the southern African Pentecostal movement, c.1908-1960. *Journal of African History*, 39, 2: 243-64.

Naudé, Piet. 1995. *The Zionist Christian Church in South Africa: A case study in oral theology*. New York: Edwin Mellen Press.

Oosthuizen, G. C., ed. 1986. *Religion alive: Studies in the new movements and indigenous churches in South Africa.* Johannesburg: Hodder & Stoughton.

Oosthuizen, G. C., M. C. Kitshoff, and S. W. D. Dube, eds. 1994. *Afro-Christianity at the grassroots: Its dynamics and strategies.* Leiden: E. J. Brill.

Petersen, Robin M. 1996. *Time, resistance and reconstruction: A theology of the prophetic and the popular.* Ph.D. Dissertation, University of Chicago.

Pillay, Gerald J. 1994. *Religion at the limits? Pentecostalism among Indian South Africans.* Pretoria: University of South Africa.

Ranger, Terence. 1987. Religion, development, and African Christian identity." In *Religion, development, and African identity,* ed. K. H. Petersen, 29–57. Uppsala: Scandinavian Institute of African Studies.

Schoffeleers, Matthew. 1991. Ritual healing and political acquiescence: The case of the Zionist churches in Southern Africa. *Africa* 60 (1): 1–25.

StatsSA. 1999. *1996 Census primary tables (Report 03-01-19).* Pretoria: StatsSA.

Sundkler, B. G. M. 1961 (1948). *Bantu prophets in South Africa.* London: Oxford University Press.

Thomas, Linda E. 1994. African Indigenous Churches as a source of socio-political transformation in South Africa. *Africa Today* 41 (1): 39–56.

West, Martin. 1975. *Bishops and prophets in a black city: African Independent Churches in Soweto, Johannesburg.* Cape Town: David Philip.

Appendix

Religious Affiliation, 2001

Affiliation[a]	*Adherents*	*% of Population*
No religion	6,767,165	15.10
Other Apostolic churches[b]	5,627,320	12.56
Zion Christian churches	4,971,931	11.09
Pentecostal/Charismatic churches	3,695,211	8.24
Catholic churches	3,181,332	7.10
Methodist churches	3,035,719	6.77
Dutch Reformed churches	3,005,697	6.71
Other Christian churches	2,890,151	6.45
Other Zionist churches	1,887,147	4.21
Anglican churches	1,722,076	3.84
Ethiopian type churches	1,150,102	2.57
Lutheran churches	1,130,983	2.52
Presbyterian churches	832,497	1.86
Baptist churches	691,235	1.54
Other African independent churches	656,644	1.47
Congregational churches	508,826	1.14
Bandla Lama Nazaretha	248,825	0.56

Apostolic Faith Mission	246,193	0.55
Other Reformed churches	226,499	0.51
Orthodox churches	42,253	0.09
African traditional belief	125,898	0.28
Islam	654,064	1.46
Undetermined	610,974	1.36
Hinduism	551,668	1.23
Other beliefs	283,815	0.63
African traditional belief	125,898	0.28
Total	44,819,774	100.00

Source: StatsSA 2004.

Notes:

a. Affiliation data includes infants, who were assigned the beliefs of their mothers.

b. Bold indicates affiliation that typically is included in enumerating AICs.

REFERENCE

StatsSA. 2004. *Census 2001 by province, gender, religion recode (derived) and population group*. Statistics South Africa. (URL: http://www.statssa.gov.za/SpecialProjects/Census2001/Census/Dialog/varval.asp?ma=Religionbyprovince&ti=Table%3A+Census+2001+by+province%2C+gender%2C+religion+recode+%28derived%29+and++population+group%2E+&path=../Database/Census%202001/Provincial%20Level/Persons/&lang=).

Glossary

Dawid Venter

African National Congress (ANC): Formed in 1912 as the South African Native National Congress, and renamed the African National Congress in 1930, the ANC was one of several African organizations involved in the struggle for political and human rights against the apartheid regime. After it was banned in 1960, the organization appeared to lose its vitality, but a combination of factors led to its resurgence in the 1970s, including overseas lobbying, growing resistance to state repression within South Africa, a decision to open its leadership to all races, increasing support (moral, financial, and logistic) from abroad, and the formation in December 1961 of an armed wing, *Umkhonto we Sizwe* ("Spear of the Nation") at the prompting of a young Nelson Mandela (b. 1918). In 1994, the ANC overwhelmingly won the first democratic elections and have been the ruling party since.

Afrikaners: Literally, "Africans" (derived from Dutch), a term that was self-applied by white settlers and their descendants who regarded South Africa as their place of origin. In 1879, an Afrikaner bond was formed to promote Dutch; white nationalists who wanted to achieve political and cultural independence from the British colonial regime coined the term at the start of the twentieth century. Afrikaners were primarily from Dutch descent, but eventually absorbed French and German Huguenots. Their language, Afrikaans, developed among slaves in the late nineteenth century at the Cape of Good Hope and bears the imprint of slaves from Indonesia (often referred to as "Malays") and Madagascar. Afrikaans apparently developed as a result of interaction between slaves and the Dutch. One of the earliest Afrikaans books was published in 1873 in Arabic script. The 2001 census identified some 5,983,423 Afrikaans-speakers in South Africa, of whom 2,536,907 were Caucasian.

analysis: To attempt to understand a subject by breaking it down into component parts.

apartheid: Literally, "separateness" (Afrikaans), the state policy of racial segregation in South Africa between 1948 and 1994. Promoted by state propagandists as safeguarding the integrity of ethnic groups, apartheid was applied in such a way as to reserve resources for whites. Those who were not legally designated as white were often forcibly removed in order to create white residential areas and game reserves. Apartheid legislation included the Land Acts (1913 and 1936, abolished 1991), Immorality Act (1927, 1950, and 1957, abolished 1985), Prohibition of Mixed Marriages Act (1949, abolished 1985), influx control (abolished 1986), Group Areas Act (1950 and 1966, abolished 1991), Population Registration Act (1950, abolished 1991), Bantu Authorities Act (1951, abolished 1984), Bantu Education Act (1953, repealed in 1979), and Separate Amenities Act (1953, abolished 1990). For a summary of apartheid laws in the mid-1980s, see http://www.newint.org/issue159/facts.htm. *See also* volume 1, chapters 1 and 13 of the Truth and Reconciliation Commission's Final Report (1998) for a more comprehensive list at http://www.soz.uni-hannover.de/isoz/truthcom/EMBARGO/.

Bambata Rebellion: The imposition of a poll tax on January 1, 1906, designed by British colonial authorities to force blacks into the agricultural and mining industries, provoked an insurrection in various places in Natal between February and August 1906. Bambata, head of the Zondi clan, played a prominent part in this rebellion against taxation. Whites blamed Ethiopians (e.g., the African Presbyterian Church, according to Pretorius and Jafta 1997, 215) for an incident on February 10, when two policemen were killed. The alleged involvement of Dinizulu ka Cetshwayo, king of the Zulu, led to his imprisonment and eventual exile to the Transvaal. Bambata was beheaded (http://www.anglo.50megs.com/bambata.htm).

Bantu: (1) A grouping of some 120 million African people that stretches from western Africa through central to southern Africa based on broadly defined shared language characteristics. Nguni, Sotho, Tsonga-Shangaan, and Venda are South Africa's major Bantu subgroups, and the sources of nine of its eleven official languages (Xhosa, Zulu, Ndebele, Pedi, Sotho, Tswana, Swati, Venda, and Tsonga). For more detail see http://www.encyclopedia.com/articles/01094.html, and *South Africa—a Country Study* by the Library of Congress at http://memory.loc.gov/frd/cs/zatoc.html. (2) 'Bantu' was adopted by successive apartheid regimes after 1948 to refer to black Africans. Due to the negative association evoked by the term Bantu Education (which aimed to educate blacks for unskilled labor only), the term gained a negative sense, so that some black South Africans prefer not to use it at all.

Betterment Scheme: "The 'betterment' and rehabilitation programmes were initiated in the 1930s and extended across South Africa, and the British colonies of southern and east Africa. They involved the separation of residential, arable, grazing and woodland and the resettlement of people in planned villages. In South Africa, as everywhere else, they provoked enormous resentment, and in many regions bitter revolt, over the culling of livestock, the cutting of arable lands, the enforced removal and concentration of settlement, and the imposition of Native/Bantu Authorities through which the state sought to enforce its policies. They were designed to improve production and conserve the soil in the African 'reserves' without altering the distribution of land" (Murray and Williams 1994).

Boer: Literally, "farmer" (Afrikaans), the term became a self-description for Afrikaners at the end of the nineteenth century. The Anglo-Boer Wars describe two successive South African wars (1880–81 and 1899–1902) by which imperial Britain took control of the independent Afrikaner states to acquire their vast goldfields. By the late twentieth century, during their struggle for political liberation, black South Africans came to apply the word pejoratively to Afrikaners in general, most of whom supported apartheid. The term *Boere* was also used more specifically for white members of the South African police force, who enforced apartheid legislation. Most notoriously, it appeared in the politically motivated Africanist slogan coined by ANC member Peter Mokaba: "Kill the Boer, kill the farmer." The slogan implicitly linked support for apartheid to the harsh treatment of disenfranchised black farm laborers.

case study: "A research design that focuses on a single example rather than a representative sample" (http://www.webref.org/sociology/C/case_study.htm).

Ciskei: The southernmost part of the region where Xhosa-speakers form the majority, adjacent to the Transkei (also Xhosa-speaking), to its north. Presently part of the eastern Cape Province. The Ciskei formed one of South Africa's so-called "homelands," which constituted rural reserves in which most of the black population were confined as labor pools.

core: In world-economy theory, a capital-intensive region, characterized by relatively higher levels of wage and of technologies, that dominates the global system and exploits the semiperipheral and peripheral zones. Examples of states currently constituting the core include the United States, Japan, Germany, and Britain.

cult: (1) Practices associated with a religious belief system—the meaning referred to in this book; (2) a small religious group characterized by opposition to certain established norms of society and dominant religious systems.

diachronic: Type of research that studies a phenomenon that occurred over a lengthy time span. By contrast, synchronic research examines a phenomenon over a shorter, more limited period.

ethnic groups: South Africa contains a myriad of ethnic groupings, of which the Zulu along the central east coastal region is the largest, followed by the Xhosa, a little to the south. Others include Tswana, Swati, Sotho, Ndebele, Venda, the Khoi, San, Afrikaners, English, Germans, Portuguese, Greeks, and Italians. Photographs depicting some of these ethnic groups can be viewed at http://www.africaimagery.co.za/CD/Cultural/.

external arena: Region that exists outside the zones of the world system.

globalization: "the process through which social and economic relationships come to stretch across the world, so that aspects of individuals' lives are influenced by organisations and networks outside the societies in which they live. The overall effect is to create a world system, in which an interconnected and interdependent system of nation-states exist" (Giddens 1989, 727).

hegemony: In world-systems theory, a condition that exists when a core state achieves dominance over its competitors as a result of productive, trade, and financial superiority; which all supports military supremacy. Military power is necessary, as hegemony historically follows war conducted between core states. The Netherlands (seventeenth century), Britain (nineteenth century), and the United States (twentieth century) have been hegemonic states (Goldfrank 2000, 171).

idiographic: A research design that seeks to provide results through investigating one particular case.

Inkatha Freedom Party (IFP): Chief Mangosuthu Gatsha Buthelezi (b.1928, currrently Minister of Home Affairs) in 1975 founded the Inkatha National Cultural Liberation Movement (*Inkatha Yenkululeko Yesizwe* in Zulu). Inkatha originally aimed to preserve Zulu culture and to continue the political and human rights campaigns of disenfranchised black South Africans. *Inkatha* refers to a coil woven from grass and worn on the head as protection when heavy loads are carried there. Although originally supporting the ANC, disagreements between *Inkatha* and the exiled ANC (e.g., on the ANC's armed campaign, economic disinvestment) came to a head in 1979. An extremely violent struggle for power ensued in KwaZulu-Natal from the early 1980s to the mid-1990s, which was exported to the region around Johannesburg in 1990. Thousands were killed, rendered homeless, or forced to flee their homes. After the IFP eventually participated in the 1994 election, which was won by the ANC, Buthelezi was given the post of minister of home affairs.

***lager* mentality:** South African term to describe the closed mind-set of the apartheid regime, which generated internal solidarity among Afrikaners—and motivated an insular stance by the government—by portraying outsiders as enemies. The term literally means to "circle the wagons," recalling the defensive military strategy used by Proto-Afrikaner *Voortrekkers* ("pioneers") to overcome Zulu forces—for example, at the Battle of Blood River (September 16, 1838).

methodology: In a narrower sense, the steps taken during the design and execution of a research project; the broader sense includes the assumptions and rationale that guides the research process.

mode of production: The general manner in which a particular society produces commodities, as characterized by the level of technological development (forces of production) and class relations (determined by ownership of the means by which goods are produced).

- **preindustrial mode of production**: Characterized by the production of material goods by human labor, which tend to be divided along gender and/or age lines;
- **industrial mode of production**: Distinguished by mass production through the widespread use of machinery in factories, associated with division between classes.

Nguni: Collective term for black southern African ethnic groupings whose languages, subgroups of the Bantu language family, overlap considerably but who differ in other ways (for example, geographic location). Includes the Northern Nguni (Zulu, Swazi), Southern Nguni (Xhosa, including the Tembu and Mpondo subgroupings), and Ndebele.

nomothetic: A research design that seeks to provide results that apply to all similar cases (i.e., that are universally valid). *See* idiographic.

Pan-Africanist Congress (PAC): Currently one of the smaller opposition political parties, the PAC was founded as a liberation organisation in April 1959 by Robert Sobukwe (1924–78), who broke away from the African National Congress. Sobukwe promoted Pan-Africanism and welcomed anyone regardless of race willing to accept African majority rule. Under leadership of Potlako Leballo, who acted as leader (1962–78), the PAC embraced an antiwhite rhetoric, ameliorated only by the opening of its leadership structures to other races after 1960. In 1960, the PAC, like the ANC ten days later, organized nonviolent resistance to pass laws. During the Sharpeville massacre, South African police shot sixty-nine unarmed protesters who responded to the PAC's call on March 21. Like the ANC, the PAC formed an internal military wing in 1959 called *Ama-afrika Poqo* (Xhosa, "the real owners of Africa"), followed in 1968 (when in exile) by the Azanian People's Liberation Army (APLA). *See* http://www.paca.org.za and http://www.si.umich.edu/fort-hare/pac_hist.htm; http://www.wits.ac.za/histp/sobuk.htm; and http://www.robben-island.org.za/ sobukwe.htm.

periphery: In world-economy theory, a labor-intensive zone exploited by both core and semiperipheral states. Most are located in the so-called Third World, for example, Mozambique.

semiperiphery: In world-economy theory, an intermediate buffer region between core and periphery states. Semiperipheral states are exploited by the core, but in turn exploit those in the periphery, for example, South Africa.

Tembu: A royal clan of the Xhosa-speaking people, to which Nelson Mandela was born. *See* Haskins 1995, 191–97; and http://www.gov.za/profiles/mandela.htm. An independent church was formed among the Tembu by Nehemiah Tile (see http://www.gospelcom.net/dacb/stories/southafrica/tile_nehemiah.html), whose successor was Jonas Goduka (see http://www.gospelcom. net/dacb/stories/southafrica/goduka_jonas.html).

tertiary data: Information based on already processed data that was not collected by the researcher who interprets it. Secondary data refers to information that exists in an already processed form, while primary data refer to information that has not been processed. Statistics collected by a census, for example, would generally be regarded as primary data. Interpretations based on census data form secondary data, and their reinterpretation comprises tertiary data. In qualitative research, recorded or transcribed interviews that have not yet been coded represent instances of primary data, as do field notes.

township: In South Africa, black ghettoes reluctantly created without economic infrastructure by apartheid urban planners to serve as labor pools for nearby (formerly) white cities and towns. The largest and most renowned township is Soweto (short for South Western Township), near Johannesburg.

Transkei: A largely rural region along the southeast coast of South Africa—populated predominantly by Xhosa-speaking people—which today (with the Ciskei) forms part of the Eastern Cape Province (for a summary on Transkeian history, see http://www.1upinfo.com/country-guide-study/south-africa/south-africa40.html). In 1976, the Transkei was given putative independence (black) by the apartheid regime—followed by Bophutatswana (1977), Venda (1979), and Ciskei (1981). Six other black "homelands" were being prepared for independence, namely KwaZulu, Lebowa, Gazankulu, QwaQwa, KaNgwane, and KwaNdebele (for an excellent summary of South Africa's political history, see http://www.1upinfo.com/country-guide-study/south-africa/south-africa40.html).

unit of analysis: The object of the research project; usually considered to be an individual, group, organization, event, or artefact.

Venda: An ethnic grouping occupying the northern parts of South Africa in areas adjoining the Sotho.

world-economy: Linkages between states that tie them into a global economy through a single division of labour between states in the core zone, on the one hand, and the peripheral and semiperipheral zones, on the other.

world-polity theory: Argues that global norms, which define the legitimacy of actors within the world system, diffuse across the system through isomorphism, a process by which an increasing number of states incorporate global norms.

world system: The integrated global whole, consisting primarily of economic networks, but also of cultural, political, and social linkages, that tie the various units (e.g., individuals, states, organizations) together in such a way that they are interconnected and interdependent to varying degrees. The interactions between the units in the system affect the internal structures of each unit. Synonymous with global system, overlaps with the concepts world-economy and world-polity.

Xhosa: A collective name for South Africa's second-largest ethnic grouping (7,907,156; StatsSA, 2004); or, for the dominant language spoken within that grouping - although many dialects occur. As an ethnie, Xhosas emerged from clans who fled southward to escape the Zulu ruler Shaka. The language and belief system of Xhosas were heavily influenced by that of the San, whom they subjugated. The Xhosa engaged in nine wars against British colonial rule along what was then the eastern border of the Cape colony, before their final defeat in 1878. The Xhosa produced several ANC leaders—for example, Oliver Tambo (1917–93), Nelson Mandela (b. 1918), and Thabo Mbeki (b. 1942)—although certain other Xhosa regions staunchly supported leaders of the Pan-Africanist Congress (such as Sabelo Phama) and of its military wing, the Azanian People's Liberation Army. For more detail on Xhosa and its dialects, see http://www.lmp.ucla.edu/profiles/profx01.htm and http://www.worldlanguage.com/Languages/Xhosa.htm?CalledFrom=210325.

Zulu: A collective name for South Africa's largest ethnic grouping (10,677,308, StatsSA, 2004); and also of the clan and chief whose name is used to define it. Zulu is the name of a son of the Malendela clan, which settled in present-day KwaZulu-Natal province (on South Africa's northeast coast) during the 16th century, among the Mtetwa Nguni group. The clan had moved as part of the successive, gradual waves of southward migration from the Central African Basin by Nguni peoples from about 500 AD on. The Nguni search for pasture and water was partly prompted by the gradual desertification of northern Africa. Between 1817 and 1828 Shaka (ca. 1787—1828), a Zulu chief, achieved dominance in the coastal region over neighboring Nguni chiefdoms such as the Ndwandwe. His successor Dingane (ca. 1795—1840), and later Cetswayo (ca. 1826—1882), became engulfed in conflict with land-seeking Boers and later the British, eventually suffering substantial defeats from each in 1839 and 1879, respectively. British colonial forces eventually subjugated the area through warfare and in 1887 established the colony of Natal. By 1977 the apartheid government had carved out a patchwork homeland in Natal, called KwaZulu (literally, place of the Zulu). But Gatsha Buthelezi, then chief minister of KwaZulu, refused to have it declared independent. For more detail, see http://www.marques.co.za/clients/zulu/indexorg.htm, http://www.warthog.co.za/dedt/tourism/culture/history/menu.htm, and *South Africa—a Country Study* (Library of Congress at http://memory.loc.gov/frd/cs/zatoc.html). *See also* Bambata Rebellion Inkatha Freedom Party, Nguni, *and* Bantu.

REFERENCES

Giddens, A. 1989. *Sociology*. Cambridge: Polity Press.

Goldfrank, Walter L. 2000. Paradigm regained? The rules of Wallerstein's world-system method. *Journal of World-Systems Research* VI (2): 150–95 (URL: http://csf.colorado.edu/jwsr/archive/vol6/number2/pdf/jwsr-v6n2-goldfrank.pdf).

Haskins, J. 1995. *From afar to Zulu—A dictionary of African cultures*. New York: Walker.

Murray, Colin, and Gavin Williams. 1994. Land and Freedom in South Africa. *Review of African Political Economy* 21: 61, editorial introduction, September; http://www.roape.org/edit_61.html).

Pretorius, Hennie L., and Lizo Jafta. 1997. 'A branch springs out'—African Initiated Churches. In *Christianity in South Africa: A political, social and cultural history*, ed. Richard Elphick and Rodney Davenport, 211—26. Cape Town: David Philip.

StatsSA. 2004. *Census 2001 by province, gender, religion recode (derived) and population group*. Statistics South Africa. (URL: http://www.statssa.gov.za/SpecialProjects/Census2001/Census/Dialog/varval.asp?ma=Religionbyprovince&ti=Table%3A+Census+2001+by+province%2C+gender%2C+religion+recode+%28derived%29+and++population+group%2E+&path=../Database/Census%202001/Provincial%20Level/Persons/&lang=).

Additional Resources

Dawid Venter

FURTHER READING

Anderson, Allan. 2000. *Zion and Pentecost: The spirituality and experience of Pentecostal and Zionist/Apostolic churches in South Africa.* Pretoria: University of South Africa.

Gunner, Elizabeth. 2002. *The Man of Heaven and the Beautiful Ones of God: Writings from Ibandla lamaNazaretha, a South African Church.* Leiden: Brill.

Hexham, Irving, Oosthuizen, Gerhardus C. (eds.). 1996, 1998, 2002. *The Story of Isaiah Shembe.* Volumes 1-3. Translation by Hans-Jürgen Becken. Lewiston: Edwin Mellen.

Kiernan, James P. 1991. Wear 'n' tear and repair: The colour coding of mystical mending in Zulu Zionist Churches. *Africa/International African Institute,* 61 (1): 26–39.

Kitshoff, M. C. (ed.). 1996. *African Independent Churches Today - Kaleidoscope of Afro-Christianity.* Lewiston: Edwin Mellen Press.

Maboea, Sello Isaiah. 2002. *The influence of life-giving power in African traditional religion and the Zionist churches in Soweto: A comparative study.* Pretoria: C. B. Powell Bible Centre, University of South Africa.

Mohr, Matthias. 1997. *Negotiating the boundary: The response of Kwa Mashu Zionists to a volatile political climate.* Hamburg: Lit Verlag; New Brunswick, NJ: Transaction Publishers.

Ngada, Nduruso H., and Rev. Kenosi Mofokeng. 2001. *African Christian witness: The movement of the spirit in African Indigenous Churches.* Pietermaritzburg: Cluster Publications.

Oosthuizen, Gerhardus. 1996. African independent/indigenous churches in the social environment: An empirical analysis. *Africa Insight* 26 (4): 308–24.

Pretorius, Hennie L. 1993. *Ethiopia stretches out her hands unto God: Aspects of Transkeian indigenous churches.* Pretoria: Institute for Missiological Research, University of Pretoria.

Schoffeleers, J. Matthew. 1991. Ritual healing and political acquiescence: The case of the Zionist churches in southern Africa. *Africa/International*

African Institute 61 (1): 1–25.
Thomas, Linda Elaine. 1999. *Under the Canopy - Ritual Process and Spiritual Resilience in South Africa.* Columbus: University of South Carolina.

AUDIOVISUAL MATERIAL

- *Umoya: The Spirit in Africa.* DVD. Includes interviews with AIC members from different denominations, historical overview, academic paper. URL: http://www.coh.arizona.edu/newandnotable/kunnie/kunnie.html.
- *Zulu Zion.* VHS. Series: *The Long search.* 1978. Subject: Isaiah Shembe's *Ibandla AmaNazaretha*, situated in sociohistorical context, with examples of dancing, pilgrimage, and services. 52 min.

WORLD WIDE WEB SITES

- *African Initiated Churches.* Web site maintained by Stephen Hayes on behalf of the South African Missiological Society. Contains online articles, discussion group, and links to databases and researchers. URL: http://www.geocities.com/Athens/Parthenon/8409/aic.htm.
- Afrika Studiecentrum, Universiteit van Leiden, the Netherlands. Offers summaries of articles. URL: http://www.asc.leidenuniv.nl/library.
- Bethel College, Ohio. Contains summaries of history, main characters, and brief descriptions of types of AICs as part of 1998 history course on African Christianity (HIS 303). URL: http://www.bethel.edu/~letnie/African Christianity/ SouthAfricaHomepage.html.
- Department of Missions and Intercultural Studies, Wheaton, Illinois. A. Scott Moreau provides an annotated bibliography for AICs (Missions 532). URL: http://www.wheaton.edu/Missions/Courses/532/biblio/aic.htm.
- Department of Religion, University of Calgary, Alberta. Irving Hexham conducts research, and provides online texts on Isaiah Shembe. URL: http://www.ucalgary.ca/~nurelweb/books/shembe/s-index.html.
- *The Dictionary of African Christian Biography.* Contains brief descriptions of AICs and other figures in African Christianity. URL: http://www.gospelcom.net/dacb/newindex.html.
- Dr. Allan Anderson's Home Page. Contains online resources and Anderson's extensive bibliographies. URL: http://artsweb.bham.ac.uk/ aanderson/ index.htm.
- St. Mary's University, Halifax, Nova Scotia. Wally Mills's History 322.0 Web site on South Africa includes full text articles on AICs and aspects of South African history, including brief descriptions. URL: http://husky1. stmarys. ca/~wmills/course322/his322.html.
- Statistics South Africa. An interactive website which allows basic statistical manipulation of census data. URL: http://www.statssa. gov.za.

RESOURCES ON AICs IN THE REST OF AFRICA

Video

- *Rise up and walk: The life and witness of the African Indigenous Churches.* 1982. Produced with the cooperation of the Organization of African Independent Churches. 28 min.
- *The sword and spirit: Ivory Coast. Let my people go.* 1988. The Harrist Church. 60 min.
- *The life and witness of African Indigenous Churches.* 1981. Covers Zaire, Swaziland, Kenya, Ivory Coast. 55 min.
- *Today's Africa: The church and the people.* 1994. AICs in the Ivory Coast and the Harrist Church. 50 min.

World Wide Web

- *African religion: Studies in anthropology and intercultural philosophy.* Site maintained by anthropologist Wim Van Binsbergen. URL: http://www.shikanda.net/african_religion/index.htm.

Index

About the Contributors

ROBERT GARNER is a Briton who has set up a Christian nongovernment organization promoting integrated development and equality of opportunity for impoverished children in southern Africa (http://www.fideo.org). Formerly a vice president with an investment bank, he has subsequently worked as an AIDS consultant in KwaZulu Natal. Garner holds a Ph.D. in social and political science from Cambridge University, Cambridge, where he distinguished himself in development studies. E-mail: Robandfideo@aol.com.

JIM KIERNAN is currently a professor in the School of Community Development and Adult Education at the University of Natal in Durban, South Africa, and an emeritus professor of social anthropology at the same university. A former Jesuit, he is an early pioneer of research on AICs. He has conducted extensive fieldwork on AICs, as demonstrated by his impressive publication record in this regard. E-mail: kiernanj@nu.ac.za.

LAWRENCIA KWARK is a Korean with considerable experience of various international religious and research nongovernmental organizations, including the Korean Network for the United Nations Conference on Human Rights of South Korea, the International Movement of Catholic Students, and the Centre L-J. Lebret. Currently working as a project officer for Latin America and Asia with the Comité Catholique contre la Faim et pour le Développement, she is completing a Ph.D. in sociology at the Ecole des Hautes Etudes en Sciences Sociales in Paris, France. E-mail: l.kwark@ccfd.asso.fr.

DAWID VENTER is a South African who has taught sociology at the

University of Missouri–St. Louis and at University of the Western Cape in South Africa. A past assistant editor of the official South African *Journal of Sociology*, Venter has concentrated on the intersections of religion, politics, and the global system. Currently a research associate in the Department of Political and International Studies at Rhodes University in Grahamstown, South Africa, Venter holds a Ph.D. in religion and a Ph.D. in sociology from the University of Stellenbosch, South Africa. E-mail: dawidventer@webmail.co.za.